Back in 7

Also by Graeme Carlé & Emmaus Road Publishing:

Eating Sacred Cows
A Closer Look at Tithing

Because of the Angels
Unveiling 1 Corinthians 11:2-16

The Red Heifer's Ashes
Mysteries of Ancient Israel

Born of the Spirit
A Study Guide for New Believers

The Revelation Series

1. Dancing in the Dragon's Jaws
The Mystery of Israel's Survival

2. Slouching Towards Bethlehem
The Rise of the Antichrists

3. Gotta Serve Somebody
The Mystery of the Marks & 666

4. Silencing the Witnesses
Jerusalem & the Ascent of Secularism

5. Threshing Hour
Armageddon & Babylon the Great

Next book:
7. Kingdom Come
Justice for All

Back in 7

The Seven Seals, Trumpets & Bowls

Graeme Carlé

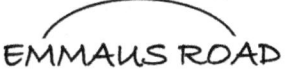

All proceeds from the sale of this book are used for the further publication of this and similar work by Emmaus Road Publishing.

© 2024 Graeme Carlé

All rights reserved including the right of reproduction in whole or in part in any form. The moral rights of the author have been asserted.

Author photo, cover,
book design and production by Olivia Carlé

ISBN 978-1-7385820-2-0
Epub ISBN 978-1-7385820-3-7

Unless otherwise stated, all Scripture quoted is from the
NEW AMERICAN STANDARD BIBLE®,
Copyright ©1995 The Lockman Foundation.
Used with permission.

Emmaus Road Publishing
PO Box 38 823, Howick, Auckland 2014, New Zealand
www.emmausroad.org.nz

Contents

Introduction 11

1. The Seventh Bowl 15
   "It is Done!"

2. The Purpose 29
   & Timing

3. The Seven Seals 42
   Business as Usual

4. God's Will 55
   For Them & Us

5. Sixth & Seventh Seals 74
   In Our Time?

6. The Seventh Trumpets 88
   Proximity Alerts

7. The Prelude 106
   Answering Prayer.

8. The First Trumpet 120
   Signs on the Earth

9. The Second Trumpet 136
   Signs in the Sea

10. The Third & Fourth Trumpets 148
    Signs in the Water & Air

11. The Fifth Trumpet 163
    The First Woe

12. A Plague 179
    To Redeem

13. The Sting 192
    Temporary Torment

14. Dangers 203
    & Antidotes
15. The Sixth Trumpet 222
    The Second Woe
16. Fire & Brimstone 239
    1st Century
17. The Horsemen 246
    Today
18. The Seventh Trumpet 266
    The Third Woe
19. Twenty-Two Signs 281
    "When You See..."
20. The Seven Bowls 297
    Tipping Point
21. Bowl by Bowl 317
    Hoping for Repentance
Epilogue 332

Bibliography 334

Index 340

Figures and Charts
(i) Greek gold phiale c. 4 BC 35
(ii) Roman priestess with phiale c. 3 AD 36
(iii) The seal of Darius the Great c. 500 BC 51
(iv) Alchon Hun horseman c. 460 AD 57
(v) Artaxeres' 1st decree 104
(vi) Bible illustration 1909 149
(vii) Desert locust (Schistocerca Gregaria) 186

(viii) Map of Euphrates River 230
(ix) Coin depicting Mithridates VI Eupator 243
(x) World population chart 260
(xi) Twenty-two signs 283

Attributions

(i) The Metropolitan Museum of Art. https://commons.wikimedia.org/w/index.php?curid=57853104

(ii) Wolfgang Sauber - https://commons.wikimedia.org/w/index.php?curid=16466402

(iii) E. A. Wallis Budge & L. W. King, *A Guide to the Babylonian and Assyrian Antiquities.* https://commons.wikimedia.org/w/index.php?curid=77750378

(iv) Detail on Hephalite bowl. The British Museum, www.britishmuseum.org/collection/object/A_1963-1210-1.

(vi) Old Believers Bible https://commons.wikimedia.org/w/index.php?curid=65373809

(vii) Adrian Pingstone, Jan 2005 https://commons.wikimedia.org/w/index.php?curid=620414

(viii) Map based on: https://commons.wikimedia.org/w/index.php?curid=12714539

(ix) By Classical Numismatic Group, Inc. http://www.cngcoins.com, CC BY-SA 2.5, https://commons.wikimedia.org/w/index.php?curid=75342103

(x) https://en.wikipedia.org/wiki/File:World-population-1750-2015-and-un-projection-until-2100.png

"There will be signs in sun and moon and stars,
and on the earth dismay among nations, in
perplexity at the roaring of the sea and the waves…

Then they will see the Son of Man coming…
But when these things begin to take place,
straighten up and lift up your heads,
because your redemption is drawing near."

- Jesus   (Luke 21:25-28)

Dedication

To Barry Smith
(1933 - 2002)

A wonderful evangelist & friend who inspired me
to search the Scriptures regarding End Times

Thanks

To good friends for their love, support, and feedback, Arthur Amon, Joanna Bain, Chris & Dianne Bryan, Olivia Carlé, Dmitry & Linda Gafiyatulin, Mohan & Amy Herath, Mike & Jill Meyer, Benjamin & Dolly Pan, Chris Pan, Shane & Melissa Pope, Murray Powell, Graham & Dianne Poskitt, Peter & Susan Ridley, Heidi Roussell, and Simone Varney.

Introduction

In Book 5, *Threshing Hour: Armageddon & Babylon the Great*, we looked at 'one hour', the last hour before the Lord returns, from Revelation 16:13 to the end of Chapter 19. However, I skipped over the last five verses of Revelation 16 (vv. 17-21) because they introduce another of Revelation's mysteries, the 7th Bowl. I decided not to show how that relates to Armageddon and Babylon the Great because the bowls, seals, and trumpets require far more explanation than a brief mention - together they reveal the will of God over the last 2,000 years as well as in our immediate future. Accordingly, they are the subject of this book.

I am also concerned that many Christians today are not expecting us to be this close to the last hour because many of the events that I and my friends were taught as predicted have not yet happened and some never will. On the other hand, as I will show in Chapter 19, the Scriptures give us twenty-two signs of the times that we are called to recognise - ten have already happened, ten are in progress today, and the only two remaining to be fulfilled are the appearance of the Antichrist and the return of Jesus Christ.

How did we miss them all? We have simply misunderstood the Scriptures.

In the early 1970s, I was startled to hear an interview with the celebrated oceanographer Jacques Cousteau (1910-1997) in which he said, "A third of the fish of the sea are threatened by mercury poisoning". In 1971, he told *Time* magazine that 'the vitality of the seas, in terms of fish and plant life, has declined some 30% to 50% in the past 20 years'.[1] I was astonished because I had just read about a third of marine life in Revelation:

---

1 https://content.time.com/time/subscriber/article/0,33009,877387,00.html, 2 May 2024.

> 8. The second angel sounded, and something like a great mountain burning with fire was thrown into the sea; and a third of the sea became blood,
> 9. and a third of the creatures which were in the sea and had life, died... (Rev 8:8-9*)[2]

Mr Cousteau's words set me on a whole new approach to Revelation. At that moment, I realised I had been harbouring a fear that God was about to do terrible things to the earth – that He was about to do them *to us* – but here was Jacques Cousteau saying we are doing this particular poisoning to ourselves. Mercury in the sea is a by-product of coal-fired power generation and mining.[3]

I suddenly saw the angel not as inflicting this disaster on us but as sounding a warning to us to recognise what we are doing to ourselves. As I searched the Old Testament, I found that in ancient Israel one of the primary purposes for trumpets was to sound the alarm. This discovery took away my fear of the Book of Revelation and I hope it will similarly help the reader.

In trying to identify what is happening in the world around us, I have quoted from a wide cross-section of sources but my hope is that you will see and search out for yourself the latest developments, scientific findings, and conclusions.

This Series

In this series, I have been showing the visions of Revelation are, like the four Gospels, concurrent rather than consecutive.[4] Here is an overview of what I have covered so far.

---

2 I have used asterisks throughout to signify 'emphasis added'.
3 Half of atmospheric mercury comes from volcanoes and half from human activity, 2/3 of which is from the combustion of coal and the production of metals such as gold, iron, and steel. The other 1/3 comes from cement, caustic soda, and batteries, as well as waste disposal, human crematoria, and biomass burning.
4 Some teach that there will be twenty-one judgements, one after the other, during a future seven year period called the Great Tribulation (e.g. https://jewishroots.net/library/end-times/twentyone_judgments.html, 6 Dec, 2023).

(i) Book 1, *Dancing in the Dragon's Jaws*

I began as I was personally led,[5] with Revelation 12 as a stand-alone vision in which the woman portrays 4,000 years of Israel's history, as can be readily understood by anyone interested in Jewish history.

For the first 2,000 years the woman, Israel, faced Satan's genocidal attacks through the Gentile empires of Egypt, Assyria, Babylon, Medo-Persia, and Greece. Jesus came in the time of the Roman Empire (Rev 12:5) but her rejection of Him led to her last 2,000 years in exile until "the times of the Gentiles" were fulfilled and she regained the Promised Land.

(ii) Books 2 & 3, *Slouching Towards Bethlehem* and *Gotta Serve Somebody*

Having established the meaning of the metaphorical "a time, times, and half a time"[6] as being the last 2,000 years, I showed how the two beasts[7] of Revelation 13 have rampaged through the Gentile nations, from John's day to ours. I also detailed how the 144,000 apostles[8] of Revelation 7 and 14 have been evangelising the world throughout this time.

---

5   I believe I was led by the Holy Spirit to first understand Revelation 12, then to Chapters 13 and 14, then to 11. I was later told by a curious seminary professor that I had unwittingly followed the chiastic structure common in ancient Jewish thinking. Jesus often used memorable chiasms which present ideas and then repeat or invert them symmetrically e.g. "the first shall be last and the last shall be first" (Matt 19:30). Also Matt 6:24, 7:6, 20:16, 23:12; Mark 2:27. A chapters-long example can be seen in the narrative of the Flood (Genesis 6-9).

6   Also referred to as 1,260 days, forty-two months, and three years and six months.

7   That is, the feral state and the spirit of antichrist which caused the Romans to deify their emperors.

8   This metaphorical number shows the original 'twelve apostles of the Lamb' (Rev 21:14) being multiplied by another twelve and then by a thousand to show that the Lamb has never stopped calling apostles so 'that He could send them out to preach' (Mark 3:14) to the Gentiles until 'a great multitude which no one could count, from *every* nation and *all* tribes and peoples and tongues' are at last worshipping the Lamb on His throne (Rev 7:9).

(iii) Book 4, *Silencing the Witnesses*

The stand-alone vision of Revelation 11 also portrays the last 2,000 years but this time looking at God's abiding testimony to Israel in the Law and the Prophets regarding Jesus, His atoning death, resurrection, and His gift of the Holy Spirit, but also the curse of the Law. I showed how John's vision illustrates Paul's teaching that Jews are still under the Old Covenant unless and until they are born again into the New (Rom 7:1-4).

I also showed the world-changing significance of the Jews regaining Jerusalem in 1967, which marked the end of "the times of the Gentiles", and the Gentiles' subsequent slow overthrow of the morality of our Judaeo-Christian heritage.

(iv) Book 5, *Threshing Hour*

The visions of the Battle of Har-Magedon at Jerusalem and the fall of Babylon the Great, i.e. the God-rejecting world, in Revelation 16-19 are explicitly set in the 'one hour' before Jesus returns so I believe these visions will be fulfilled very quickly and soon.

You see then I have been opening up Revelation from the middle i.e. as a chiasm or chiasmus (see Footnote 5).

I began with Chapter 12, then 13, then 7 and 14, then 11, then 16-19. In this book, we will look at Chapters 5-6, 8-10, and 15-16, leaving Chapters 20-22 to Book 7, *Kingdom Come*.

We will begin at what may seem a strange starting point with the seventh and last bowl. However, as noted in the introduction, it is described in the verses I skipped over in the last book (Rev 16: 17-21) so I am simply completing that chapter.

1
The Seventh Bowl
"It is Done!"

Threshing Hour ended with the last battle at Har-Magedon which I believe could be imminent but, as John describes it, that is also the time of the 7th Bowl:

> 16. And they gathered them together to the place which in Hebrew is called Har-Magedon.
> 17. Then the seventh angel poured out his bowl upon the air, and a loud voice came out of the temple from the throne, saying, "It is done!" (Rev 16:16-17*)

The 'loud voice...from the throne' (v. 17) echoes Jesus' cry from the cross, "It is finished!" (John 19:13). In 30 AD, Jesus was taking on Himself all the wrath of God for all the sins of all who will repent and trust in Him; here, John sees the last of the bowls of wrath poured out on all who will not.[9]

So why are there seven and what happened with the previous six bowls?

The Seventh Bowl

Seven can have the metaphorical meaning of 'perfect, complete, or just'[10] and John sees the seven bowls will be God's just punishment of the whole world:

> Then I saw... seven angels who had seven plagues, which are *the last, because in them the wrath of God is finished.*
> (Rev 16:1*)

---

[9] We see here the two Days of Judgement as explained in Book 1, *Dancing in the Dragon's Jaws*, pp. 129-130.
[10] *Gotta Serve Somebody*, p. 147.

The 7th Bowl poured out 'upon the air' (Rev 16:17) will have a staggering effect on the earth:

> 18. And there were flashes of *lightning* and sounds and peals of *thunder;* and there was a *great earthquake,* such as there had not been since man came to be upon the earth, so great an earthquake was it, and so mighty.
> 19. The great city was split into three parts, and the *cities of the nations fell.* Babylon the Great was remembered before God, to give her the cup of the wine of His fierce wrath.
> 20. And *every island* fled away, and the *mountains* were not found. (Rev 16:19-20*)

This unprecedented earthquake (v. 18) will be the last ever on the old earth, impacting not only every city everywhere (v. 19) but also the whole 'world' known as Babylon the Great (v. 19), as established in Book 5. When the armies of all the nations gather to fight at Har-Magedon, against Jerusalem the city of God, He will shake *their* cities until *they* fall. 'Every island' (v. 20) and all 'the mountains' (v. 20) will disappear on that day.

In the sky above, the thunderstorm of v. 18 will be utterly catastrophic:

> 21. And huge hailstones, about one hundred pounds each [Grk, talantiaios, talent-like in weight], came down from heaven upon men; and men blasphemed God because of the plague of the hail, because its plague was extremely severe. (Rev 16:21)

The largest hailstone officially recorded was an agglomerate,[11] measured in 2010 in South Dakota, USA, as weighing 1.94 pounds (0.88 kg). It was 20.3 cm (8 in) in diameter, only 2.5 cm (1 in) smaller in diameter than a soccer ball. It made a 25

---

[11] Formed by many smaller hailstones sticking and freezing together. Scientists classify any larger than 15 cm (6 in) as 'gargantuan', noting that this size has penetrated roofs and multiple floors in houses.

cm (10 in) pit in the ground,[12] which is unsurprising because they can fall at up to 160 km/h (100 mph).

Imagine then hailstones fifty times heavier than that - no one would survive this hailstorm.

Some take this to be hyperbole or symbolic of cosmic upheaval of every kind and we will consider that soon. However, I believe that it is literal - it is the last plague in which 'the wrath of God is finished' (Rev 15:1); after it, the voice from the throne declares, "It is done!" (Rev 16:17). It is the end of what Jesus called "the present age" (Mark 10:30) and Paul, 'this present evil age' (Gal 1:4) - it is Judgement Day for the whole world and is immediately followed by Judgement Day for every individual.[13]

Jewish History 101

As frightening as this 7th Bowl may seem for us today, the Jewish disciples in John's 1st century audience would have instead recognised it as their coming vindication and liberation - this is just what happens when God Himself steps into a battle and it ends!

As I will show in Chapter 18, ancient Israel actually celebrated His thunder and lightning, hailstones, and earthquakes throughout their national history. They sang of them in the Song of Deborah (Judg 5:4-5, 19-21) and in their psalms[14] because God's targeted hailstones were remembered every year at Passover as liberating them from slavery in Egypt (Ex 9:22-26); His hailstones enabled them to conquer the Promised Land (Jos 10:10-11). When David sang of his deliverance from Saul, he used earthquakes and

---

12 https://phys.org/news/2020-04-gargantuan-hail-argentina-world.html, 27 June, 2023.
13 We will look at this properly in Chapter 20 in comparing temporal and eternal judgements.
14 Psalms 78:47-48, 105:32-33, and 148:8.

hailstones as a metaphor for God's intervention, and compared his escape to the Exodus (Psa 18:12-17).

So as usual, we ask are these literal or metaphorical?

John's earthquake and hailstones could be as metaphorical as David's but I believe they will be literal, especially in the light of Haggai's prophecy. Haggai was one of the last of Israel's prophets and in 520 BC (Hag 1:1), he predicted that the earth's last earthquake will be uniquely cataclysmic:

> 6. "For thus says the LORD of hosts, 'Once more in a little while, I am going to shake the *heavens and the earth, the sea also and the dry land.*
> 7. "'I will shake *all the nations*; and they will come with the wealth of all nations, and I will fill this house with glory...'" (Hag 2:6-7*)

The author of Hebrews gives us the inspired interpretation as understood by John's 1st century Jewish audience:

> 26. ...He has promised, saying, "YET ONCE MORE I WILL SHAKE NOT ONLY THE EARTH, BUT ALSO THE HEAVEN."
> 27. This expression, "Yet once more," *denotes the removing of those things which can be shaken,* as of created things, so that those things which cannot be shaken may remain.
> 28. Therefore, since we receive *a kingdom which cannot be shaken*, let us show gratitude... (Heb 12:26-28*)

As the material world disintegrates around us, we will indeed be thanking God that we are in His 'kingdom which cannot be shaken' (v. 28)!

Let us be very clear - those 1st century Jewish disciples would have easily recognised John's description of the 7th Bowl as fulfilling Haggai's prophecy that the heavens, 'the dry land' with all its cities and its highest mountains, and 'every island' in the sea will be 'removed':

18. and there was a great earthquake, such as *there had not been* since man came to be upon the earth, so great an earthquake was it, and so mighty…
19. …and the cities of the nations fell…
20. And every island fled away, and the mountains were not found. (Rev 16:18-20*)

When 'heaven and earth pass away' like this, it will be Judgement Day. Unfortunately, none of the four traditional views of Revelation fully recognise it as such - Preterists see this as referring to the destruction of Jerusalem in 70 AD, Historicists as the start of the Millennium, while Futurists and Idealists see it as the beginning of the seven trumpets and seven bowls. We therefore have some work to do to get back on track.

In the chapters that follow, we will consider each of the seven bowls (Rev 16:1-21), seven seals (Rev 6:1-17, 8:1), and seven trumpets (Rev 8:2-9:21, 11:15) but first I want to restate and re-emphasise my overall approach.

The 1st Century Jewish Teenager Approach

There are three keys to understanding the seals, trumpets, and bowls that we must grasp to catch up with John's original 1st century audience:

(i) Historical *Jewish* images

The events of the 7th Bowl are not random or chaotic but prefigured in spectacular episodes in Israel's past including the Exodus, the gaining of the Promised Land, and God's interventions in their battles. This should alert us to see all the seals, trumpets, and bowls through the eyes of those to whom John was writing i.e. 1st century Jewish disciples and/or Gentiles taught by those Jewish disciples.

Paul explained this necessity to the Romans:

> Then what advantage [Gk *perissos*, super-abundance] has the Jew? Or what is the benefit of circumcision? *Great in every respect.* First of all, that they were entrusted with *the oracles of God*. (Rom 3:1-2*)

'The oracles of God' are the Hebrew Scriptures which they had collected over 1,500 years! Writing to Timothy, Paul reminded him of what would have been common among Jewish disciples:

> ...from childhood you have known the sacred writings... All Scripture is inspired by God and profitable for teaching... (2 Tim 3:15-16)

They had learned the images and metaphors 'from childhood', giving them a head-start in learning God's way of talking and behaving throughout their previous 2,000 year history. They had *lived* in 'the covenants, the Law, the temple service, and the promises' (Rom 9:4). By their teenage years, they would have experienced first-hand a dozen cycles of their annual feasts and fasts which re-enact their unique nation's escapes from annihilation and which foreshadow the Messiah's coming and His work.

Paul urged the Roman disciples to learn from Israel's recorded history and experiences of God (Rom 15:4); he wrote to the Greeks to learn from the temptations faced by the Hebrews in the wilderness:

> 6. Now these things happened as *examples for us*, so that we would not crave evil things as they also craved...
> 11. Now these things happened to them as *an example,* and they were written for our *instruction,* upon whom the ends of the ages have come. (1 Cor 10:6 & 11*)

I am a Gentile so I have spent five decades learning everything I can from our Jewish Scriptures and now advocate for what I call the '1st Century Jewish Teenager Approach' to Revelation, as described in Book 5.[15]

---
15 *Threshing Hour*, pp. 12-13.

(ii) The *purpose* of seals, trumpets, and bowls

These particular images are also not random or new to the Jews but metaphors drawn from their history and daily life: they had to break *seals* to open official documents and personal correspondence; they gathered to the sound of the priests blowing *trumpets* in their festivals; they heard the warnings of the prophets regarding God's *bowls of wrath* in the Scriptures read aloud every Sabbath.

We therefore need to familiarise ourselves with and identify the purpose of these images to catch up with John's original audience; if we do not, we will miss the whole point of the revelation as I will show in the next chapter.

(iii) They are not *consecutive*

I was taught that the three series of seven seals, seven trumpets, and seven bowls are consecutive but they are not - each series refers to a different time period but all three end in Judgement Day.

Understanding this will enable us to identify the strengths and flaws in the four traditional views of Revelation.

Simultaneous Ending

We have just seen how the 7th Bowl is Judgement Day. Now look at the 6th and 7th Seals:

> 12. I looked when He broke *the sixth seal*, and there was a great earthquake; and the sun became black as sackcloth made of hair, and the whole moon became like blood;
> 13. and the stars of the sky fell to the earth...
> 14. The sky was split apart... and *every mountain and island* were moved out of their places. (Rev 6:12-13*)

As we just saw, this also happens with the 7th Bowl:

> 20. And *every island* fled away, and *the mountains* were not found. (Rev 16:20*)

John's vision of the 6th Seal continues:

> 15. Then the kings of the earth and the great men and the commanders and the rich and the strong and every slave and free man hid themselves in the caves and among the rocks of the mountains;
> 16. and they said to the mountains and to the rocks, "Fall on us and *hide us from the presence* of Him who sits on the throne, and from the wrath of the Lamb;
> 17. for *the great day* of their wrath *has come*, and who is able to stand?" (Rev 6:15-17*)

We see then that the 6th Seal, i.e. "the great day of the wrath" of God and of the Lamb, is also Judgement Day and, as we will see in Chapter 3, the 7th Seal is 'silence in heaven for about half an hour' (Rev 8:1) before every individual hears their fate.

Now consider the *7th Trumpet* when Jesus is proclaimed as King:

> 15. Then the seventh angel sounded; and there were loud voices in heaven, saying, "The kingdom of the world has become the kingdom of our Lord and of His Christ; and He will reign forever and ever…" (Rev 11:15)

This is when He raises and judges the dead:

> 18. "And *the nations* were enraged, and *Your wrath came*, and the time came for *the dead to be judged*, and the time to reward Your bond-servants the prophets and the saints and those who fear Your name, the small and the great, and to destroy those who destroy the earth."
> 19. And the temple of God which is in heaven was opened; and the ark of His covenant appeared in His temple, and there were flashes of *lightning* and sounds and peals of *thunder* and *an earthquake* and *a great hailstorm*.
> (Rev 11:18-19*)

The 7th Trumpet is therefore also Judgement Day.

We see then that the seven seals, the seven trumpets, and the seven bowls are not consecutive but all culminate in Judgement Day[16] and this tells us a great deal about the Book of Revelation. Revelation is frequently read as if it is chronological, as if every vision follows the next in its fulfilment. The effect has been to render the book completely incomprehensible to most modern readers. Imagine if the four gospels of Jesus' life, death, and resurrection were read the same way!

However, each series *begins* at a different time because of their *purpose*. As I will show, the seals reveal one time period (the last 2,000 years), the trumpets are blown in another (the last 80-100 years), and the bowls are poured out in another (the last 'hour').

"Then I Saw…"

My *New American Standard Bible* has John using the word 'then' 47 times,[17] 46 times to begin a new sentence and only once to describe a time,[18] giving the impression of consecutive events. However, he was recording the order in which *he saw or heard* the Revelation. For example, 9 times he says, 'Then I saw…'; 4 times he says, 'Then I looked…'; and 6 times he says 'Then I heard…'

John's recording the visions consecutively does not mean the events in them followed one after the other. As you can see for yourself, the seven seals, trumpets, and bowls all culminate in Judgement Day, just as the four gospels all culminate in the crucifixion and resurrection of Jesus.

---

16 As I will show in Book 7, there are also five depictions of Jesus' second coming and victory but there will not be five last battles (Rev 6:15-17, 11:15-19, 16:12-16, 19:11-20, and 20:8-9), just one, and that will be very brief.

17 *NIV* has 54 times, *NKJV* 63 times, while the *KJV* has only 2, preferring 'And…' instead.

18 '…in the days of…, then…' (Rev 10:7).

My wife Olivia recently suggested a way to illustrate this. She and I had enjoyed binge-watching a television series called '24', an award-winning American crime drama.[19] It is about a US counter-terrorist federal agent Jack Bauer responding to terrorist attacks and presidential assassination attempts and each season covers 24 consecutive hours in his life. Several interrelated plots in each episode are followed for one hour, depicting events as happening in real time, and to emphasise that, a digital clock is kept on-screen so you can feel the tension as if an eye-witness.

The series frequently used split-screens to show two, three, or four scenes occurring at the same time. Of course, this is only possible on a screen; we cannot read two, three, or four passages of writing simultaneously but it does illustrate what John was doing in writing Revelation and what occurs in the gospels.

As I have been showing throughout these studies and recapped in the Introduction, we are supposed to read Revelation as a series of visions describing overlapping time periods:

(i) Revelation 12 spans 4,000 years of Jewish history, from Joseph's dreams in 19th century BC Egypt until today.

(ii) Revelation 11, 13, and 14 span the last 2,000 years

(iii) Revelation 16-19 reveal the last "hour" and I believe we are living in it.

In this book, I will show that:

(i) The seven seals were to reveal God's will from 30 AD until Jesus returns (i.e. the last 2,000 years and counting).

---

19 Broadcast between 2001 and 2014, it comprised 204 episodes over nine seasons and was a joint production by Imagine Television and 20th Century Fox Television.

(ii) The seven trumpets were to warn of the world conditions that every one of us can see for ourselves today as occurring over the last 80-100 years with the seventh being Jesus' return.

(iii) The seven bowls are yet to come but will be very brief with the second, third, and seventh occurring instantaneously at His return.

Traditional Views of Timing

As you may know, there are four main ways of interpreting Revelation which result in very different timing for the seals, trumpets, and bowls:

(i) Preterist

From the Latin, *praeter*, meaning 'past'. Preterists believe Revelation was mostly fulfilled by the year 70 AD and the fall of Jerusalem.

For example, Preterists believe that the 6th Seal's reference to 'the kings of the earth and the great men and the commanders and the rich and the strong and every slave and free man' hiding in 'the caves and among the rocks of the mountains' (Rev 6:15) was describing the Jews hiding from the Roman invasion. The sun becoming black, the moon like blood, the stars falling to the earth, and the removal of 'every mountain and island' (Rev 6:12-17) are interpreted as symbolic.

This view and the Futurist view are widely held by post-Reformation Catholics.

(ii) Historicist

For Historicists, the seals, trumpets, and bowls are consecutive and fulfilled by specific events over last 2,000 years. They believe that the 6th Seal refers to the collapse of the Roman Empire when the Goths and Vandals invaded between 375 and 418 AD. Most believe the effect on sun, moon, and stars is symbolic[20] which means they can interpret Babylon the Great as the Roman Catholic Church. This was the standard view of the Reformers and their Protestant followers.

(iii) Futurist

Futurists believe that Revelation is mostly yet to be fulfilled. They see the 6th Seal as predicting literal volcanic eruptions and/or nuclear war that will so pollute the atmosphere that the sun will darken, the moon turn red, and massive meteors will shower the earth. This will then be followed by the 7th Seal, then the seven trumpets, then the seven bowls.

First held by post-Reformation Catholics, this view became the dominant Protestant perspective in the 19th century through J.N. Darby and the Scofield Study Bible and in the 20th century as illustrated in Hal Lindsay's *The Late, Great Planet Earth*[21] and Tim LaHaye and Jerry Jenkins' *Left Behind* novels, movies, and video games.[22]

(iv) Idealist

To Idealists, Revelation is continually fulfilled metaphorically. Widely held since Augustine in the 4th century, this view sees no particular historical events other than the Second Coming and Judgement Day, looking instead for 'timeless…

---

20 However, some Seventh Day Adventists think the earthquake occurred in 1775, the darkening in 1780, the meteorites appeared in 1883, and they are waiting for the Lord's return (www.bibleinfo.com/en/questions/seventh-seal-of-revelation, 27 May, 2023).

21 Lindsey, Hal, with Carlson, Carole C., *The Late, Great Planet Earth*, Grand Rapids, MI; Zondervan, 1970.

22 This view is often referred to as Dispensationalism, the belief that history is divided into seven 'dispensations', i.e. ages, in which God interacts with His chosen people in different ways. I instead see history as shaped by eight everlasting covenants, as described in *Silencing the Witnesses*, pp. 312-338.

truths about the nature of reality or human existence that either are continuously present or continually recur'.[23] In this view, the 6th Seal refers to the end of the age when Christ returns to judge the world, bringing cosmic upheaval of every kind.

Each of the four approaches obviously has merit or no one would hold to them.[24] All four agree that Jesus will return and the seals, trumpets, and bowls appear to be escalating judgements. However, if any of these views is completely correct, the other three are necessarily incorrect.

My 1st Century Jewish Teenager Approach accepts none of the four completely, all of them partially, and shows where each is correct and where each is incorrect, as you will see.

Summary

(i) The 7th Bowl is the Battle of Har-Magedon in which God's wrath will be poured out on the armies gathering to take Jerusalem from Israel during which 'heaven and earth pass away'. It is the last temporal judgement, i.e. within time, and is immediately followed by Judgement Day, i.e. for eternity.

(ii) Jesus' Jewish disciples would have readily recognised the accompanying hailstones and earthquakes from their history of God intervening on their behalf, reassured that these would target His opponents as in the Exodus, the taking of the Promised Land, and the battle at Megiddo. Deborah's famous song, three psalms, and every Passover celebrated these extraordinary events.

---

23 Millard J. Erickson, *A Basic Guide to Eschatology: Making Sense of the Millennium*, Grand Rapids, MI; Baker Books, 1998, p. 30.

24 Each view also has 'partial' followers and each is being continually modified today. For example, https://cbtseminary.org/modified-idealist-revelation-1, 27 Dec, 2022.

(iii) These disciples would also have readily recognised, either directly or as prompted by the letter to the Hebrews, that the 7th Bowl's unprecedented shaking of heaven, earth, and sea will fulfill Haggai's prophecy of Judgement Day.

(iv) In the 1st Century Jewish Teenager Approach, there are three keys to understanding the seven bowls, seals, and trumpets: their Jewish history, their purpose, and their timing.

(v) The 7th Bowl is the last judgement on the old earth but so are the 6th and 7th Seals and the 7th Trumpet - all three series of seven culminate in Judgement Day. They are not consecutive but partially contemporaneous. This overlapping is a major feature of Revelation as can be seen by its five depictions of the Second Coming - there are not five last battles but one.

(vi) Recognising this will help us identify what is correct and what is incorrect in each of the four traditional interpretative approaches to Revelation: the Preterist, Historicist, Futurist, and Idealist perspectives.

2
Purpose
& Timing

Once the purpose of these seals, trumpets, and bowls is clear, their timing will become obvious. I therefore aim in this chapter to give a general overview of their purpose which we will apply in the following chapters.

Seals

In Biblical days, scrolls were rolled up to be stored and wax or clay seals were added for privacy and/or authentication.

(i) Privacy

Seals on scrolls closed them off from public sight, to be read only by the authorised recipient or at the right time, hence the angel's instructions to Daniel:

> "But you, Daniel, roll up and *seal the words* of the scroll until the time of the end..." (Dan 12:4, *NIV*[25] *)

John's Book of Revelation in the 1st century, however, was an open scroll because it was the right time for anyone to read it so:

> ...he said to me, "*Do not seal up the words* of the prophecy of this book, for the time is near" (Rev 22:10*)

In fact, this book is actually to bless everyone who reads or hears it (Rev 1:3).

---

[25] The *NASB* renders this as 'until the end of time' but that could mean the scroll would never be opened in this life which would make it pointless as revelation.

(ii) Authentication

Seals were also to authenticate scrolls, as we see in King Ahasuerus's instruction to Mordecai:

> 8. "Now you write to the Jews as you see fit, in the king's name, and *seal it* with *the king's signet ring*; for a decree which is written in *the name of the king* and *sealed with the king's signet ring* may not be revoked."
> 9. So the king's scribes were called… and it was written according to all that Mordecai commanded…
> 10. He wrote in the name of King Ahasuerus, and sealed it with the king's signet ring, and sent letters by couriers on horses… (Est 8:8-10*)

The king's seal confirmed the scrolls expressed his irrevocable will on any matter.

The Seven Seals

What then are we to make of the scroll John sees in the heavenly throne-room, sealed with seven seals?

> 1. I saw in the right hand of Him who sat on the throne a book written inside and on the back, sealed up with seven seals.
> 2. And I saw a strong angel proclaiming with a loud voice, "Who is worthy to open the book and to break its seals?"
> 3. And no one in heaven or on the earth or under the earth was able to open the book or to look into it.
> 4. Then I began to weep greatly because no one was found worthy to open the book or to look into it… (Rev 5:1-4)

This scroll was sealed by God Himself, authenticated as revealing His will, but only One 'in heaven or on the earth or under the earth' can open it - Jesus:

> 5. and one of the elders said to me, "Stop weeping; behold, the Lion that is from the tribe of Judah, the Root of David,

> has overcome so as to open the book and its seven seals"…
> 7. And He came and took the book out of the right hand of Him who sat on the throne. (Rev 5:5-7)

There are seven seals because, as on Creation's seventh day, seven symbolises perfection and completion (Gen 1:31, 2:2-3). Here is the point: the seven seals authenticate the scroll in Revelation as revealing the perfect and complete will of God *for John's audience* in the 1st century and for all of us right *up to Judgement Day*. As will become obvious, the first five seals portray not what God is doing but what, in His sovereignty, He is allowing to occur. I will also show that they are not consecutive but concurrent while the last two *are* Judgement Day.

Trumpets

Most cultures, old and new, have some form of horn or trumpet for music and celebration, alarms, and battlefield communication. They attract attention, as Jesus taught in His famous metaphor:

> "…when you give to the poor, do not sound a trumpet before you, as the hypocrites do in the synagogues and in the streets, so that they may be honored by men…"
> (Matt 6:2)

However, we Gentiles need to know how they were used in Jewish history.

(i) General use

Israel had two silver trumpets to make announcements:

> 2. "Make yourself two trumpets of silver, of hammered work you shall make them; and you shall use them for summoning the congregation and for *having the camps set out…*

7. "When convening the assembly, however, you shall blow without sounding an alarm." (Num 10:2 & 7*)

They blew them to warn of imminent attack (Neh 4:18-20) and as an act of faith to call on God:

> "When you go to war in your land against the adversary who attacks you, then you shall sound *an alarm* with the trumpets, that you may be *remembered* before the LORD your God, and be saved from your enemies." (Num 10:9*)

Trumpets were also for celebration, to invoke God in their festivals and new moons:

> "Also in the day of your gladness and in your appointed feasts, and on the first days of your months, you shall blow *the trumpets* over your burnt offerings, and over the sacrifices of your peace offerings; and they shall be *as a reminder* of you before your God. I am the LORD your God." (Num 10:10*)

The seventh month's first day was particularly sanctified by the trumpets (Num 29:1), giving them ten days to prepare for the Day of Atonement (Num 29:7).

The purpose of Revelation's trumpets is likewise to gain our attention. But why? Are we to gather, move on, celebrate, prepare, or be alert to attack? As I will demonstrate, the first six trumpets are *alarms* regarding 'the signs of the times' (Matt 16:1-3), all to prepare us for the seventh at Jesus' return.

(ii) Proclaiming freedom

Every fifty years, a shofar, i.e. a trumpet made from a ram's horn, was to be blown in the forty-ninth year (Lev 25:8) of their calendar:

> 9. "You shall then sound *a ram's horn* abroad on the tenth day of the seventh month; on the Day of Atonement you

> shall sound a horn all through your land.
> 10. "'You shall thus consecrate the fiftieth year and *proclaim a release through the land to all its inhabitants*. It shall be a jubilee for you, and each of you shall return to his own property, and each of you shall return to his family." (Lev 25:9-10*)

This shofar proclaimed that the coming year would be "a jubilee" (v. 10), freeing them from all their debts and restoring them to any lost family land, ensuring that every generation could have a fresh start with resources.

The Seven Trumpets

There is also extraordinary significance in John seeing and hearing seven trumpets which no 1st century Jewish teenager would have missed.

(i) Conquering Jericho

One of the greatest victories in their long and storied history was due to seven trumpets bringing down the walls of Jericho:

> 4. "...seven priests shall carry *seven trumpets* of rams' horns before the ark; then on the seventh day you shall march around the city and the priests shall blow the trumpets. 5. "It shall be that when they make a long blast with the ram's horn, and when you *hear the sound of the trumpet*, all the people shall shout with a great shout; and the wall of the city will fall down flat, and the people will go up every man straight ahead." (Josh 6:4-5*)

Just as Israel laid siege to the seemingly impregnable walls of the great Canaanite city, in Revelation God is laying siege to the whole world - its "walls" will come tumbling down at the 7th Trumpet, which also announces the resurrection for Judgement Day.

As I will show, the first six of John's trumpets have been sounding increasingly loudly over the last hundred years.

(ii) The Resurrection

If we are alive on that day, we will not be resurrected but we will be transformed:

> 51. Behold, I tell you a mystery; we will not all sleep, but we will *all be changed,*
> 52. in a moment, in the twinkling of an eye, *at the last trumpet*; for the trumpet will sound, and the dead will be raised imperishable, and we will be changed.
> (1 Cor 15:51-52*)

Paul rephrased this for the Thessalonians:

> 16. For the Lord Himself will descend from heaven with a shout, with the voice of the archangel and *with the trumpet of God*, and the dead in Christ will rise first.
> 17. Then we who are alive and remain will be caught up together with them in the clouds to meet the Lord in the air, and so we shall always be with the Lord. (1 Thess 4:16-17*)

Some argue that Paul's naming of this trumpet as 'the last' does not necessarily mean it is John's 7th Trumpet but there is no other trumpet mentioned in Revelation after the seventh. When we come to look at that in Chapter 13, the parallel will be obvious.

We will also see that, like the seals, the six trumpets are not consecutive but concurrent. And, I believe, began sounding over the last fifty to one hundred years.

Have you heard them?

The Bowls

The Greek word John uses, *phiale,* was translated by the *KJV* as 'vial' so we still hear of 'the vials of wrath' today. However, today a vial is a 'small, usually cylindrical glass vessel for holding liquid medicines etc',[26] like a test tube with a cap whereas the Greek meant 'a broad shallow bowl [or] deep saucer',[27] in this instance made of gold (Rev 15:7).

Fig (i) Gold phiale c. 4 BC Greece

These were not just any kind of bowl. The Romans called them *patera* and they were used in Greek and Roman temples for pouring out libations, i.e. drink offerings to their gods, as you can see in this Greek statue (see photo). They could be ceramic, as in black-glaze terracotta,[28] or metal, i.e. gold, silver, or bronze, depending on the wealth of the family.

Libations were an essential part of ancient Greek and Roman religion and daily life as shown in their art and coins, with the most dutiful offering them every morning and evening and to begin meals. They mostly used wine and water but also honey, oil, or milk. The ritual consisted of pouring the liquid from a jug into a *phiale* while praying; they then poured a portion from the *phiale* onto an altar and drank

---
26   *Concise Oxford Dictionary*, p. 1196.
27   (Strong's G5357) www.biblestudytools.com/lexicons/greek/nas/phiale.html, 8 Feb, 2023.
28   www.artic.edu/artworks/87663/phiale-shallow-bowl-for-pouring-ritual-libations, 9 Feb, 2023.

the rest. John's Gentile audience would have known the significance of *phiale* but his Jewish listeners would have recognised another layer of meaning, dating back over 1,500 years. His golden bowls came from the Tabernacle of Moses (Ex 25:29) and Solomon's Temple (1 Chron 28:17) and featured in a very famous feast in 539 BC, famous because it led to the 'writing on the wall' of a Babylonian palace.

Fig (ii) Roman priestess with phiale c. 3 AD

Belshazzar's Feast

When the Babylonians razed Jerusalem and the Temple in 586 BC, their army returned to Babylon with much booty. Some forty years later, Daniel the prophet recorded that they not only desecrated the holy vessels but used them to worship their idols:

> 1. Belshazzar the king held a great feast for a thousand of his nobles...
> 2. ...he gave orders to bring the gold and silver vessels which Nebuchadnezzar his father had taken out of the temple which was in Jerusalem, so that the king and his nobles, his wives and his concubines might drink from them.
> 3. Then they brought the gold vessels that had been taken out of the temple, the house of God which was in Jerusalem; and the king and his nobles, his wives and his concubines drank from them.
> 4. They drank the wine and praised the gods of gold and silver, of bronze, iron, wood and stone. (Dan 5:1-4*)

But they were interrupted:

> 5. Suddenly the fingers of a man's hand emerged and began writing opposite the lampstand on the plaster of the wall of the king's palace, and the king saw the back of the hand that did the writing.
> 6. Then the king's face grew pale and his thoughts alarmed him, and his hip joints went slack and his knees began knocking together. (Dan 5:5-6)

Belshazzar's 'seeing the writing on the wall' is proverbial to this day as portending a calamity because the unearthly hand wrote a cryptic note that Daniel interpreted for him:

> 26. "This is the interpretation of the message: 'MENE'-- God has numbered your kingdom and put an end to it.
> 27. " 'TEKEL'--you have been weighed on the scales and found deficient.
> 28. "'PERES'--your kingdom has been divided and given over to the Medes and Persians." (Dan 5:26-28)

The explanation was blunt:

> 23. "…you have *exalted yourself* against the Lord of heaven; and they have brought the vessels of His house before you, and you and your nobles, your wives and your concubines have been drinking wine from them; and you have praised the gods of *silver and gold, of bronze, iron, wood and stone, which do not see, hear or understand*. But the God in whose hand are your life-breath and all your ways, you have not glorified." (Dan 5:23*)

Belshazzar and his empire fell to Darius's Medo-Persian army and he was slain 'that same night' (Dan 5:30).

Would John's Jewish audience have made the connection with Belshazzar's feast? John even paraphrased Daniel 5:23 so that they could:

> 20. The rest of mankind, who were not killed by these

plagues, did not repent of the works of their hands, so as not to worship demons, and *the idols of gold and of silver and of brass and of stone and of wood which can neither see nor hear* nor walk (Rev 9:20*)

John's vision of the bowls is predicting that just like Belshazzar, his thousand nobles, and their wives and concubines in 539 BC, *the whole world* will still be rejecting our Creator and worshipping deaf, dumb, blind, and immobile idols right up until Judgement Day.

The Seven Bowls

John's vision of seven bowls also contains three metaphors very familiar to the Jews in his 1st century audience:

(i) Pouring out of wrath

When we fail to control our anger, our outbursts or fits of anger are called 'deeds of the flesh' (Gal 5:19-20). God's anger, however, is never uncontrolled - it is His righteous response to injustice and always restrained by His love and patience. 'Wrath' can seem today to be an old-fashioned word for anger but it has an implicit sense of 'punishment or vengeance as a manifestation of anger'[29] and God only pours out His wrath as punishment for wrongdoing:

> "Now I will shortly *pour out My wrath* on you and spend My anger against you; judge you according to your ways and bring on you all your abominations." (Ezek 7:8*)

> "[Israel] did not walk in My statutes, nor were they careful to observe My ordinances... they profaned My sabbaths. So I resolved to *pour out My wrath* on them, to accomplish My anger against them in the wilderness." (Eze 20:21*)[30]

---

29 *The American Heritage® Dictionary of the English Language*, 5th Edition.
30 See also Psalm 79:6; Jeremiah 6:11, 10:25; Ezekiel 14:19, and Hosea 5:10.

(ii) Metaphorical cups

Another familiar metaphor for them was God giving cups to be drunk by those He is judging. For example, Jeremiah prophesied:

> 15. For thus the LORD, the God of Israel, says to me, "Take this *cup of the wine of wrath* from My hand and cause all the nations to whom I send you to drink it.
> 16. "They will drink and stagger and go mad because of the sword that I will send among them." (Jer 25:15-16*)

Jeremiah says he gave it to the kings of Judah, Egypt, Philistia, Edom, Moab, Arabia, and all the surrounding nations (vv. 18-26) prior to the Persians conquering them all.

Zechariah prophesied as we saw in Book 5[31] that prior to the Battle of Har-Magedon, God's cup will be the holy city and He will judge all who are foolish enough to besiege it:

> "Behold, I am going to make Jerusalem *a cup that causes reeling* to all the peoples around… And in that day I will set about to destroy all the nations that come against Jerusalem" (Zech 12:2 & 9)

Jesus drank the cup of God's wrath on the cross so that we could be forgiven. He had to agonise in prayer three times to steel His resolve to accept it:

> 39. And He went a little beyond them, and fell on His face and prayed, saying, "My Father, if it is possible, let *this cup pass* from Me; yet not as I will, but as You will"…
> 42. He went away again a second time and prayed, saying, "My Father, if this cannot pass away unless I drink it, Your will be done"…
> 44. And He… went away and prayed a third time, saying the same thing once more. (Matt 26:39-44*)

---

31 *Threshing Hour,* pp. 66-67.

(iii) Seven meaning complete

As shown in Book 3, 'seven' can be a metaphor that means:

> ...justly, completely, or perfectly. It originates from the seventh day or Sabbath, when God rested from all His works - He had finished Creation to the state of goodness or perfection, i.e. nothing was wrong or lacking (Gen 1:31). God's striking Israel seven times was to punish their sins perfectly, and the blood being sprinkled seven times was to make perfect atonement for them.[32]

Seven bowls therefore signify, as noted earlier, God's complete and final temporal punishments on the earth before He delivers His eternal judgement:

> Then I saw another sign in heaven, great and marvelous, seven angels who had seven plagues, which are the *last*, because in them the wrath of God is *finished*. (Rev 15:1*)

> Then the seventh angel poured out his bowl upon the air, and a loud voice came out of the temple from the throne, saying, "*It is done!*" (Rev 16:17*)

Like the seals and trumpets, the bowls are not consecutive but concurrent. They will also be very brief, as I will show in Chapter 21.

Summary

(i) Jesus opens the seals on the scroll to reveal the will of God regarding what He will *allow* to happen until Judgement Day.

(ii) The trumpets are alarms, signs of the times, alerting us to what we have done, to where we are up to within mankind's history. Most have taken place over the

---

32   *Threshing Hour*, pp. 66-67.

last 80-100 years and the seventh will announce Jesus' return and the Resurrection for Judgement Day.

(iii) The bowls are God's temporal judgements that precede and confirm the certainty and reasons for Judgement Day and eternal judgement.

3
The Seven Seals
Business as Usual

As noted earlier, the four schools of interpretation, Preterist, Historicist, Futurist, and Idealist, attribute different timings for the seven seals. Preterists believe the seals refer to events before 70 AD; Historicists, that they refer to eras over the last 2,000 years; Futurists, that they refer to future events; and Idealists, that the seals refer not to events or eras but to overall trends.

Idealists therefore see the 1st Seal as the gospel going forth; seals two to four represent the disintegration of human civilisation and the natural realm due to the rejecting of the gospel; the 5th Seal reveals that believers will suffer until the 6th Seal which is the Second Coming.

I believe the Idealists are almost right but with a small twist – the first five seals are not revealing new trends or the disintegration of human civilisation but rather, saying, "It's business as usual" until the 6th and 7th.

We will look at each seal but let us first establish their 1st century context.

Burning Questions

Consider John's original audience in c. 95 AD – what would they really want to know?

(i) "When is Jesus coming back?"

It had been sixty-five years since Jesus had ascended to the right hand of the Father but promising to return. It had been thirty years since Peter had died, teaching that He could come tomorrow or in a thousand years' time (2 Pet 3:8-9). Likewise Paul, but adding that 'the apostasy comes first, and the man of lawlessness is revealed' (2 Thess 2:3-8). Now John is seemingly about to die, so what can he add?

(ii) "Has God given up on Jerusalem and the Jews?"

As mentioned earlier, in 30 AD, the disciples were all Jewish so a burning question for them was the crisis facing their fellow-countrymen and their nation:

> 6. So when they had come together, they were asking Him, saying, "Lord, is it at this time You are restoring the *kingdom to Israel*?" (Acts 1:6*)

Jesus answered them:

> 7. ... "It is not for you to know times or epochs which the Father has fixed by His own authority;
> 8. *but you will receive power* when the Holy Spirit has come upon you; and you shall be My witnesses both in Jerusalem, and in all Judea and Samaria, and even *to the remotest part of the earth.*" (Act 1:6-8*)

By 95 AD, they had seen the power of the Holy Spirit and the gospel spreading throughout the Roman Empire but not 'to the remotest part of the earth' (v. 8). That would not be until 1814, when the gospel finally reached New Zealand and the Pacific Islands at the furthest point on earth from Jerusalem.

The Jewish disciples had also seen Israel and their city of Jerusalem face devastating judgement in 70 AD, just as Jesus had predicted (Luke 21:20-24), and it must have seemed to many then, as it still does to some Biblical scholars today, that God had finally forsaken the Jewish nation. However, as we saw in Book 1's exposition of Revelation 12, and in Book 4's exposition of Revelation 11:1-13, God has not and never will give up on Jerusalem and the Jews. He promises to preserve Israel as "a nation" as long as the sun, moon, and stars exist (Jer 31:35-37).

(iii) "Why are we still being killed?"

This was a perfectly reasonable question to ask, given that Jesus has 'all authority in heaven and earth' (Matt 28:18). John hears even the martyrs in heaven asking about this:

> 9. ... I saw underneath the altar the souls of those who had been slain because of the word of God, and because of the testimony which they had maintained;
> 10. and they cried out with a loud voice, saying, "How long, O Lord, holy and true, will You refrain from judging and avenging our blood on those who dwell on the earth?" (Rev 6:9-10)

The divine answer is that many more are yet to be martyred (Rev 6:11), overcome (Rev 13:7), persecuted and exiled (Rev 1:9), imprisoned and enslaved (Rev 13:9-10). The disciples would therefore just have to wait while God works out His purpose for the whole human race.

(iv) "What will happen after John dies?"

John is very old and the last of the Twelve – what will happen after he is gone? There had also been a misunderstanding:

> ...this saying went out among the brethren that that disciple [John] would not die; yet Jesus did not say to him that he would not die, but only, "If I want him to remain until I come, what is that to you?" (John 21:23)

John knows he *will* die and the disciples are not to worry

because, as we saw in Book 3,[33] the Twelve were only the beginning, the foundation, of 12 x 12 x 1,000 apostles who will complete the eternal city of God, New Jerusalem. We will look at them again in Chapter 5, when we consider the gap between the 6th and 7th Seals.

The First Four Seals

The seals are opened to answer the third question, "If Jesus has 'all authority in heaven and earth', why are we still being killed?" They reveal the express *will of God* from when Jesus received 'all authority in heaven and on the earth' – He alone can open the seals - until He returns to change everything. In other words, what He will *allow* to happen on the earth in the meantime.

Consider this: what had changed in the whole world with Jesus' coming? Nothing, politically. Israel had not been redeemed from Roman domination and although the kingdom was growing day by day, individual by individual, it was yet to affect the principalities and powers in 'the kingdom of the world' (Rev 11:15).[34]

So what was God's will for John's audience in the 1st century?

The first four seals reveal four horsemen, the famous Four Horsemen of the Apocalypse:

> 1. Then I saw when the Lamb broke one of the seven seals, and I heard one of the four living creatures saying as with a voice of thunder, "Come."
> 2. I looked, and behold, a white horse, and he who sat on it had a bow; and a crown was given to him, and he went out conquering and to conquer. (Rev 6:1-2)

---

33   *Gotta Serve Somebody*, pp. 147.
34   I will cover this in detail in my forthcoming *The Pearl in Plain Sight: Kingdom, Christendom & Colonisation*.

We are not told who the royal archer is, whom he will conquer, or where this will take place. He is followed by a swordsman:

> 3. When He broke the second seal, I heard the second living creature saying, "Come."
> 4. And another, a red horse, went out; and to him who sat on it, it was granted to take peace from the earth, and that men would slay one another; and a great sword was given to him. (Rev 6:3-4)

Wherever he goes, men will kill each other. The third horseman is unarmed but his scales are to weigh out a scarcity of food:

> 5. When He broke the third seal, I heard the third living creature saying, "Come." I looked, and behold, a black horse; and he who sat on it had a pair of scales in his hand.
> 6. And I heard something like a voice in the center of the four living creatures saying, "A quart of wheat for a denarius, and three quarts of barley for a denarius; and do not damage the oil and the wine." (Rev 6:5-6)

The fourth horseman is the most frightening:

> 7. When the Lamb broke the fourth seal, I heard the voice of the fourth living creature saying, "Come."
> 8. I looked, and behold, an ashen horse; and he who sat on it had the name Death; and Hades was following with him. Authority was given to them over a fourth of the earth, to kill with sword and with famine and with pestilence and by the wild beasts of the earth. (Rev 6:7-8)

It is easy to assume that the fourfold command, 'Come' (vv. 1, 3, 5, 7), means the horsemen are being introduced to the world, that each seal is the beginning of a new tribulation, but consider:

(i) Was conquering (v. 2) new to them in the 1st century?

(ii) Was warfare (v. 4)?

(iii) Or famine (v. 5-6)?

(iv) Or Death and Hades (v. 8)?

Of course not. For 1st century disciples, these events and tribulations were 'business as usual'.

The Fifth Seal

The 5th Seal was also not a new event nor a future era:

> 9. When the Lamb broke the fifth seal, I saw underneath the altar the souls of those who had been slain because of the word of God, and because of the testimony which they had maintained;
> 10. and they cried out with a loud voice, saying, "How long, O Lord, holy and true, will You refrain from judging and avenging our blood on those who dwell on the earth?"
> (Rev 6:9-10)

John's audience were all too familiar with martyrdom, having lost many including their major leaders. John hears the martyrs, impatient for vindication, but they will all have to wait until death and Hades are destroyed when the Lord returns to raise the dead. In the meantime, many more will be martyred.

The first five seals reveal that Jesus coming as Messiah and receiving 'all authority in heaven and on the earth' was *not* to end conquering armies, warfare, famine, and murderous persecution of His followers. These will all continue until He returns to reign.

None of this was new to John. Sixty-five years earlier, when Jesus was asked when He would return, He had replied:

6. "You will be hearing of *wars* and *rumors of wars*. See that you are not frightened, for those things must take place, but that is not yet the end.
7. "For nation will rise against nation, and kingdom against kingdom, and in various places there will be *famines* and earthquakes.
8. "But all these things are merely the beginning of birth pangs.
9. "Then they will deliver you to tribulation, and will *kill you*, and you will be hated by all nations because of My name." (Matt 24:6-9*)

In the plainest of words, Jesus said there will be conquering armies (v. 7), warfare, actual and threatened (v. 6), famines (v. 7), and martyrs (v. 9) until He returns. John's five seals and four horsemen are simply illustrating this in graphic style.

Zechariah's Scroll

As shown in Book 4,[35] several of John's visions can only be understood in the light of Zechariah's visions from six hundred years earlier: John's 'measuring' of the Temple (Rev 11:1-2) echoes Zechariah's vision of a man measuring Jerusalem (Zech 2:1-5); John's two witnesses being 'the two olive trees and the two lampstands that stand before the Lord of the earth' (Rev 11:4) references Zechariah's two olive trees which continuously feed a lampstand (Zech 4:2-3) and 'are standing by the Lord of the whole earth' (Zech 4:14).[36]

Zechariah also saw a scroll. In his vision, however, the scroll is not sealed but open for all to read. It is also flying and it is enormous:

---

35 *Silencing the Witnesses.*
36 I was able to show these witnesses would have been clearly understood by a 1st century Jewish audience as symbolising the Law and the Prophets, giving unending light to the Jewish nation regarding Jesus as Messiah, their great need of Him due to their clearly defined sinfulness, and the reason behind the destruction of the Second Temple and Jerusalem, as well as all subsequent misfortunes.

> 1. Then I lifted up my eyes again and looked, and behold, there was a flying scroll.
> 2. And he said to me, "What do you see?" And I answered, "I see a flying scroll; its length is twenty cubits and its width ten cubits." (Zech 5:1-2)

That is, ten metres long and five metres wide.[37] The angel explains:

> 3. Then he said to me, "This is the curse that is going forth over the face of *the whole land*; surely *everyone who steals* will be purged away according to the writing on one side, and *everyone who swears* will be purged away according to the writing on the other side.
> 4. "I will make it go forth," declares the LORD of hosts, "and it will enter the house of *the thief* and the house of *the one who swears falsely by My name*; and it will spend the night within that house and consume it with its timber and stones." (Zech 5:3-4*)

Zechariah's scroll was to reveal God's wrath against dishonesty throughout "the whole land" of Israel (v. 3) in the 6th century BC, in behaviour and in speech. This was the time of Israel's restoration from the Babylonian exile: the Temple was being rebuilt, Jerusalem was being rebuilt, but God was not going to allow corruption to sneak back in among them.

John's scroll, however, reveals God's will for the whole world in John's time, in the 1st century.

Zechariah's Horsemen

> 8. I saw at night, and behold, a man was riding on a red horse, and he was standing among the myrtle trees which were in the ravine, with red, sorrel and white horses behind him.
> 9. Then I said, "My lord, what are these?" And the angel

---

[37] For comparison, the Great Isaiah Scroll, 1QIsaa of the Dead Sea Scrolls, is 7.34 metres long and only ¼ metre wide (or high – it is read from the side).

who was speaking with me said to me, "I will show you what these are."
10. And the man who was standing among the myrtle trees answered and said, "These are those whom the LORD has sent to patrol the earth." (Zech 1:8-10)

He only mentions one rider but there were at least four since the other 'red, sorrel, and white horses' (v. 8) would not be sent without them. In Jewish thinking, four symbolises 'the four corners of the earth' (Rev 7:1) - north, south, east, and west – and they are sent "to patrol the earth" (v. 10).

The horses' colours are translated by the *NASB, KJV,* and *NKJV* as red, sorrel, and white. Sorrel means chestnut brown so the *NIV* has 'red, brown and white'. However, *The Jewish Study Bible*[38] has them as 'bay, sorrel, and white' and notes that the Septuagint adds 'dappled' to the second 'bay'. We are not told the significance of the colours - although the white horse was a rarity in those days, the leading horseman is riding a common red.[39] We are told they were sent by the Lord 'to patrol the earth' (v. 10) and report to Him:

11. So they answered the angel of the LORD who was standing among the myrtle trees and said, "We have patrolled the earth, and behold, all the earth is peaceful and quiet." (Zech 1:11)

It was "peaceful and quiet" in 520 BC because the Babylonians had been defeated by the Medo-Persians who had ended

---

38 *The Jewish Study Bible*, feat. Jewish Publication Society, Oxford University Press, 2004, p. 1251.
39 Genetic studies of horse colours today show that all variations and patterns stem from just two colours: chestnut brown (often called red) and black. The 'bay' is the most common variation - a chestnut body with 'black points', i.e. a black mane, tail, ear edges, and lower legs. The 'red' simply has no black points. Dappling and greying occurs due to a lack of pigmentation in either skin or hair – a grey horse, for example, has black skin but white or mixed black and white hairs. There is also fading due to age and sunlight. The white horse is rare, having white hair and fully or mostly unpigmented skin. Born white, they cannot fade so they remain white for life but the vast majority of what are called white horses are actually grey with a fully white hair coat.

Israel's exile and were allowing the restoration of Jerusalem and the rebuilding of the Temple.

Zechariah's Four Chariots

Zechariah then sees four chariots drawn by similarly coloured horses:

> 1. Now I lifted up my eyes again and looked, and behold, four chariots were coming forth from between the two mountains; and the mountains were bronze mountains.
> 2. With the first chariot were red horses, with the second chariot black horses,
> 3. with the third chariot white horses, and with the fourth chariot strong dappled horses. (Zech 6:1-3)

Chariots were used for hunting and were also fearsome weapons of war in the ancient world, devastating to foot soldiers because of their speed and providing a platform for an archer and/or a warrior wielding a spear or battle-axe. The great powers, the Egyptians, Assyrians, Babylonians, Persians, Greeks, and Romans, made extensive use of them; Solomon established 'chariot cities' (1 Kin 10:26) to protect his kingdom's borders and his capital, Jerusalem (1 Kin 9:15-19).

Fig (iii) The seal of Darius the Great c. 500 BC

In Zechariah's day, the Medo-Persians had used them to build the greatest, most extensive empire ever seen, with Greek historian Herodotus (484-c.425 BC) commenting:

> The armoured Persian horsemen and their death-dealing chariots were invincible. No man dared face them.[40]

What then of Zechariah's heavenly chariots? They represent the truly invincible armies of God:

> 4. Then I spoke and said to the angel who was speaking with me, "What are these, my lord?"
> 5. The angel replied to me, "These are the *four spirits of heaven*, going forth after standing before the Lord of all the earth…" (Zech 6:4-5*)

Emerging from between two bronze mountains (v. 1), which represent God's righteous judgements (Psa 36:6), the chariots drawn by the red, black, and white horses went north while the chariot drawn by the dappled went south (v. 6), the Lord explaining:

> 8. "See, those who are going to the land of the north have appeased My wrath in the land of the north." (Zech 6:8)

Zechariah is prophesying in Israel and Israel has always been invaded from the north and the south (e.g. Dan 11:40-41); the sea is to the west and their only harbour then at Joppa was too small, while to the east was the Arabian Desert. Accordingly, the ancient empires to their east – the Assyrian, Babylonian, and Medo-Persian Empires – skirted around the desert to attack from the north. Only the Egyptians came from the south.

It may therefore be that Zechariah's four chariots were to illustrate God's protection of Israel from the Egyptian,

---

[40] A hundred years later, in 331 BC, Alexander the Great's Greek armies did dare and overcame them at the Battle of Gaugamela.

Assyrian, Babylonian, and Medo-Persia Empires; what is beyond doubt, however, is that He has dealt with all of Israel's enemies so they can rebuild Jerusalem and the Temple.

The Chariots of God

As Herodotus recorded, the Medo-Persians were renowned for their chariots but Zechariah is seeing that their defeating of "the land of the north", the Babylonians, was not due to their might and power but to the hand of God and His heavenly armies.

Six centuries earlier, Elisha's ministry began when he saw 'a chariot of fire and horses of fire' accompanying Elijah when he was taken up into heaven (2 Kin 2:11). This became so normal to him that he later reassured his attendant:

> 15. Now when the attendant of the man of God had risen early and gone out, behold, an army with horses and chariots was circling the city. And his servant said to him, "Alas, my master! What shall we do?"
> 16. So he answered, "Do not fear, for those who are with us are more than those who are with them."
> 17. Then Elisha prayed and said, "O LORD, I pray, open his eyes that he may see." And the LORD opened the servant's eyes and he saw; and behold, the mountain was full of *horses and chariots of fire* all around Elisha.
> (2 Kin 6:15-17*)

We too can be reassured of God's sovereignty in every situation as we read of the horses John saw but let us first summarise what we have seen so far.

Summary

(i) John's original audience in 95 AD had many very natural concerns. Even though Jesus had been raised from the dead with "all authority in heaven and on earth" in 30 AD, He had left them - when was He coming back?

(ii) The Roman Empire still ruled over them, having razed the holy city of Jerusalem and the Temple in 70 AD. His Jewish disciples wanted to know, has God abandoned Israel? Why were Paul, Peter, John's brother James, Jesus' brother James, and innumerable disciples still being martyred? What would happen after John, the last of the Twelve died?

(iii) Jesus' opening of the seven seals of God's scroll was, like Zechariah's scroll, to reveal His will for His people until He returns. Nothing in the first five seals was new to them – conquering, warfare, famine, death and Hades, believers being killed for their faith - it was business, or life, as usual.

(iv) The dreaded four horsemen are actually to give us hope, just as Zechariah's did for the Jews in 6th century BC. They reassure us that God is not only acutely aware of every empire and power on earth but, as we will see in the next chapter, He has set limits for them, appointed tasks for them, and will bring them all to an end as we saw in Book 5, *Threshing Hour: Armageddon & Babylon the Great*.

4
God's Will
For Them & Us

First Seal – White Horse

> 1. Then I saw when the Lamb broke one of the seven seals, and I heard one of the four living creatures saying as with a voice of thunder, "Come."
> 2. I looked, and behold, a white horse, and he who sat on it had a bow; and a crown was given to him, and he went out conquering and to conquer. (Rev 6:1-2)

Today, commentators are divided over whether the rider is Jesus, the gospel, the Roman Empire, or the Antichrist[41] but like John, we are not told his identity. Why? Because he is just *an image*, but a very familiar image to John's intended audience in the seven churches in 1st century Asia Minor.

These churches were at the eastern edge of the Roman Empire and their next door neighbours for hundreds of years both before and after then were the Parthians and the Scythians who were renowned for developing horse archery.

The Parthians

As depicted over the page in Fig (iv), their tactics included the Parthian shot which required superb equestrian skills - while in real or feigned retreat at full gallop, the archer would turn

---

[41] Preterists interpret the rider as symbolising the Roman Empire, with Nero as the Antichrist, sending Vespasian to suppress the Great Jewish Revolt in 67 AD. Historicists, however, believe it is the gospel going forth from various dates in the 1st century: 30 AD, 73 AD, or 96 AD. Futurists believe it is the future Antichrist reviving the Roman Empire after the Secret Rapture of the church, whereas Idealists see it as the gospel of the conquering Christ throughout the ages.

his upper torso to shoot at the pursuing enemy. Hands fully occupied by the composite bow (which they had invented) and without stirrups (which they later invented), the rider relied solely on pressure from his legs to stay mounted and to guide the horse.

In 53 BC, at the Battle of Carrhae, the Parthians' mounted archers had defeated Rome in one of the most crushing defeats in Roman history, killing their general, Marcus Crassus,[42] his son, Publius, and 20,000 soldiers, as well as capturing 10,000 more.[43]

Twenty years later, Rome's most famous poet, Virgil, (70-19 BC) dreamed of the day when Augustus would defeat them:

> With backward bows the Parthians shall be there,
> And, spurring from the fight, confess their fear.
> A double wreath shall crown our Caesar's brow...[44]

Virgil read this to Augustus when he returned from defeating Antony and Cleopatra at the Battle of Actium in 31 BC but it was never to be. The crown was won instead by the Parthians.

'Went Out Conquering...'

Sir William Ramsay (1851-1939) was a Scottish archaeologist and New Testament scholar and considered to be the foremost authority of his day on the history of Asia Minor. He wrote:

> The writers of that period often mention the Parthian terror on the East, and their devastating incursions were

---

42 One of the Republic's richest men as well as a consul, Crassus had secretly aligned with Julius Caesar and Pompey, two other generals and consuls, to thwart the Senate's control and steer the Republic before Julius Caesar took sole control. They have been referred to as First Triumvirate but modern scholars dispute the term.
43 Plutarch, *The Life of Crassus*, 31:7. http://penelope.uchicago.edu/Thayer/E/Roman/Texts/Plutarch/Lives/Crassus*.html, 12 Nov, 2018.
44 *The Third Book of the Georgics*, lines 48-50; *The Works of Virgil*, Vol 2, trans. Dryden, 1792, p. 5.

so much dreaded at that time that Trajan undertook a Parthian war in 115 AD.[45]

Accordingly, Sir William interpreted the rider as the king of the Parthians. He went on:

> Colour was also an important and significant detail. The Parthian king in vi. 2 rides on a white horse. White had been the sacred colour among the old Persians, for whom the Parthians stood in later times; and sacred white horses accompanied every Persian army. The commentators who try to force a Roman meaning on this figure say that the Roman general, when celebrating a Triumph, rode on a white horse. This is a mistake; the general in a Triumph wore the purple and gold-embroidered robes of Jupiter, and was borne like the god in a four-horse car.[46]

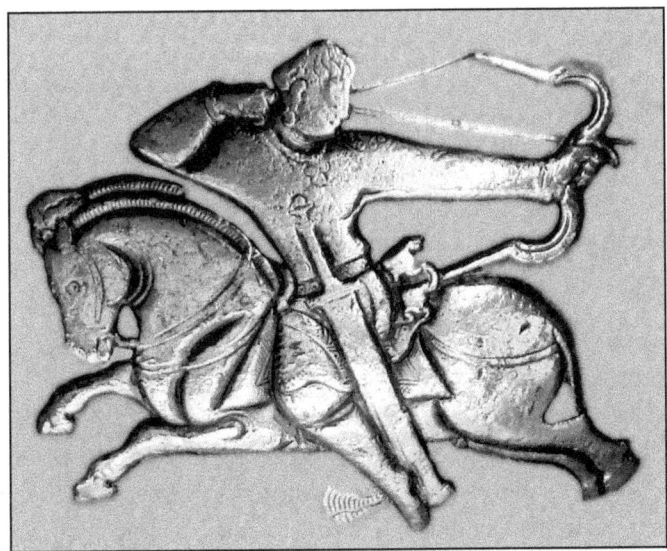

Fig (iv) Hephthalite image of Parthian shot c. 470 AD

---

45 W. H. Ramsay, *The Letters to the Seven Churches*, p. 58.
46 Ibid.

The Parthian Empire (247 BC – 224 AD) rivalled Rome's, extending from the Euphrates to the Indus rivers, i.e. most of today's Iran, Iraq, and Afghanistan. Their successors, the Sassanid Empire (224-651 AD), were also famous archers on horseback, and they defeated Galerius in 298 AD.

John's white horse, being rare, is worthy of a king and signifies the victory described in the rider's commission and coronation – he is sent forth 'conquering and to conquer'.

We see then that John's first horseman would have been easily recognised by his 1st century audience as the ever-present threat to Rome's primacy. The second, third, and fourth horsemen naturally followed – war, famine, death, and Hades, just as they always have done. Rome was eventually sacked in 451 AD but *conquering armies have never ceased*, just as Jesus said.

Second Seal – Red Horse

> 3. When He broke the second seal, I heard the second living creature saying, "Come."
> 4. And another, a red horse, went out; and to him who sat on it, it was granted to take peace from the earth, and that men would slay one another; and a great sword was given to him. (Rev 6:3-4)

Again, what would this have meant to John's 1st century hearers?

We saw earlier in Zechariah's vision that there is no obvious significance in the horse being red and we are not told of any here either. The most common colours in horses are chestnut brown (usually called red) and black so John's audience would have frequently seen red and black horses.

As for the rider taking 'peace from the earth' (v. 4), consider the context: John's intended audience were living in the time of the *Pax Romana*, i.e. Roman Peace, the golden age of Rome ushered in by Augustus Caesar in 27 BC. For hundreds of years before then, the Roman Republic had faced constant warfare, both within and without. Plutarch, the 1st century historian, observed that they had appointed Julius Caesar (100-44 BC) as dictator for life:

> ... in the hope that the government of a single person would give them time to breathe after so many civil wars and calamities. This was indeed a tyranny avowed, since his power was not only absolute, but perpetual too.[47]

However, he was assassinated by Brutus and his co-conspirators and Rome was plunged into yet another civil war until his grand-nephew Octavian overcame all rivals and was granted the title Augustus Caesar in 27 BC:

> To many, Augustus, for his achievements, was a god on earth; only a supra-human being could have brought stability out of chaos. Not surprisingly, therefore, Augustus found himself the object of acclamations of divinity.[48]

As shown in Book 2,[49] this was the beginning of the antichrist regimes in Rome. Augustus allowed the populace in Pergamum to worship *Dea Roma et Augustus,* i.e. Rome and himself. In the imagery of Revelation 13, this was the second beast (the spirit of antichrist) causing the people to worship the first beast (at that time, Rome) and the image of that beast (the emperor).

It was during the Pax Romana - a two hundred year period of unprecedented peace, stability, and economic prosperity - that the empire reached its greatest extent and a population of some 70 million people. It ended with the death of Marcus Aurelius, the last of the Five Good Emperors, in 180 AD. He

---

47 *Lives of Noble Greeks and Romans,* Plutarch (50-120 A.D).
48 David Colin Arthur Shotter, *Augustus Caesar,* New York; Routledge, 2nd edition, 2005, p. 72.
49 *Slouching Towards Bethlehem,* pp. 97-100.

was succeeded by his son Commodus whose disastrous reign was portrayed in the movie, *Gladiator*.[50]

John's intended audience in 95-96 AD were therefore living in the middle of this 'peace' and would have understood his vision as revealing that the Pax Romana would be 'taken from the earth'. All subsequent audiences were to understand that any peace created by any conquering empire will only be short-term, just as Jesus taught:

> 6. "You will be hearing of wars and rumors of wars. See that you are not frightened, for those things must take place, but that is not yet the end.
>
> 7. "For nation will rise against nation, and kingdom against kingdom, and in various places there will be famines..." (Matt 24-6-8*)

Third Seal – Black Horse

As surely as night follows day, famines follow wars[51] due to the disruption of normal food production:

> 5. When He broke the third seal, I heard the third living creature saying, "Come." I looked, and behold, a black horse; and he who sat on it had a pair of scales in his hand. 6. And I heard something like a voice in the center of the four living creatures saying, "A quart of *wheat* for a denarius, and three quarts of *barley* for a denarius; and do not damage the *oil* and the *wine*." (Rev 6:5-6*)

The rider was measuring a shortage of wheat and barley and the heavenly voice was describing price increases that

---

50 An epic historical drama directed by Ridley Scott and co-produced and released in 2000 by DreamWorks Pictures and Universal Pictures. It starred Russell Crowe, Joaquin Phoenix, Connie Nielsen, and Oliver Reed in his final role.

51 The USSR's World War II death toll of 26.6 million included 9 million due to famine and disease (Michael Ellman and S. Maksudov, *Soviet Deaths in the Great Patriotic War: A Note*, Europe-Asia Studies, Vol. 46, No. 4, 1994).

John's 1st century audience would have readily understood; "a quart of wheat", i.e. a litre, was a day's ration for a man,[52] with women and children eating about two thirds of that, while "a denarius" was a day's wages (e.g. Matt 20:2). Well-to-do people ate wheat bread; the poorer ate barley bread so for a labourer to feed a family of four daily with "three quarts of barley" would take all of his daily wage.

Famine was an integral part of Roman history. As Rome's population grew, they became dependent on grain from Egypt and olive oil from Libya. As the Empire contracted, they lost the grain-producing lands in Germany, Egypt, and Britain, becoming unable to maintain the food supply which had ensured domestic stability. Between 400 and 800 C.E., the population of the city of Rome fell by over 90 percent, largely because of famine.[53]

As for the wine, Italian viticulture produced an abundance of cheap wine for Rome[54] and the oil supply was secure, originating in an area of North Africa, today's Libya, once called the "Green Sea" because it was like a green sea of olive trees. These olive orchards were highly productive with trees larger than those of Mediterranean Europe.

The heavenly command to "not damage the oil and wine" would limit what the first two riders could do. Five hundred years earlier during the Peloponnesian War (431-404 BC), the Spartans annually attacked Athenian lands, burning farms and felling olive trees and vineyards.[55] The Athenians often responded in kind and this crippled the rural Greek economy for at least forty years while young olive trees matured.

As mentioned earlier, the horse being black would have been normal to John's audience but not so with the fourth horse.

---

52 *Athenian Democracy*, ed. P. J. Rhodes, Oxford University Press, 2004, p. 128.
53 http://people.uvawise.edu/pww8y/Supplement/-ConceptsSup/PopulationSup/History.html, 4 Nov, 2018.
54 Peter Garnsey, *The Land*, in *Cambridge Ancient History: The High Empire A.D. 70–192*, Cambridge University Press, 2000, vol. 11, p. 695.
55 www.worldhistory.org/Peloponnesian_War, 1 Dec, 2022.

Fourth Seal – Ashen Horse

The opening of the 4th Seal reveals a horse of dreadful colour with a dreadful rider:

> 7. When the Lamb broke the fourth seal, I heard the voice of the fourth living creature saying, "Come."
> 8. I looked, and behold, an ashen horse; and he who sat on it had the name Death; and Hades was following with him. Authority was given to them over a fourth of the earth, to kill with sword and with famine and with pestilence and by the wild beasts of the earth. (Rev 6:7-8)

The horse ridden by this grim personification of death is described in Greek as *chlōros*, green. The *KJV* and *NIV* therefore describe it as 'pale', the pallid colour of a corpse. It is as if the horse is dead and with Death comes Hades, the place of the dead.

As fearful as this image is in any age, was it predicting a new development in the 1st century? Was it about to appear to them, or to others in the distant future? Obviously, death and Hades have been around since the Fall so what is the point of this vision?

Remember the context - the One who opens this seal has conquered death and emerged victorious from Hades, saying:

> "Do not be afraid; I am the first and the last, and the living One; and I was dead, and behold, I am alive forevermore, and *I have the keys of death and of Hades.*" (Rev 1:17-18*)

This seal is to reveal the will of God - *Jesus' resurrection does not mean the immediate or imminent end of death and Hades.* They will not be dealt with until He returns on Judgement Day, as John records:

> And I saw the dead, the great and the small, standing before the throne... And death and Hades gave up the

> dead which were in them; and they were judged, every one of them according to their deeds. *Then death and Hades* were thrown into the lake of fire. This is the second death, the lake of fire. (Rev 20:12-14*)

In the Meantime…

What then of their terrible effect in the meantime?

> Authority was given to them over a fourth of the earth, to kill with sword and with famine and with pestilence and by the wild beasts of the earth. (Rev 6:8)

Did this change anything on the earth? These four means of death – sword, famine, pestilence, wild beasts – were familiar to Jews in John's 1st century audience because, some five hundred years earlier, Ezekiel had prophesied similarly against Jerusalem:

> For thus says the Lord GOD, "How much more when I send My four severe judgments against Jerusalem: *sword, famine, wild beasts* and *plague* to cut off man and beast from it!" (Ezek 14:21*)

So too had Jeremiah:

> "I will send *the sword, the famine and the pestilence* upon them until they are destroyed from the land which I gave to them and their forefathers." (Jer 24:10)

Those 'four severe judgements' came about in 586 BC through the Babylonians invading the region and the southern kingdom of Judah was not spared as they had been in 701 BC (2 Kin 19:34-36).

In Ezekiel and Jeremiah's time, the judgements were directed against Jerusalem and the people of Israel to drive them from the Promised Land, sending the survivors, the godly remnant, into exile in Babylon. In Revelation, these judgements are directed against 'a fourth of the earth' i.e. of *all the nations of the earth* but with a clear limit and not to 'destroy them from the land'.

'A Fourth of the Earth'

As dreadful as this sounds, it actually means the sword, famine, pestilence, and wild animals will *not* kill three quarters of the earth's population – they will instead die of old age and the more usual causes. Was this to begin in the 1st century? Of course not - it had always been happening. Did anything change when Jesus came? Not in regard to violent deaths.

(i) Wars since Jesus came

Vast numbers have always died all over the earth due to wars and famines but, looking at just the last two thousand years, as we saw in Book 2:

> ...in 8th Century China, after the An Lushan rebellion against the Tang Empire, some 36 million people disappeared from census figures between 753 and 764 A.D. In the 12th and 13th Centuries, 30 million Persian, Arab, Hindu, Russian, Chinese and European men, women and children were put to death for resisting the Mongol Khans... In the 14th Century, Tamerlane (Timur the Lame) killed between 15 and 20 million in Central Asia and northern India, while in China, the Ming overthrow of the Yuan Dynasty led to 30 million perishing. In 17th Century China, the Manchu emperors killed 25 million or 17% of China's population. Two centuries later, they put down the Taiping Rebellion at a cost of another 20-30 million deaths.[56]

As Islam spread:

---

56 *Slouching Towards Bethlehem*, p. 125.

> Indian historian, K.S. Lal estimates that in India between 1000-1500 A.D., 60-80 million Hindus were killed by the Muslim invaders. Although the invasion began in 732 A.D., Prof. Lal's work is based on populations, starting from the conquest of Afghanistan in 1000 A.D. which culminated in the annihilation of its entire Hindu population. To this day the region is called Hindu Kush or "Hindu slaughter".[57]

In the 20th century, the four years of World War I (1914-1918) saw the deaths of 15 million[58] and in the six years of World War II (1939-1945), another 66 million.[59] We will consider the 20th century's many other wars in Chapter 17.

(ii) Famines since Jesus came

As mentioned above, famine was an integral part of Roman history, especially in the final collapse of the Empire. *A Brief History of Population Growth*, issued by the University of Virginia, notes that between 400 and 800 AD, the population of the city of Rome fell by over 90%, largely because of plagues and famine.[60] After that:

> Large-scale famine also occurred in the Byzantine Empire in 927, in Japan in 1232, Germany and Italy in 1258, England in 1294 and 1555, all of Western Europe in 1315, Russia in 1603, Bengal in 1669 and 1769, Ireland in 1845-49, and China and India in 1876 and 1879. Tens of millions died in these events, sometimes reducing local populations by as much as one third or more.[61]

In the 20th century, famines were often caused by political

---
57 Ibid, p. 159.
58 https://necrometrics.com/20c5m.htm#WW1, 23 Nov, 2023.
59 https://necrometrics.com/20c5m.htm#Second, 23 Nov, 2023.
60 https://people.uvawise.edu/pww8y/Supplement/-ConceptsSup/PopulationSup/History.html, 19 Jan, 2024.
61 Ibid.

autocrats. In Russia, for example, Vladimir Lenin came to power in the 1917 revolution:

> Food shortages were a critical source of social unrest and political instability during the first year of Soviet power. Through the course of the civil war, efforts by the Soviet government to acquire sufficient foodstuffs to support the Red Army and the urban population assumed massive proportions... The resulting famine affected at least twenty million people... [and] an estimated five million people died as a result of the famine, succumbing to outbreaks of cholera and typhus that proved fatal owing to weakened resistance.[62]

Non-Soviet sources put the figures at 30 million affected with 9 million dying. Ten years later, Joseph Stalin punished Ukraine for resisting his collectivisation plans, exporting so much grain from this former 'breadbasket of Europe' in 1932 and 1933 that between 7 and 10 Ukrainians died of starvation.[63]

China also saw mass starvation: between 1906-1907, 25 million died in the second largest famine in history due to catastrophic floods; between 1928-1930, 6 million people died due to a famine triggered by drought but made worse by local warlords and harsh taxes; in 1943, 5 million more died due to the Japanese invasion and grain seizures by the Chinese army to feed its troops and finance the war. However, their worst famine, and the worst in recorded history, was between 1958-1962 and caused by Mao Zedong's Great Leap Forward which enforced agricultural collectivisation and steel production, and led to 45 million dying of starvation.[64] Another 2 or 3 million were summarily

---

62 http://soviethistory.msu.edu/1921-2/famine-of-1921-22, 4 Nov, 2018.
63 Reported to Stalin as 8-9 million. R.J. Rummel, www.hawaii.edu/powerkills/USSR.TAB4A.GIF, 20 Jan, 2024.
64 Frank Dikotter, *Mao's Great Famine: The History of China's Most Devastating Catastrophe, 1958-62*, New York; Walker & Co, 2020, p. 333.

executed for disobedience.[65]

Dr Stephen Devereux of the Institute of Development Studies records over 30 major famines in the 20th century and summarises:

> China, the Soviet Union and, more recently, India and Bangladesh [have] apparently eradicated mass mortality food crises [in stark contrast] with sub-Saharan Africa, where famines precipitated by adverse synergies between natural triggers (drought) and political crises (civil war) have become endemic since the late 1960s.[66]

(iii) Plagues since Jesus came

In Jesus' day, as Dr Jonathan Kennedy notes, the Roman Empire was 'filthy, stinking and disease-ridden'. Dr Kennedy directs the global public health programmes at Barts and the London School of Medicine and Dentistry and in his *Pathogenesis: How Germs Made History*,[67] he writes of the great plagues that weakened Rome from the inside:

(a) The Antonine Plague (165-180 AD)

Probably smallpox, this plague killed 5-10 million throughout the empire, i.e. 25-33% of the population, including two emperors, Lucius Verus in 169 AD and Marcus Aurelius in 180 AD.[68]

(b) The Plague of Cyprian (250-270 AD)

Probably Ebola,[69] this one also killed two emperors, Hostilians

---

65   Ibid, p. 298.
66   *Famines in the 20th Century*. www.ids.ac.uk/files/dmfile/wp105.pdf, 14 Dec, 2023..
67   Jonathan Kennedy, *Pathogenesis: How Germs Made History*, London; Torva, 2023.
68   www.worldhistory.org/Antonine_Plague, 27 Apr, 2023.
69   www.theatlantic.com/science/archive/2017/11/solving-the-mystery-of-an-ancient-roman-plague/543528, 27 Apr, 2023.

in 251 and Claudius II Gothicus in 270 AD. The death-toll is unknown but it raged from Ethiopia to Greece to Syria and reportedly killed 5,000 a day in Rome. Historians comment that:

> Only the nascent Christian church benefitted from the chaos. The illness claimed the lives of emperors and pagans who could offer no explanation for the cause of the plague or suggestions for how to prevent further illness much less actions for curing the sick and dying. Christians played an active role in caring for the ill as well as actively providing care in the burial of the dead. Those Christians who themselves perished from the illness claimed martyrdom while offering non-believers who would convert the possibility of rewards in the Christian afterlife. Ultimately this episode not only strengthened but helped to spread Christianity throughout the furthest reaches of the empire and Mediterranean world.[70]

(c) The Plague of Justinian (541-750 AD)

Probably bubonic plague, this plague spread through China, North India, North Africa, and Europe.[71] Death-toll estimates for Europe vary from 15-100 million, i.e. 25–60% of their population.

Dr Kennedy concludes that the massive death-tolls led to the end of the Roman Empire, the rise of Christianity, and the Muslim conquest of the Middle East.

Six hundred years later in the 14th century, Europe faced the Black Death:

> It's estimated that somewhere in the region of 60% of the population of Europe (about 50 million out of 80 million people) died from the plague between 1346 and 1353.[72]

---

70 www.worldhistory.org/article/992/plague-of-cyprian-250-270-ce, 27 Apr, 2023.
71 www.worldhistory.org/article/782/justinians-plague-541-542-ce, 27 Apr, 2023.
72 Interview with Dr Kennedy. www.theguardian.com/society/2023/apr/02/microbes-germs-history-humanity-pathogenesis-jonathan-kennedy-interview, 27 Apr, 2023.

The New World was not spared either as 15th and 16th century European explorers and colonisers took their diseases with them. In Book 2,[73] I quoted Jared Diamond's overview from his 1998 Pulitzer Prize-winning *Guns, Germs and Steel*:

> ...one of the key factors in world history: diseases transmitted to peoples lacking immunity by invading peoples with considerable immunity. Smallpox, measles, influenza, typhus, bubonic plague, and other infectious diseases endemic in Europe played a decisive role in European conquests...Throughout the Americas, diseases introduced with Europeans spread from tribe to tribe far in advance of the Europeans themselves, killing an estimated 95% of the pre-Columbian Native American population.

The spreading of disease was not a one-way street however - the Europeans had never before encountered malaria and yellow fever which devastated Scotland's attempt at colonising Panama in 1707[74] and Ferdinand de Lesseps' canal project there in the 1880s.

Dr Kennedy notes:

> ...it wasn't just the New World that was profoundly affected by pathogens. On the west coast of Africa, explorers and would-be colonialists died in droves from malaria and yellow fever.[75]

This initially prevented them from colonising the African interior until quinine was discovered in the 17th century and helped prevent death from malaria.

In the 20th century, the Spanish Flu Pandemic (January

---

73   *Slouching Towards Bethlehem*, p. 142.
74   www.historic-uk.com/HistoryUK/HistoryofScotland/The-Darien-Scheme, 15 May, 2023.
75   https://theconversation.com/diseases-gave-us-the-rise-of-christianity-the-end-of-the-aztecs-and-public-sanitation-how-might-future-plagues-change-human-history-201569, 27 Apr, 2023.

1918 – December 1920) infected 500 million people around the world and killed 50 to 100 million,[76] i.e. 3-5% of the world's population, making it one of the deadliest natural disasters in human history.

In our times, the COVID-19 coronavirus has infected an estimated 700 million and killed 7 million.[77]

(iv) Killed by animals since Jesus came

John's 1st century audience knew all-too-well about the Roman circuses which featured *damnatio ad bestias*,[78] the execution of criminals by wild animals. However, the bigger picture includes us today.

The fall of Adam and Eve from their dominion over the earth (Gen 1:26-31) led to the animal kingdom fighting back, from the brute force of the big cats, bears, and bulls on the land, hippos and crocodiles in waterways, and sharks in the sea, to the insidious poison of snakes, scorpions, spiders, and jellyfish, to the diseases spread by tsetse flies and mosquitoes.

The 4th Seal reveals that Jesus' overcoming death has not yet removed the Adamic curse of sickness and death from the earth. He will not remove the curse until He returns and raises the dead:

> Then he showed me a river of the water of life, clear as crystal, coming from the throne of God and of the Lamb... On either side of the river was the tree of life... and the leaves of the tree were for the healing of the nations. There will no longer be any curse... (Rev 22:1-3*)

---

76 www.britannica.com/event/influenza-pandemic-of-1918-1919, 1 May, 2023.
77 www.worldometers.info/coronavirus/coronavirus-death-toll, 15 Dec, 2023.
78 Latin, condemnation to beasts.

Fifth Seal – The Martyrs

As mentioned earlier, the 5th Seal was also not a new event nor predicting a future era but describing a very present reality in the 1st century:

> 9. When the Lamb broke the fifth seal, I saw underneath the altar the souls of those who had been slain because of the word of God, and because of the testimony which they had maintained;
> 10. and they cried out with a loud voice, saying, "How long, O Lord, holy and true, will You refrain from judging and avenging our blood on those who dwell on the earth?"
> (Rev 6:9-10)

John and his audience had lost family members, friends, and many of their major leaders. John hears the martyrs, impatient for vindication, but they will have to wait until the Lord returns to raise the dead, judge the killers, and destroy death and Hades.

However, there is a great consolation for us in John's vision - he sees their souls metaphorically 'underneath the [heavenly] altar'.

Why there? Because under the Law of Moses, every sacrificial animal was to be killed 'at the doorway of the Tent of Meeting that [the offerer] may be accepted before the LORD' (Lev 1:3). Its blood was to be poured out at the base of the bronze altar with a portion sprinkled on the altar (Lev 1:5). With sin offerings, some of the blood was also to be placed on the horns of the golden incense altar:

> "He shall put some of the blood on the horns of the [golden incense] altar which is before the LORD in the tent of meeting; and all the blood he shall pour out at the base of the [bronze] altar of burnt offering which is at the doorway of the tent of meeting."
> (Lev 4:18, clarification added)

As we will see in Chapters 11 and 13, these details are essential to also understand the 6th Trumpet and the seven bowls. Here with the 5th Seal, however, the astonishing symbolism would have been unmistakeable to the Jews in John's 1st century audience.

In Book 3, I put this in context:

> This was the era of the Colosseum and the Roman circuses which routinely featured criminals and Christians facing *damnatio ad bestias* (i.e. execution by wild animals)[79]

So while the watching Romans saw the martyrs as criminals, condemned for not worshipping the Empire and their successive emperors, John was revealing that their deaths were actually their vindication. They were fully 'accepted before the LORD'.

In Revelation 12, John further revealed their deaths were not losses but victory over 'the accuser of our brethren' (Rev 12:10):

> "And they overcame him because of the blood of the Lamb and because of the word of their testimony, and they did not love their life even when faced with death." (Rev 12:11*)

The 5th Seal is also explaining, however, that until the Lord returns as King, many more will be martyred:

> 11. And there was given to each of them a white robe; and they were told that they should rest for a little while longer, until the number of their fellow servants and their brethren who were to be killed even as they had been, would be completed also. (Rev 6:11)

John therefore urged his audience to hold fast to Jesus regardless of any outcome:

---

[79] *Gotta Serve Somebody*, p. 190.

> If anyone is destined for captivity, to captivity he goes; if anyone kills with the sword, with the sword he must be killed. Here is the perseverance and the faith of the saints. (Rev 13:10*)

When did martyrdom start? Abel was the first, killed for his faith and righteousness by his brother Cain (Heb 11:4, 1 John 3:12) and nothing has changed fallen mankind since then. When will God judge and avenge the martyrs' blood? At the 6th Seal.

Summary

(i) The first horseman is not identified but was a very familiar image to John's 1st century audience in the eastern fringe of the Roman Empire. Even though the Pax Romana was at its apex, the Parthians remained famously undefeated just over the border. John's vision illustrated the inevitable fall of Rome and ultimately every other empire on earth.

(ii) The second, third, and fourth horsemen naturally followed – war, famine, and death - just as they always have done, with Hades claiming their victims. Jesus' coming and resurrection earned forgiveness of sins for all believers but was not to immediately transform the whole world.

(iii) While a quarter of the earth's population dying due to wars, famines, plagues, and wild animals is awful, it is actually normal in our fallen world. The good news is that three quarters do not die violently.

(iv) The 5th Seal revealing believers being martyred for their faith is also nothing new - the first was Abel at the hands of his brother, Cain.

5
Sixth & Seventh Seals
In Our Time?

The first five seals reveal the will of God for John's 1st century audience as well as for us. However, we may well see in our time what John's audience could only hear about – the opening of the 6th and 7th Seals.

Sixth Seal – The Second Coming

> 12. I looked when He broke the sixth seal, and there was a great earthquake; and the sun became black as sackcloth made of hair…
> 16. and they said to the mountains and to the rocks, "Fall on us and hide us from the presence of Him who sits on the throne, and from the wrath of the Lamb;
> 17. for the great day of their wrath has come, and who is able to stand?" (Rev 6:12-17*)

"The great day of their wrath" (v. 17) is the Day that Jesus returns as Judge.[80] John describes in graphic detail the effect on heaven and earth:

> 12. …*the sun* became black as sackcloth made of hair, and *the whole moon* became like blood;
> 13. and *the stars* of the sky fell to the earth, as a fig tree casts its unripe figs when shaken by a great wind.
> 14. The sky was split apart like a scroll when it is rolled up, and *every mountain and island* were moved out of their places. (Rev 6:12-14*)

As we have to ask so many times, is this literal or metaphorical?

---
80 We will look at this in detail in Book 7, *Kingdom Come: Justice for All*.

Some scholars, the Preterists,[81] believe it was metaphorical and fulfilled at the fall of Jerusalem in 70 AD. I will respond to this later.

If literal, will "the stars of the sky" (v. 13) really fall on the earth? Today we talk of falling or shooting stars to describe pieces of space debris that burn up as they pass through the Earth's atmosphere. They can be really bright and leave a streak across the sky for a minute or two[82] so yes, they can be described as such, but no, they are not literally stars. However, all the literal stars in the literal heavens will be replaced in the recreation of the Universe[83] that Peter describes as happening on the Day of the Lord (2 Pet 3:7-13).

John is watching the end of the old heaven and earth as the sun disappears, the moon turns blood-red, meteoroids and meteorites[84] fall while 'the sky was split [separated from the land] and rolled up like a scroll' (*Amplified Bible*).[85]

No Hiding Place

When He appears, the earth shakes so violently that 'every mountain and island' (v. 14) will move and unbelievers will desperately want to hide from Him:

---

81 For example, Daniel Morais. www.revelationrevolution.org/revelation-6-a-preterist-commentary, 18 Jun, 2022.

82 Properly termed meteoroids, they can be as small as a piece of sand and as large as a boulder. If smaller, astronomers call them interplanetary dust; if larger than a boulder, they are asteroids. The streak in the sky is called a fireball or bolide. Any that survive passage through the atmosphere are called meteorites. There are about thirty meteor showers annually, the brightest and most popular being the Leonids, the Geminids, and the Perseids. https://solarsystem.nasa.gov/asteroids-comets-and-meteors/meteors-and-meteorites/geminids/in-depth, 26 May, 2022.

83 With modern technology enabling us to see and understand far more of Universe than the ancients ever could, we should be far more impressed with this Day.

84 See Footnote 81.

85 The *NASB* translation of Rev 6:14 as 'the sky was split apart' does not make sense because a rolled-up scroll does not split apart. Other translations use 'departed' (*KJV*) or 'receded' (*NIV, NKJV*). However, the Greek *apochorizo* does mean 'to separate, part asunder' (Strongs G673) as used elsewhere to describe Paul and Barnabas separating (Acts 15:39). I therefore prefer the *Amplified*.

> 15. Then the kings of the earth and the great men and the commanders and the rich and the strong and every slave and free man *hid themselves* in the *caves* and among *the rocks* of the mountains;
> 16. and they said to the mountains and to the rocks, "Fall on us and *hide us from the presence* of Him who sits on the throne, and from the wrath of the Lamb;
> 17. for *the great day* of their wrath *has come*, and who is able to stand?" (Rev 6:15-17*)

I first heard these words as an atheistic teenager in the 1960s in the song, 'Sinner Man', recorded by The Seekers, The Weavers, and, in its most famous civil-rights version, by Nina Simone as she denounced the Ku Klux Klan.[86] Based on a 19th century Negro/African American spiritual, the song warns against leaving it too late to turn to God but when my friends and I roared it out in our local folk-club, we were completely oblivious to its imminent reality.

In John's vision, 'the kings' and 'commanders' (Grk, *chiliarchos*, commander of a thousand soldiers) of verse 15 will be trying to hide because, as I showed in Book 5,[87] they will have gathered at Har-Magedon. It is in this last battle for Jerusalem that they will face 'the great day' (v. 17) of 'the wrath of the Lamb' (v. 16).

The rich, the strong, the slave, the free man - all will be called to give an account because this is the Day that Isaiah predicted in the 6th century BC:

> 19. Men will go into *caves of the rocks*
> And into *holes* of the ground
> Before the terror of the LORD
> And the splendor of His majesty,
> When He arises to make the earth tremble. (Isa 2:19*)

---

86 She had learned it in revival meetings in her childhood when her Methodist-minister mother used it to urge repentance.
87 *Threshing Hour: Armageddon & Babylon the Great.*

Not only will they try to hide themselves but also their idols:

> 20. In that day men will cast away to the moles and the bats
> Their idols of silver and their idols of gold, Which they made for themselves to worship,
> 21. In order to go into the caverns of the rocks and the clefts of the cliffs
> Before the terror of the LORD and the splendor of His majesty,
> When He arises to make the earth tremble. (Isa 2:20-21)

So will this hiding be literal or metaphorical?

While in ancient times, men could hide from invading armies in caves, cellars, and cisterns, on the Last Day all concealment will be imaginary i.e. metaphorical - there is no hiding from God.

The 144,000

Before the seventh seal is opened, however, Revelation 7 answers a natural question for John's audience - 'what is the situation of Christians while the disasters of Revelation 6 are unfolding',[88] what is happening to believers in the midst of all of this?

While the first five seals reveal that it is 'business as usual' with God not intervening to stop us doing what we do to each other until the 6th Seal, Revelation 7 reveals what He *has* been doing all along:

> 1. After this I saw four angels standing at the four corners of the earth, holding back the four winds of the earth, so that no wind would blow on the earth or on the sea or on any tree.
> 2. And I saw another angel ascending from the rising of the sun, having the seal of the living God; and he cried out with a loud voice to the four angels to whom it was

---

88   Laurie Guy, *Unlocking Revelation*, Bletchley, UK; Paternoster Press 2016, p. 100.

> granted to harm the earth and the sea,
> 3. saying, "Do not harm the earth or the sea or the trees until we have sealed the bond-servants of our God on their foreheads."
> 4. And I heard the number of those who were sealed, one hundred and forty-four thousand sealed from every tribe of the sons of Israel… (Rev 7:1-4*)

The four angels, as we will see when we come to the seven trumpets, will be allowed to 'harm the earth and the sea' (v. 2) by no longer restraining man but first, God sets apart the 144,000.

As I showed in Book 3,[89] the seven identifying features given in Revelation 14:1-5 reveal the 144,000 to be apostles,[90] evangelising missionaries that have already been sent out by the Lord to *every nation over the last 2,000 years*. John sees the fruit of their ministry on Judgement Day:

> 9. After these things I looked, and behold, a great multitude which no one could count, from *every nation and all tribes and peoples and tongues*, standing before the throne and before the Lamb, clothed in white robes, and palm branches were in their hands;
> 10. and they cry out with a loud voice, saying, "Salvation to our God who sits on the throne, and to the Lamb."
> (Rev 7:9-10*)

The number 144,000 (12 x 12 x 1,000) is not literal but a metaphor based on the Twelve whom Jesus first set apart:

> And He appointed twelve, so that they would be with Him and that He could *send them out to preach* (Mark 3:14*)

---

[89] *Gotta Serve Somebody*, pp. 156-174.
[90] Contrary to what is often taught today, the Greek *apostolos*, lit. sent one, refers to the itinerant nature of their work and can be translated as missionary, regardless of what that work is. The work of the first twelve was evangelism (Mark 3:14); others like Paul and Barnabas were sent as prophets and teachers (Acts 13:1-3); the work of the two unnamed apostles in 2 Corinthians 8:23 was to carry financial gifts to Jerusalem.

The twelve apostles were the first evangelists, being sent out to preach the gospel as a full-time occupation. Leaving their fishing nets, they became 'fishers of men' (Matt 4:18-20).

John was the last survivor of the Twelve and he saw they were only the beginning of the ministry of apostles - their names are on the twelve *foundation* stones of the wall of New Jerusalem (Rev 21:14). This was the answer to the question in Chapter 3, "What will happen after John dies?"

We do not know how many of the multitudes of new disciples had become apostles by the close of the New Testament text but at least another ten were named as such[91] and two more were unnamed (2 Cor 8:23).[92] At the very minimum, therefore, the number of apostles had doubled. We are not told how many evangelists, prophets, or teachers there were by then but they too had obviously multiplied.

Of course, evangelism is never confined to evangelists any more than prophecy is to prophets (Num 11:29, Acts 2:17-18, 1 Cor 14:31). God's intention has always been that all of His people would be evangelical priests (Ex 19:6, 1 Pet 2:9), mediating between our holy God and sinful man. Evangelists and prophets are simply so gifted, motivated, and effective that they are recognised as such and may be financially supported to also leave their nets to become fishers of men.

Start to Finish

The first generation of the 144,000 began their ministry in the 1st century and they have gone through all of the earth. Consider China after 1948:

> Mao Zedong came to power then, outlawing Christianity, expelling all the European apostles (those we today call

---

91 Matthias (Acts 1:26), Paul and Barnabas (Acts 14:4), James the Lord's brother (Gal 1:19) Silvanus (a.k.a. Silas) and Timothy (1 Thess 2:6, cf. 1:1), Apollos (1 Cor 4:6-9), Epaphroditus (Phil 2:25), Andronicus and Junia (Rom 16:7).
92 Others had been found to be false apostles (2 Cor 11:13, Rev 2:2).

'missionaries') and persecuting about 3.3 million Catholics and 750,000 Protestants. There are now estimated to be 21 million Catholics and 84 million Protestants, almost 8% of the population![93] How did that happen? Where did all these believers come from? From thousands, perhaps tens of thousands, of Chinese apostles going from house to house, city to city, preaching the gospel to them.[94]

When will the 144,000 finish?

> "This gospel of the kingdom shall be preached in the whole world as a testimony to all the nations, and then the end will come." (Matt 24:14)

As mentioned in Book 1,[95] for the first time in all of recorded history, it is possible to preach in 'every nation and all tribes and peoples and tongues' (Rev 7:9) and we may well have done so.

The 144,000 coming 'from every tribe of the sons of Israel' (Rev 7:14) is also a metaphor, as I showed in Book 3,[96] with the two missing tribes, Ephraim and Dan, typifying those who like Judas turned away and needed to be replaced.

In summary, John saw the calling of the 144,000 to God's redeeming work at the same time as the opening of the first six seals:

(i) The first five reveal it will be 'business as usual' in God's not preventing man's inhumanity to man until Jesus returns.

---

[93] In Book 1, *Dancing in the Dragon's Jaws*, p. 38, I noted the Chinese government had recently acknowledged 130 million Christians or 10% of their population. That 2008 news report has since been disputed so I now accept Paul Hattaway's more careful 2011 figure of 105 million. www.asiaharvest.org/pages/Christians%20in%20China/Provinces/=CHINA=.htm, 31 Aug, 2011.
[94] *Gotta Serve Somebody*, p. 158.
[95] *Dancing in the Dragon's Jaws*, pp. 176-178.
[96] *Gotta Serve Somebody*, pp. 172-181.

(ii) The opening of the 6th Seal shows He will intervene to end it all.

(iii) In the meantime, Jesus has commissioned another 12x12x1,000 apostles/missionaries to evangelise all the nations of the earth. When He returns, they will have made disciples from 'every nation and all tribes and peoples and tongues'.

We also see the perfect love, patience, and justice of God in His ensuring that the whole earth has heard the offer of His forgiveness before He judges us.

The Seventh Seal - Silence

Revelation Chapter 8 resumes the opening of the seals:

> When the Lamb broke the seventh seal, there was *silence* in heaven for about half an hour… (Rev 8:1*)

In the mid-1970s, I went to see Ingmar Bergman's movie *The Seventh Seal* which is considered a classic of world cinema and one of the greatest movies of all time.[97] It tells the story of a disillusioned medieval knight and his squire returning from the Crusades to find Sweden in the grip of the Black Death.

When he meets the hooded figure of Death face-to-face, he challenges him to a game of chess to delay the inevitable:

> As the fateful game progresses, and the knight and his squire encounter a gallery of outcasts from a society in despair, Bergman mounts a profound inquiry into the nature of faith and the torment of mortality. One of the most influential films of its time, *The Seventh Seal* is a stunning allegory of man's search for meaning and a work of stark visual poetry.[98]

---

97 Filmed in 1957, 'it established Bergman as a world-renowned director' and many scenes have become 'iconic through homages, critical analysis, and parodies'. https://en.wikipedia.org/wiki/The_Seventh_Seal, 1 July, 2023.
98 www.criterionchannel.com/sight-and-sound-directors-greatest-films-of-all-time/season:1/videos/the-seventh-seal, 1 July, 2023.

At the beginning and end of the movie, Bergman quotes Revelation 8:1 to establish his theme which is the 'silence of God'.

I found the plot unrelentingly bleak and having just met the Lord, I had been delighted to find that He *does* speak, through both inner promptings and the Scriptures, leading me to put things right with people I had hurt. Later, I learned that if we do not first obey Him by repenting, He will not continue the conversation (Matt 21:23-27) - repentance actually enables us to hear and understand Him (Luke 7:29-30).

I also began to realise that He had been speaking wordlessly to me through all of Creation (Rom 1:20), especially the stars at night when, as an atheist, I first began praying:

> 1. The heavens are telling of the glory of God;
> And their expanse is declaring the work of His hands.
> 2. Day to day *pours forth speech*,
> And night to night reveals knowledge.
> 3. There is *no speech*, nor are there *words*;
> Their *voice* is not heard.
> 4. Their line has gone out through all the earth,
> And their utterances to the end of the world… (Psa 19:1-4*)

I also learned from another famous movie in the 1970s, Franco Zefferelli's *Brother Sun, Sister Moon*, that in real life, one disillusioned soldier returning from an Italian war turned instead to God and became known as St Francis of Assisi (1181-1226).

"Silence in the Court"

Heaven is usually full of animated conversation and music[99] but on the Last Day, there will be half an hour of silence. When God sits to judge, everyone listens:

---

[99] We will look at this properly in Book 7, *Kingdom Come: Justice for All.*

> "The LORD is in His holy temple; let all the earth be silent before Him" (Hab 2:20. Also Zeph 1:7)

We will all be there at the pleasure of the King, waiting for Him to speak.

Secondly, He does not pass judgement until He has heard all the witnesses, every explanation, and every extenuating circumstance. Even though He is omniscient and has no personal need, for our sake He follows the due process that He required of Israel in courts of justice (Deut 19:15-19).

In the same way, on Judgement Day we will all be given opportunity to explain, defend, and justify ourselves, just as Isaiah prophesied:

> "Coastlands, *listen* to Me *in silence*, and let the peoples gain new strength;
> Let them come forward, *then let them speak*;
> Let us *come together* for *judgment*." (Isa 41:1)
>
> *All the nations* have gathered together
> So that the peoples may be *assembled*…
> Let them *present their witnesses* that they may be justified,
> Or let them hear and say, "It is true." (Isa 43:9*)

We see then the process will be:

(i) "All the nations" will have "assembled"

As covered in Book 5,[100] the armies of the United Nations will have gathered around Jerusalem to take it away from Israel and to "gloat over Zion" (Mic 4:11) only to find God has actually been gathering them as "sheaves to the threshing floor" (Mic 4:12) to be judged.

To this gathering will be added everyone ever born, the dead having been resurrected (John 5:28-29). Everyone trusting Jesus has *already been judged as guilty* but forgiven:

---

100   *Threshing Hour: Armageddon & Babylon the Great*, pp. 48-56.

> "Truly, truly, I say to you, he who *hears* My word, and *believes* Him who sent Me, has eternal life, and *does not come into judgment*, but has passed out of death into life." (John 5:24*)

So we will all be there but believers will have nothing to fear.

(ii) We will all "listen… in silence" as He, the Judge, explains the process.

(iii) Anyone claiming innocence can try to justify themselves with "their witnesses".

(iv) If they have nothing to say, they will have to "hear" and they will confess what "is true".

Everything Known

Before anyone speaks, however, something truly astonishing will have happened. Jesus said that everything will 'come to light', explaining:

> "For nothing is hidden that will not become evident, nor anything secret that will not be known and come to light. (Luke 8:17)

Even private conversations will become public:

> 2. "But there is nothing covered up that will not be revealed, and hidden that will not be known.
> 3. "Accordingly, whatever you have said in the dark will be heard in the light, and what you have whispered in the inner rooms will be proclaimed upon the housetops." (Luke 12:2-3)

In the full light of eternity, everyone will know everything. We will even know the secret and mixed motives of everyone's hearts:

> Therefore do not go on passing judgment before the time, but wait until the Lord comes who will both bring to light the things hidden in the darkness and disclose the motives of men's hearts; and then each man's praise will come to him from God. (1 Cor 4:5*)

It will be completely unnecessary for anyone to explain themselves. As comforting as that will be for those needing vindication, it will be terrifying to anyone not yet forgiven. This is why Isaiah's prophecy above continues with God's extravagant promise:

> 25. "I, even I, am the one who wipes out your transgressions for My own sake,
> And I will not remember your sins.
> 26. "Put Me in remembrance, let us argue our case together;
> State your cause, that you may be proved right."
> (Isa 43:25-26)

The Judge of all is also Love. He does not want to humiliate anyone, only to forgive and accept anyone who will come to Him, facing their sins and sinfulness:

> "Come now, and let us reason together,"
> Says the LORD,
> "Though your sins are as scarlet,
> They will be as white as snow;
> Though they are red like crimson,
> They will be like wool." (Isa 1:18)

This is all for the present. On that Day, it will be too late and there will be no excuses.

"Speechless"

Paul noted that his own people, the Jews, who have had a 3,500 year head-start on us today to think of something, anything, will have nothing to say:

> Now we know that whatever the Law says, it speaks to those who are under the Law, so that *every mouth may be closed* and all the world may become accountable to God (Rom 3:19*)

'All the world' will also have nothing to say because everything will be known by everyone and at long, long last, justice will finally be seen to be done in front of everyone.

We also see this process illustrated in the parable of the king's wedding feast for his son. He invites everyone from everywhere and all he requires is that they come to honour his son and that they change their clothes:

> 11. "But when the king came in to look over the dinner guests, he saw a man there who was not dressed in wedding clothes,
> 12. and he said to him, 'Friend, how did you come in here without wedding clothes?' And the man was speechless.
> 13. "Then the king said to the servants, 'Bind him hand and foot, and throw him into the outer darkness; in that place there will be weeping and gnashing of teeth.'"
> (Matt 22:11-13*)

The man was offered the friendship and hospitality of the king but he refused to change - 'the man was speechless' because he had no excuse or reasonable explanation.

Biblically, clothing symbolises righteousness and we all have to remove the "filthy garment" of our unrighteous actions (Isa 64:6), ask God's forgiveness (1 John 1:9), and put on 'the fine linen [of] righteous acts' (Rev 19:8). We too will have no excuse.

Summary

(i) The seven seals were to reveal the will of God - the first five seals describe events already occurring in John's time, which have always occurred, and will continue to occur until Jesus returns.

(ii) His resurrection as the Prince of Peace with "all authority in heaven and on earth" did not mean the end of warring empires or famines or death by plagues or wild animals; the Adamic curse will remain until He returns to raise the dead and create the new heavens and earth. Believers will continue to be persecuted and killed until that Day.

(iii) In the meantime, just as He sent out the Twelve to preach the gospel of His Kingdom to Israel, John's vision shows Jesus sending out and accompanying the 144,000, i.e. tens of thousands of new apostles, to every nation on the earth.

(iv) The 6th and 7th Seals reveal what will initially happen on Judgement Day. In Book 7, *Kingdom Come: Justice for All*, we look at what happens afterwards in proper detail.

6
The Seven Trumpets
Proximity Alerts

As noted in the Introduction, in the 1970s I was startled to hear Jacques Cousteau state that "a third of the fish in the sea are threatened by mercury poisoning" because I had just read that number in Revelation (Rev 8:9).

This set me on a whole new approach to Revelation - I realised the angel is not inflicting anything on us - he is *blowing a trumpet* (Rev 8:8), i.e. sounding a warning to us. Today, our motor vehicles have proximity alerts to warn of nearby objects and our aircraft have GPWS (Ground Proximity Warning Systems) - the seven trumpets are God's proximity alerts that we are nearing Judgement Day. And like our proximity alerts, they will keep sounding right up to impact.

Even teenagers in John's 1st century Jewish audience knew the reason for Israel's trumpets so let us catch up with them.

Sounding Trumpets

In the wilderness, God commanded Israel:

> 2. "Make yourself two trumpets of silver, of hammered work you shall make them; and you shall use them for summoning the congregation and for having the camps set out...
> 9. "When you go to war in your land against the adversary who attacks you, then you shall sound an alarm with the trumpets...
> 10. "Also in the day of your gladness and in your appointed feasts, and on the first days of your months, you shall blow the trumpets over your burnt offerings, and over the sacrifices of your peace offerings..." (Num 10:2, 9-10*)

Back in 7

The trumpets were sounded to summon the people or to signal the time to move on (v. 2), as 'an alarm' and call to arms (v. 9),[101] and for rejoicing (v. 10). They were also sounded for the troops to stand down after a battle (2 Sam 2:28).

In Israel's history there were two famous victories that particularly featured trumpets: Joshua's battle for Jericho (Josh 6:20), as mentioned earlier, and Gideon and his three hundred men whose trumpets and torches panicked a vast army of Midianites and Amalekites into defeat (Jud 7:16-22).

In the case of Revelation's seven trumpets, we will see the first six are not to summon, move on, or rejoice, but there are clearly reasons for alarm and to prepare for action. The first five trumpets are alarms, given when particular circumstances occur, the sixth announces a great battle, the Battle at Har-Magedon described in Book 6, and the seventh announces the end of that battle, the summoning of God's people, a moving on, and great rejoicing!

Each trumpet sounding is *a sign of a particular time.*

"Signs of the Times"

In the 1st century, Jesus called on Israel and their leaders to recognise the times in which they were living, telling them that the "signs of the times" were as easily recognisable as the daily weather:

> 1. The Pharisees and Sadducees came up, and testing Jesus, they asked Him to show them a sign from heaven.
> 2. But He replied to them, "When it is evening, you say, 'It will be fair weather, for the sky is red.'
> 3. "And in the morning, 'There will be a storm today, for the sky is red and threatening.' Do you know how to discern the appearance of the sky, but cannot discern *the signs of the times*?" (Matt 16:1-3*)

---

101 Paul also refers to the use of trumpets in battle (1 Cor 14:8).

I have always liked Jesus using this analogy because I was taught as a child that we can all predict the weather with a rhyme:

> Red sky at night, shepherds' delight;
> Red sky in the morning, shepherds' warning.[102]

They were in Galilee (Matt 15:39) and Jesus had already been 'throughout all Galilee… in their synagogues… and healing every kind of disease and every kind of sickness among the people' (Matt 4:23). The people had 'brought to Him all who were ill, those suffering with various diseases and pains, demoniacs, epileptics, paralytics; and He healed them' (Matt 4:25) but this had not satisfied the Pharisees and Sadducees.

Jesus saw the state of their hearts, Luke recording that He also rebuked them as hypocrites (Luke 12:56). Instead of seeking only more miraculous cures, they should have *recognised the significance* of these "signs of the times" (v. 3).

(i) Signs of Messiah's arrival

The people of Israel had been waiting 2,000 years for the Messiah to come. As revealed in Revelation Chapter 12 and covered in Book 1,[103] He was the whole reason for their existence as a nation; they were to bless 'all the families of the earth' (Gen 12:3c) by bringing forth Eve's Seed to free the earth from Satan's power (Gen 3:15).

Their forefather and namesake Jacob/Israel had prophesied in Egypt that Messiah would come from the tribe of Judah:

> "The scepter shall not depart from Judah,
> Nor the ruler's staff from between his feet,
> Until Shiloh[104] comes,

---

102 A variation applies this to sailors.
103 *Dancing in the Dragon's Jaws*, pp. 8-19.
104 A Messianic title meaning 'He whose it is'. Ezekiel uses a similar phrase: "until He comes whose right it is, and I will give it to Him" (Ezek 21:27).

And to Him shall be the obedience of the peoples."
(Gen 49:10)

Four hundred years later, when the Hebrew slaves escaped from Egypt in 1446 BC, they also heard from a Mesopotamian prophet Balaam:

"I see him, but not now;
I behold him, but not near;
A star shall come forth from Jacob,
A scepter shall rise from Israel…" (Num 24:17)

Four hundred years later again, in about 1000 BC, David, Israel's greatest king, also sang and prophesied of God's covenantal promises that the Messiah would be one of his descendants, i.e. of the tribe of Judah, of the family of David.[105]

Two hundred years later, Micah predicted He would be born in David's home village of Bethlehem:

"But as for you, Bethlehem Ephrathah,
Too little to be among the clans of Judah,
From you One will go forth for Me to be ruler in Israel.
His goings forth are *from long ago*,
From the days of eternity" (Mic 5:2*)

One hundred years later in about 700 BC, Isaiah added that He would be God in human form:

6. For a child will be born to us, a son will be given to us;
And the government will rest on His shoulders;
And His name will be called Wonderful Counselor,
Mighty God, Eternal Father, Prince of Peace.
7. There will be no end to the increase of His government or of peace,
On the throne of David and over his kingdom,

---

105 *Silencing the Witnesses*, pp. 201-216.

To establish it and to uphold it with justice and righteousness
From then on and forevermore… (Isa 9:6-7*)

In 550 BC, Daniel predicted a date range of His coming (Dan 9:25)[106] which Jesus fulfilled when He was baptised in the Jordan River in 26 AD and announced:

"The time is fulfilled, and the kingdom of God is at hand…" (Mark 1:15)

God the Father had also audibly proclaimed Jesus as His Son at the Jordan, as had John the Baptist (Matt 3:11-17, John 1:29-34) whom 'everyone considered to have been a real prophet' (Mark 11:32). John's message had reached all of 'Jerusalem… and all Judea and all the district around the Jordan' (Matt 3:5).

The leaders of Israel, the chief priests and the scribes, knew all of this even from His birth. When the wise men came hundreds of miles from the East to worship Him in 5 BC,[107] it had caused a great stir:

3. When Herod the king heard this, he was troubled, and all Jerusalem with him.
4. Gathering together all the chief priests and scribes of the people, he inquired of them where the Messiah was to be born.
5. They said to him, "In Bethlehem of Judea; for this is what has been written by the prophet…" (Matt 2:3-5*)

(ii) Signs of Messiah's ministry

Jesus told His home synagogue in Nazareth that He was/is the Anointed One and why (Luke 4:16-21). He turned

---

106 We will look at the four decrees at the end of this chapter. See also *Dancing in the Dragon's Jaws*, pp. 93-96.
107 Date established in *Dancing in the Dragon's Jaws*, p. 96.

water into wine in Cana (John 2:1-11) and healed lepers, telling them to have the priests authenticate their healing (Matt 8:1-4, Luke 17:14). He cast out many demons (Matt 8:16, 28-34), opened blind eyes (Matt 9:27-31), healed the deaf and mute (Matt 9:32-33, Mark 7:32-37) and the lame (Matt 15:30-31). He had also raised the dead (Luke 7:11-17), a miracle performed previously only by Elijah and Elisha[108] with whom He openly aligned Himself (Luke 4:16-27).

In summary, Jesus fulfilled all the "signs of the time" of Messiah's arrival.

Accordingly, when John the Baptist was in prison and in doubt, Jesus reminded him of these signs. John had sent two messengers to ask:

> 20. ..."Are You the Expected One, or do we look for someone else?"
> 21. At that very time He cured many people of diseases and afflictions and evil spirits; and He gave sight to many who were blind.
> 22. And He answered and said to them, "Go and report to John *what you have seen and heard*: the blind receive sight, the lame walk, the lepers are cleansed, and the deaf hear, the dead are raised up, the poor have the gospel preached to them." (Luke 7:19-22*)

John had good reason to wonder if he had been wrong in identifying Jesus as Messiah because instead of being proved right, he had been imprisoned by Herod Antipas (Luke 3:20) and would soon be executed (Mark 6:17 ff.).

Jesus reassured John by pointing to what his two disciples had "seen and heard" (Luke 7:22) and quoting five[109] of Isaiah's messianic prophecies:

> 4. Say to those with anxious heart, "Take courage, fear not. Behold, your God will come with vengeance;

---

108   1 Kings 17:22, 2 Kings 4:20-36, 13:20-21.
109   Besides Isaiah 35, there are Isaiah 29:18-19, 32:3-4, 42:6-7, 61:1-3.

> The recompense of God will come,
> But He will save you."
> 5. Then the eyes of the blind will be opened
> And the ears of the deaf will be unstopped.
> 6. Then the lame will leap like a deer,
> And the tongue of the mute will shout for joy… (Isa 35:4-6)

John would indeed be recompensed (v. 4) but first, both he and Jesus would be executed as Jesus well knew (Matt 17:12-13).

Jesus clearly expected His audience to recognise these signs of the time of Messiah's arrival as predicted in their sacred Scriptures, and that time lasted three and a half years.

(iii) The rejecting of Messiah

After rebuking the Pharisees and the Sadducees, Israel's teachers, for refusing to discern "the signs of the times" as readily as the daily weather, He added:

> 4. "An evil and adulterous generation seeks after a sign; and a sign will not be given it, except the sign of Jonah." And He left them and went away. (Matt 16:4*)

On an earlier occasion, He had defined this "sign of Jonah" as His being rejected, crucified, and resurrected:

> 38. Then some of the scribes and Pharisees said to Him, "Teacher, we want to see a sign from You."
> 39. But He answered and said to them, "An evil and adulterous generation craves for a sign; and yet no sign will be given to it but the sign of Jonah the prophet;
> 40. for just as Jonah was three days and three nights in the belly of the sea monster, so will the Son of Man be three days and three nights in the heart of the earth[110]
> 41. "The men of Nineveh will stand up with this generation at the judgment, and will condemn it because they repented at the preaching of Jonah; and behold, something greater than Jonah is here." (Matt 12:38-41*)

---

[110] I covered the "three days and three nights" prophecy in *Dancing in the Dragon's Jaws*, p. 36-37.

'The men of Nineveh', wicked Assyrians and despised Gentiles, had recognised the truth in Jonah's message and repented, shaming these Jewish leaders who were still refusing to listen to Jesus.

Ironically, when they did listen to Him and His claim to be the Messiah, they condemned Him to death for blasphemy (Matt 26:63-66)! This sign of their utterly rejecting and killing Him proved to be their nation's fourth 'abomination of desolation'[111] and triggered the destruction of Jerusalem forty years later.

Jesus wept at Israel's failure to recognise the time of His coming and the terrible consequences:

> 41. When He approached Jerusalem, He saw the city and wept over it,
> 42. saying, "If you had known in this day, even you, the things which make for peace! But now they have been hidden from your eyes.
> 43. "For the days will come upon you when your enemies will throw up a barricade against you, and surround you and hem you in on every side,
> 44. and they will level you to the ground and your children within you, and they will not leave in you one stone upon another, because you did not *recognize the time of your visitation.*" (Luke 19:41-44*)

(iv) The siege of Jerusalem

Days before He was crucified in 30 AD, Jesus predicted many future "signs of the times" that the disciples were to watch for so they could recognise what was happening or about to happen.

The most relevant to them then was to help them and their families escape the destruction of Jerusalem forty years later:

---

111   *Slouching Towards Bethlehem*, pp. 265-275.

> "...when you see Jerusalem surrounded by armies, then recognise that her desolation is near. Then those who are in Judea must flee to the mountains, and those who are in the midst of the city must leave, and those who are in the country must not enter the city; because these are days of vengeance, so that all things which are written will be fulfilled. (Luke 21:20-22*)

That "sign of the time" was the siege: "When you see…, then recognise… and flee".

It seems a strange warning that "those who are in the midst of the city must leave, and those who are in the country must not enter the city" – how could they if the city was "surrounded by armies"? It turned out that Emperor Nero who had ordered Jerusalem's destruction committed suicide and the horrendous siege (66-70 AD) was temporarily lifted. The disciples had two years to flee for their lives and all who did were spared.

(v) Two signs of Messiah's return

Deeply shocked by Jesus' predicting the destruction of Jerusalem and their fabulous Temple (Mark 13:1-2), they asked Him for more "signs of the times":

> "Tell us, *when* will these things happen, and *what will be the sign of Your coming*, and of *the end of the age*?" (Matt 24:3*)

Having answered regarding Jerusalem's desolation, Jesus then spoke of the wars, famines, plagues, and martyrdom described in the first five seals of Revelation's scroll continuing as usual (Matt 24:6-9). In other words, none of these were "signs of the times" of His return or "of the end of the age" (v. 3).

Instead, He said, we should watch for two particular signs of His return - the gospel reaching every nation (Matt 24:14) and the fig tree growing leaves:

> 32. "Now learn the parable from the fig tree: when its branch has already become tender and puts forth its leaves, you know that summer is near;
> 33. so, you too, when you see all these things, recognise that He is near, right at the door." (Matt 24:32-33*)

I showed in Book 1[112] how Jesus described Israel as an unfruitful fig tree that would be cut down if still unfruitful after His three and a half years' ministry (Luke 13:6-9). Just before His arrest, He cursed a fig tree for not bearing fruit and it 'withered from the roots' (Mark 11:20) - this had to be symbolic 'for it was not the season for figs' (Mark 11:13), as they all knew. It also graphically illustrated the curse in the Law that God would 'uproot them from their land' (Deut 29:28).

For that fig tree to again grow leaves means it has been resurrected from the dead. Paul also referred to Israel's 'acceptance' as being 'life from the dead' (Rom 11:15, 25).

Israel's restoration in the Promised Land is the spiritual, symbolic fig tree being brought back from the dead, this time to bear much good fruit. This restoration has been occurring for over *a hundred years*[113] and you can see it for yourself - have you recognised it as a major sign of our times? It also fulfils the mystery of the second return of Elijah, another major sign of our times.[114]

(vi) The seven trumpets

The seven trumpets are six "signs of the time" of Jesus' impending return which is heralded by the seventh. Accordingly, all who love Him should feel a mixture of sadness and delight to see them - sadness because of what they are but delight because of what they signify and presage.

---

112   *Dancing in the Dragon's Jaws*, pp. 55-61.
113   The Jewish population in the land has grown from some 50,000 in 1917 to 7.2 million today and the Hebrew language has come back from the dead; Israel became a nation again in 1948 and regained Jerusalem in 1967. See Book 1 of this series, *Dancing in the Dragon's Jaws*, for a full analysis of this miraculous restoration.
114   Ibid, pp. 128-147. See also the 'great earthquake' of Revelation 11:13, explained in *Silencing the Witnesses*, pp. 280 ff.

There is no doubt that John's 1st century Jewish hearers would have seen them as wonderful and reassuring. As noted in Chapter 2, they had the Jewish advantage that Paul talked about – they had heard of the seven trumpets before, prefigured in Joshua's battle for Jericho. After the Israelites had marched around Jericho seven times on the seventh day, Joshua commanded the seven priests to blow the seven trumpets, the vast walls crumbled and the great city was captured (Joshua 6:1-21).

To a 1st century Jewish disciple, then, the trumpets proclaim that God will overwhelmingly win the titanic battle for the earth because every kind of defence will be demolished – at the 7th Trumpet, the saints will win the day.

In contrast to the seals which reveal 'business as usual' in our wars and persecutions right up until Judgement Day, the first four trumpets are to draw our attention to what we are doing *to the earth, the sea, the water, and the sky*. The fifth and sixth trumpets are to alert us to *particular consequences* to mankind and we need to recognise each of these signs of the times, not as a single event but as occurring over a season.

Recognising Seasons

As noted above, Jesus told us to look for the resurrection of the fig tree, Israel. However, He warned we will not be given exact timing:

> 36. "But of that *day and hour* no one knows, not even the angels of heaven, nor the Son, but the Father alone." (Matt 24:36*)

We are instead to recognise seasons:

> 32. "Now learn the parable from the fig tree: when its branch has already become tender and puts forth its leaves, you know that *summer* is near;
> 33. so, you too, *when you see* all these things, *recognize* that He is near, right at the door… (Matt 24:32-33*)

Fig trees do not put forth their leaves in a single "day and hour" but over weeks in late spring, announcing that "summer is near" (v. 32). Summer is the time of ripening harvest and climaxes in the threshing and winnowing of the grain as well as the picking of the olives, figs, grapes, and pomegranates over several months.

We are therefore to recognise "times" and "seasons" and Israel's four seasons[115] are:

(i) Spring - March to May

(ii) Summer - June to August

(iii) Autumn - September to November

(iv) Winter - December to February

To put Jesus' words in context then, He was speaking just before He was crucified on 6th April, 30 AD[116] and fig trees begin leafing up in late March. The disciples would therefore have been looking at the new season's leaves and perhaps some breba fig buds[117] before Jesus cursed that fig tree outside Jerusalem for its fruitlessness and it withered (Mark 11:12-14).

We are supposed to recognise Israel's resurrection as the fig tree budding again and therefore a proximity alert, a major sign of spring that Jesus is "near, right at the door" (Matt 24:33). However, He is not going to get ripe figs until the end of summer, harvest-time being August and September and, as covered in Book 1, Israel's restoration has been taking place over the last hundred years.

Luke records Jesus as also referring to all deciduous trees:

---
115   https://seasonsyear.com/Israel, 23 Mar, 2023.
116   Date established in *Dancing in the Dragon's Jaws*, p. 96.
117   Some varieties produce breba figs, leftover buds on the previous year's shoots which ripen three months later in June while the main crop develops on the current year's shoots, ripening in late summer and autumn. Brebas are not usually harvested but can be eaten if necessary. Regarding the fig tree that Jesus cursed, Mark noted 'it was not the season for figs' (Mark 11:13) but Jesus may have been looking for breba figs.

> "Behold the fig tree *and all the trees*; as soon as *they* put forth leaves…" (Luke 21:29*)

I explained this in Book 5[118] as predicting the resurgence of indigenous languages and cultures in every nation - here in New Zealand, we have witnessed an extraordinary renaissance of the Maori language and culture since the 1970s.

All of this means that no one event is to be seen in isolation as a particular "day and hour" but we are supposed to see everything happening in a metaphorical season. In real time, that may be in one "generation".

"This Generation"

Jesus went on to say:

> 33. so, you too, when you see all these things, recognize that He is near, right at the door.
> 34. "Truly I say to you, this generation will not pass away until all these things take place. (Matt 24:33-34*)

In the Scriptures, "generation" (Grk, *genea*) can have three distinct meanings: a period of 40 years, a period of 100 years, or 'a race of people, possessed of similar characteristics…(of a bad character)'.[119]

The third option, that people of good or bad character will be here till the end, seems a truism so I was taught in the 1970s that Jesus meant the first option of 40 years, as in:

> …He made them wander in the wilderness forty years, until the entire generation of those who had done evil in the sight of the LORD was destroyed. (Num 32:13*)

This meant Jesus was to return before 1988. Obviously He

---

118 *Threshing Hour*, pp. 203-204.
119 W.E. Vine, *Expository Dictionary of the New Testament*, p. 42. For example: "the sons of this age are more shrewd in relation to their own kind [Grk, *genea*] than the sons of light" (Luke 16:8).

did not so that only leaves the second option - 100 years - as in God's promise to Abraham, then known as Abram:

> God said to Abram, "Know for certain that your descendants will be strangers in a land that is not theirs, where they will be enslaved and oppressed four hundred years... Then in the fourth generation they will return here..." (Gen 15:13 & 16*)

This was because Abram was going to be 100 years old when he finally produced Isaac, the promised son (Gen 17:17). As it turned out, Israel were in Egypt for 430 years (Ex 12:40-41).

If we start counting from Israel's national rebirth in 1948 as the budding of the fig tree, "all these things" should "take place" by 2048. However, I believe some of the signs were fulfilled by 1945 in World War II. My personal belief is therefore that He will return some time before 2045.

How do you see it?

Today's Technology

It is also worth noting that in the last fifty years it has become possible for the first time in human history for us to learn and keep track of all of these events occurring all around the world. Some therefore quote Daniel's prophecy:

> "But as for you, Daniel, conceal these words and seal up the book until the end of time [NIV, the time of the end]; many will go back and forth, and knowledge will increase." (Dan 12:4* NASB)

In the 17th century, Sir Francis Bacon thought this was predicting the age of world exploration and great discoveries in science.[120] In the 19th century, some thought it meant 'Christian missionaries, and ministers of the gospel... [and]

---

120 *Novum Organum*, 1.93, 1620. Quoted in the commentary in the *Cambridge Bible for Schools and Colleges*, ed. J. J. Perowne. 1914. University Press.

the times when the gospel would be preached to the world at large.'[121]

However, everywhere else in the Scriptures that this phrase "go back and forth" is used literally (Jer 5:1, Amos 8:12) and metaphorically (Zech 4:10, 2 Chron 16:9), it means to diligently seek or search. In this instance, the searching is to understand Daniel's prophecies and, as we have seen throughout this series, John's Revelation has vastly increased our knowledge of these. Also, as noted in Chapter 2, I believe the *NIV* has the better translation of this verse and it predicts our New Covenant era.

Nevertheless, there is no doubt that the invention of the electric telegraph in 1837, audio amplification in 1906, broadcast radio in 1920, and electronic television in 1928 introduced the whole world to an unprecedented era of mass communication. As covered in Book 4,[122] in 1967 the world's first live global television link broadcast The Beatles' *All You Need is Love* to an audience of over 400 million in 25 countries; in 1969, the Internet was born;[123] in 1991, the World Wide Web became accessible to the public.

Today, for the first time in history, "this generation" can "see all these things"; it seems to me that our generation will not pass away until all these things take place (Matt 24:34).

Deliberate Ambiguity

So why does God keep the timing of Jesus' return ambiguous? Firstly, He wants to *create* a particular attitude within us, and secondly, He wants us to *keep* that attitude within us. We know this because Jesus prayed for us to hear:

> At that very time He rejoiced greatly in the Holy Spirit, and said, "I praise You, O Father, Lord of heaven and earth, that

---

121   E.g. Albert Barnes, *Notes on the Whole Bible*, 1832.
122   *Silencing the Witnesses*, pp. 255-256.
123   Gromov, Gregory, *The Roads and Crossroads of Internet's History*. www.netvalley.com/cgi-bin/intval/net_history.pl?chapter=1, 4 June, 2023.

> *You have hidden* these things from the *wise and intelligent* and have *revealed* them to *infants*. Yes, Father, for this way was well-pleasing in Your sight. (Luke 10:21*)

God deliberately hides "these things" from all who trust in their own wisdom and intelligence but He reveals them to anyone willing to humble themselves and to learn as "infants" do, by listening to Him and trusting Him to be right.

> 5. Trust in the LORD with all your heart
> And do not lean on your own understanding.
> 6. In all your ways acknowledge Him,
> And He will make your paths straight. (Prov 3:5-6)

When tempted by the devil, Jesus quoted Moses,[124] emphasising that we need to stay humble and keep listening:

> But He answered and said, "It is written, 'Man shall not live on bread alone, but on every word that proceeds out of the mouth of God.'" (Matt 4:4)

I wrote about this in Book 1[125] as 'the certainty of uncertainty'.

Jesus' First Coming

Consider the time that Israel were given to expect Jesus' first coming:

> "So you are to know and discern that from the issuing of a decree to restore and rebuild Jerusalem until Messiah the Prince there will be seven weeks and sixty-two weeks; it will be built again, with plaza and moat, even in times of distress." (Dan 9:25)

The word "weeks" here is literally 'sevens'[126] which in this instance is seven years. "Seven weeks and sixty-two weeks" is

---

[124] Deuteronomy 8:3.
[125] *Dancing in the Dragon's Jaws*, pp. 125-126.
[126] Heb, *sabuim*; Grk, *heptad*, "periods of seven" (Strong's H7620).

therefore 69 x 7 = 483 years.

As covered in Book 1,[127] there were four decrees "to restore and rebuild Jerusalem" - which one were they to "know and discern" as the beginning of the 483 years? Was it Cyrus's in 538 BC? Darius's in 520 BC? Or one of Artaxerxes' two, in 458 BC and 444 BC?

In hindsight we can readily see it was Artaxerxes' first decree in 458 BC which was followed 483 years later by Jesus being baptised in the Jordan in 26 AD, there being no year 0. However, God was deliberately vague, telling Daniel and therefore all of Israel only that it would be one of the four. They were therefore to expect Messiah sometime between 56 BC, if Cyrus's, and 36 AD, if Artaxerxes' second decree i.e. *anytime in a ninety-one year period.*

It is therefore perfectly consistent for God to give our generation a one-hundred year period too.

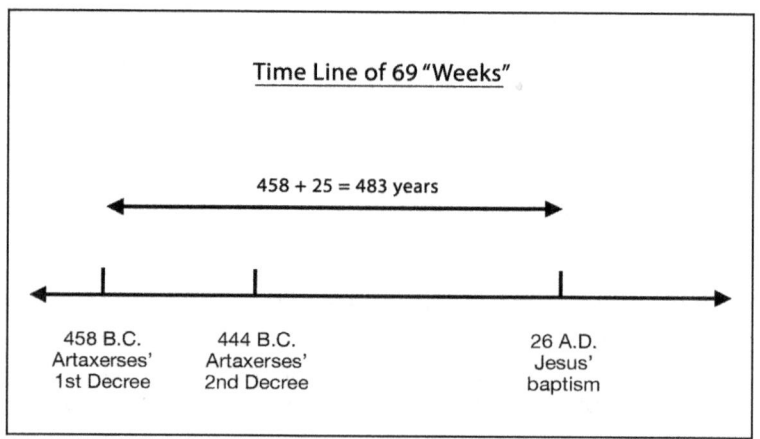

Fig (v) Artaxeres' first decree

---

127   Ibid, pp. 96-97, 194-195.

Summary

(i) The seven trumpets are alarms, the first five being "signs of the times" and the last two announcing the beginning and the end of the Battle of Har-Magedon. Signs of the times are events or situations that we need to recognise because they are to alert us to the times we are living in.

(ii) John's 1st century audience would have found the seven trumpets wonderfully reassuring because, as every Jewish teenager would have known, the legendary walls of Jericho came down after the sounding of seven trumpets and Israel entered the Promised Land.

(iii) In 26 AD, every Jew was supposed to recognise "the time of your visitation", i.e. Messiah's arrival, because of the previous 2,000 years of prophecies, including His appearing when Daniel predicted, His miraculous signs, His love and compassion for the vulnerable, His being rejected and killed, and His resurrection.

(iv) For Jewish disciples living in Jerusalem in 66 AD, their lives depended on recognising the imminent razing of Jerusalem and the Temple - the sign of that time was the Roman siege of the city.

(v) In the 20th century, we were supposed to recognise the restoration of Israel as the fig tree growing leaves and therefore a major sign of Jesus' imminent return.

(vi) The seven trumpets are alarms: the first four are to draw our attention to what we are doing to the earth, the sea, the freshwater, and the sky; the fifth and sixth trumpets, to what we are doing to ourselves; the seventh trumpet announces Jesus' return.

7
The Prelude
Answering Prayer

Before the trumpets are sounded, John sees what is often described as an interlude, an interruption, a parenthesis, or a prelude. I see it as a prelude, an introductory reassurance:

> 2. And I saw *the seven angels* who stand before God, and *seven trumpets* were given to them.
> 3. Another angel came and stood at the altar, holding a golden censer; and much incense was given to him, so that he might add it to *the prayers of all the saints* on the golden altar which was before the throne.
> 4. And the smoke of the incense, with the prayers of the saints, went up before God out of the angel's hand.
> 5. Then the angel took the censer and filled it with *the fire* of the altar, and threw it to the earth; and there followed peals of thunder and sounds and flashes of lightning and an earthquake. (Rev 8:2-5*)

Incense & Fire

John had already explained the symbolism of the incense:

> When He had taken the book, the four living creatures and the twenty-four elders fell down before the Lamb, each one holding a harp and golden bowls full of incense, which are the prayers of the saints. (Rev 5:8*)

As every 1st century Jewish teenager would know, every morning and evening for one and a half thousand years, the priests had offered a particular holy incense on the golden altar as an offering to God in the Holy Place (Ex 30:6-8). Strictly prescribed (Exo 30:34-38), it was a 'sweet' aroma, a beautiful fragrance to Him (Ex 25:6), which tells us how much He enjoys our prayers when we call on Him in Jesus' name (John 16:23-24).

John seeing the burning incense and fire 'thrown to the earth' (v. 5) reveals God is at last answering 'the prayers of all the saints' (v. 3) who have cried out for justice on the earth.

Not so well known, however, is that these prayers include *Jesus' intercession* to make atonement for our sins. This is revealed in Aaron's personal need of incense as a matter of life and death.

(i) For Aaron

The daily offering of incense took place in front of the veil of the Tabernacle and Temple which concealed the Holy of Holies where God manifested His presence; once a year, however, Aaron and his successors as high priests had to offer some *inside* the veil.

On the Day of Atonement, Aaron was to sprinkle blood on the ark of the covenant in the Holy of Holies to atone for himself, his household, and for all of Israel (Lev 16:1-11). However, he could not enter without incense and fire:

> 12. "He shall take a firepan full of coals of *fire* from upon the altar before the LORD and two handfuls of finely ground sweet incense, and bring it inside the veil.
> 13. "He shall put the incense on the fire before the LORD, that the *cloud of incense may cover* the mercy seat that is on the ark of the testimony, otherwise he will die."
> (Lev 16:12-13*)

God is holy. Not even Aaron as Israel's high priest could enter His presence without his sins first being covered by the 'cloud of incense' smoke (v. 13).

Contrast this with Jesus.

Our great high priest did not need any literal incense for Himself because He is sinless. Instead, He offered metaphorical incense in the Holy of Holies i.e. His prayers interceding for you and me, for all who trust in Him:

> Therefore He is able also to save forever those who draw near to God through Him, since He always lives to make intercession for them. (Heb 7:25*)

(ii) For Israel

Aaron had also been commanded to use incense and fire to stop a deadly plague:

> 46. ..."Take your censer and put in it fire from the altar, and lay *incense* on it; then bring it quickly to the congregation and *make atonement* for them, for wrath has gone forth from the LORD, the plague has begun!"
> 47. Then Aaron took it as Moses had spoken, and ran into the midst of the assembly, for behold, the plague had begun among the people. So he put on the incense and made atonement for the people.
> 48. He took his stand between *the dead and the living*, so that the plague was checked. (Num 16:46-48*)

The whole congregation of Israel had rebelled against God, siding with Korah against Moses and Aaron (Num 16:19) so thousands died but all for whom this atonement was made were spared.[128]

John's 1st century Jewish audience would have readily understood the significance of the incense and fire before the trumpets are sounded and been reassured that:

(a) God always hears the prayers of the saints.

Not only has He always heard and loved hearing us but He has stored up our prayers to be answered at the proper time.
These prayers for justice are about to be answered by 'the

---

[128] Think too of the seraph touching Isaiah's lips with 'a burning coal... from the altar' to make atonement for him (Isa 6:6-7).

fire of the altar', a great thunderstorm, and earth-shaking results (Rev 5:5).

(b) God distinguishes between the righteous and the unrighteous.

We were all unrighteous but in His death and resurrection, Jesus made atonement for everyone who trusts in Him and in what He does for us. As we will see, He *will* protect us.

Exodus Revisited

This is graphically and profoundly demonstrated in the Book of Exodus.

Many have recognised the parallels between the plagues that struck Egypt in the 15th century BC and the plagues that John describes in Revelation as afflicting the whole earth but few have recognised just how significant these are. We can pray with the psalmist:

> Open my eyes, that I may behold
> Wonderful things from Your law. (Psa 119:18)

To understand Revelation, we need to understand three of the wonders revealed to the liberated Hebrew slaves:

(i) God's faithfulness to His covenants

The plagues in Egypt were to reveal that God was answering the prayers of His people *according to His promises* made to Abraham, Isaac, and Jacob (Ex 2:24, 33:1), to release them from Pharaoh's power and give them the Promised Land.

God is releasing us from Satan's power over the whole world to give us a new heaven and new earth, just as He promised in the New Covenant.

(ii) They were no better than anyone else

The Hebrews were to recognise that this was not because they were good people - there are no good people. God was going to judge the Canaanites for their wickedness and give the land to the Hebrews whom *He had made righteous* through the Passover lamb:

> "It is not for *your* righteousness or for the uprightness of *your* heart that you are going to possess their land, but it is *because of the wickedness of these nations* that the LORD your God is driving them out before you, in order to confirm the oath which the LORD swore to your fathers, to Abraham, Isaac and Jacob." (Deut 9:5*)

Paul explained to the Gentiles in Corinth:

> Christ our *Passover* also has been sacrificed. Therefore let us celebrate the feast, not with old leaven, nor with the leaven of malice and wickedness, but with the unleavened bread of sincerity and truth. (1 Cor 5:7-8*)

Just as the Hebrew slaves of old had to trust in their sacrificial lamb, we all have to trust in Jesus' death for us; just as the Hebrews had to clear out of their homes leavened bread, we all have to truly and sincerely clear our own hearts of any malice, i.e. hatred, and any wicked attitude.

(iii) Gentiles could join them

As I will show, the ten plagues were to redeem everyone who believed Moses including slaves of other nationalities and any free Egyptians renouncing their nation's idolatry - 'a mixed multitude also went up with them' (Ex 12:38).

In the same way, John saw:

> ...a *great multitude* which no one could count, from every nation and *all tribes* and *peoples and tongues*, standing

before the throne and before the Lamb, clothed in white robes… and they cry out with a loud voice, saying, "Salvation to our God who sits on the throne, and to the Lamb." (Rev 7:9-10*)

The Ten Plagues

The ten plagues took place over at least six weeks; some estimate 4 or 5 months.[129]

Each of the ten could have been avoided - all God required of Pharaoh and the Egyptians was that they free their Hebrew slaves. Before He judged anyone, God gave Moses two spectacular Messianic[130] miracles as credentials: turning his staff into a snake, then back into a staff (Ex 4:1-5), and turning his hand leprous, then healing it (Ex 4:6-8). If, however, Pharaoh refused to believe, a third sign promised judgement: turning 'some water from the Nile' into blood (Ex 4:9).

At this point, no one had been judged. In the ten plagues, however, God would judge not only Pharaoh and his people for enslaving the Hebrews but 'all the gods of Egypt' (Ex 12:12).

The first three were more disruptive than devastating and affected everyone, Egyptians and Hebrews alike:

(i) Turning the Nile 'to blood' (Ex 7:18-19)

In the 5th century BC, Herodotus wrote that the land of Egypt was 'given them by the river',[131] noting that:

> …there are no men, neither in the rest of Egypt, nor in the whole world, who gain from the soil with so little labour; they have not the toil of breaking up the land with the plough, nor of hoeing, nor of any other work

---

[129] https://jesusalive.cc/ten-plagues-length, 24 Dec, 2022.
[130] These are so extraordinary that I unpack their metaphors on our website, https://emmausroad.org.nz/moses-messianic-signs, 8 Apr, 2024.
[131] Herodotus 2.1.5, https://penelope.uchicago.edu/Thayer/E/Roman/Texts/Herodotus/2A*.html, 19 Dec, 2023. Emphasis added.

which other men do to get them a crop; *the river rises of itself*, waters the fields, and then sinks back again; thereupon each man sows his field...[132]

He saw this as a great mystery:

> ...the Nile comes with a rising flood for an hundred days from the summer solstice, and when this tale of days is complete sinks again with a diminishing stream, so that the river is low for the whole winter till the summer solstice again. Concerning this matter none of the Egyptians could tell me anything, when I asked them *what power the Nile has* to be contrary in nature to all other rivers.[133]

The Nile enabled ancient Egypt's cities to flourish in the desert, providing not only water for irrigation and fertile silt in its annual floods but also the means of transporting materials for building projects such as the Pyramids. As renowned Egyptologist Toby Wilkinson puts it, 'without the Nile, there would be no Egypt'.[134]

Pharaoh had seen a little water from the Nile turned to blood in Moses' third sign – now he saw the whole river.

This plague killed all the fish and the river stank (Ex 7:21) which affected everyone and they were forced to dig new wells around the Nile (v. 24) until it ceased. However, when Pharaoh's magicians 'did the same with their secret arts' (v. 22), he showed 'no concern even for this' (v. 23).

(ii) Frogs (Ex 8:2-4)

Aimed primarily at Pharaoh (Ex 8:12), the plague of frogs even entered his bedchamber (v. 3) but it affected everyone

---

132 Ibid, para 14.
133 Ibid, para 19. Emphasis added.
134 Toby Wilkinson, *The Nile: Travelling Downriver Through Egypt's Past and Present*, New York; Knopf Doubleday Publishing Group, 2015.

because, when they died, the land stank (v. 14). Pharaoh initially softened but changed his mind when it ended (v. 15).

(iii) Gnats or lice (Ex 8:16-17)

Lice[135] seems more likely than gnats because they afflicted man and beast (v. 17) and gnats usually do not. Pharaoh still would not listen (v. 15).

The next seven plagues, however, affected people differently, based on their location and/or their faith in Moses' warnings.

(iv) Swarms of flies (Ex 8:21)

The Hebrew *arov* means literally swarms[136] so some Jewish commentators[137] take it to mean swarms of wild animals. However, our translations today follow the Septuagint's *kunomuias*, dog-flies, which bite man and beast.

This time, God's warning included a promise of protection for the Hebrews:

> 21. "…behold, I will send *swarms of flies* on you and on your servants and on your people and into your houses; and the houses of the Egyptians will be full of swarms of flies, and also the ground on which they dwell.
> 22. "But on that day *I will set apart the land of Goshen*, where *My people are living*, so that no swarms of flies will be there, in order that you may know that I, the LORD, am in the midst of the land.
> 23. "I will put a division between My people and your people…" (Ex 8:21-23*)

---

135 *NAS, NIV, ESV,* and *CEV* translate the Heb *ken* as gnats; *KJV, NKJV,* and *ASV* as lice; *The Jewish Study Bible* as 'vermin', possibly 'lice or mosquitoes'.
136 *KJV, NKJV, ASV, NIV,* and *NAS* translate Heb *arob* as flies; *The Jewish Study Bible* as insects.
137 E.g.www.chabad.org/holidays/passover/pesach_cdo/aid/1653/jewish/The-Ten-Plagues.htm#4, 19 Dec, 2022.

Four hundred years earlier, the children of Israel had been given the land of Goshen (Gen 45:10). Now this area was spared this plague; for the Egyptians, however, the 'great swarms' of biting dog-flies entered their houses and 'the land was laid waste' (Ex 8:24). The vast numbers would have made them unbearable.

Again Pharaoh softened (v. 28) but changed his mind when it stopped (v. 32).

(v) Death of livestock (Ex 9:3)

Again God's warning promised protection for the Hebrews:

> 3. "...behold, the hand of the LORD will come with a very severe pestilence on your livestock which are in the field, on the horses, on the donkeys, on the camels, on the herds, and on the flocks.
> 4. "But the LORD will make a distinction between the livestock of Israel and the livestock of Egypt, so that nothing will die of all that belongs to the sons of Israel." (Exo 9:3-4)

Pharaoh checked to see if the Hebrews were indeed spared but remained unconvinced (v. 7).

(vi) Boils (Ex 9:9)

This severe skin inflammation was 'on all the Egyptians' and their surviving livestock (vv. 10-11) but not on the Hebrews or their livestock. Pharaoh still refused to free them.

(vii) Unprecedented hailstorm (Ex 9:18)

The warning of this plague included a promise of protection for every Egyptian who believed it:

> 18. "Behold, about this time tomorrow, I will send a very heavy hail, such as has not been seen in Egypt from the day it was founded until now.
> 19. "Now therefore send, bring your livestock and whatever you have in the field to safety. Every man and beast that is found in the field and is not brought home, when the hail comes down on them, will die." (Ex 9:18-19)

Some Egyptians did believe:

> 20. The one among the servants of Pharaoh who feared the word of the LORD made his servants and his livestock flee into the houses;
> 21. but he who paid no regard to the word of the LORD left his servants and his livestock in the field. (Ex 9:20-21)

As promised, 'the LORD sent thunder and hail, and fire ran down to the earth' (Ex 9:23):

> 25. The hail struck all that was in the field through all the land of Egypt, both man and beast; the hail also struck every plant of the field and shattered every tree of the field.
> 26. Only in the land of Goshen, where the sons of Israel were, there was no hail. (Ex 9:25-26)

The Egyptians' wheat and spelt were unaffected because it was early in the season (v. 32) and, again, Goshen and the Hebrews were spared. Again, Pharaoh agreed to free them (vv. 27-28) but when the storm ceased, he changed his mind (v. 34).

(viii) Locusts (Ex 10:4-6)

On hearing Moses' warning of the locusts, Pharaoh agreed to temporarily release only the men to worship in the wilderness while keeping their families hostage (vv. 9-11) so God followed through on the threat. The Egyptians had seen locust plagues before but this one was unprecedented in intensity (v. 6) and ferocity:

> 13. ...the LORD directed an east wind on the land all that day and all that night; and when it was morning, the east wind brought the locusts.
> 14. The locusts came up over all the land of Egypt and settled in all the territory of Egypt; they were very numerous. There had never been so many locusts, nor would there be so many again.
> 15. For they covered the surface of the whole land, so that the land was darkened; and they ate every plant of the land and all the fruit of the trees that the hail had left. Thus nothing green was left on tree or plant of the field through all the land of Egypt. (Exo 10:14-15)

When Pharaoh acknowledged he had sinned (vv. 16-17), Moses prayed (v. 18):

> 19. So the LORD shifted the wind to a very strong west wind which took up the locusts and drove them into the Red Sea; not one locust was left in all the territory of Egypt. (Ex 10:19)

However, Pharaoh still would not release the Hebrews. This devastation of the crops would not have affected them much because after the tenth plague, they were finally able to leave.

(ix) Thick darkness (Ex 10:21-23)

This judgement lasted three days:

> 22. ...Moses stretched out his hand toward the sky, and there was thick darkness in all the land of Egypt for three days.
> 23. They did not see one another, nor did anyone rise from his place for three days, but all the sons of Israel had light in their dwellings. (Ex 10:22-23)

Described as "a darkness which may be felt" (v. 21), this plague is thought by some to be a natural phenomenon called a *khamsin* which occurs when a hot southerly wind from the Sahara keeps aloft dense concentrations of sand and dust. It can block out sunlight, last three days, and, travelling in streaks, it could have bypassed the Hebrews in Goshen.

However, Pharaoh would have known this too. Also, there is no mention of any wind, despite both east and west winds being described in the previous plague. And why would only Israel have 'light in their dwellings'?

I therefore see this as a supernatural darkness that affected only the Egyptians, prefiguring a future supernatural darkness from the 5th Bowl (Rev 16:10), as we will see later.

(x) The death of the first-born (Ex 12:12)

Israel were spared this plague provided they had placed the blood of the Passover lamb on the lintels and doorposts of their homes (Ex 12:7) and remained inside (Ex 12:22). We looked at this in detail in Book 3 regarding God's marks of ownership, not only on their doorways but also on their hands and foreheads (Ex 13:9 & 16).[138]

Repentance

The ten plagues were a very public punishment of Pharaoh and his people and their gods. Some Egyptians began to repent and believe the word of God that Moses proclaimed from at least the seventh plague. We are not told what they were thinking during the last three but after the tenth, as mentioned earlier, a multitude of them left Egypt with the fleeing Hebrews.

God accepted them and He instructed Israel to include them:

> 14. "If an alien sojourns with you, or one who may be among you throughout your generations, and he wishes

---

138   *Gotta Serve Somebody*, pp. 39-44.

> to make an offering by fire, as a soothing aroma to the LORD, just as you do so he shall do.
> 15. "As for the assembly, there shall be one statute for you and for the alien who sojourns with you, a perpetual statute throughout your generations; as you are, so shall the alien be before the LORD." (Num 15:14-15)

One and a half thousand years later in Jesus' time, the Jews had a particular hatred of the Samaritans who were descendants of the Gentiles moved into the land of Israel by the Assyrians from the 8th century BC. It took another major revelation before Peter recognised how God had always wanted to include the Gentiles,[139] as he told the Roman Cornelius and his household:

> "God has shown me that I should not call any man unholy or unclean… I most certainly understand now that God is not one to show partiality, but in every nation the man who fears Him and does what is right is welcome to Him." (Act 10:28, 34-35)

It also took a major dispute in the Early Church nineteen years later before Paul, Barnabas, and Peter were finally able to persuade Jesus' half-brother James that Gentiles were to be welcomed as believers in Jesus without their becoming Jews.[140]

God has obviously not changed. He still welcomes all who will repent and trust in Jesus, even to the very last minute.

As we will see with the seven trumpets, God's intention is to reveal to the whole world the awful consequences of our continuing to live in opposition to Him and His way. His hope is that we will come to our senses like the prodigal son and turn back to Him (Luke 15:11-18).

Let us now summarise before we consider the trumpets.

---

[139] Nehemiah's rejection of intermarrying with Gentiles (Neh 13:23-27) in the 5th century BC was to preserve the Jews as a distinct people until Messiah came when it became unnecessary.
[140] Acts 15:1-29, Galatians 2:1-21.

Summary

(i) Before the seven trumpets sound, John sees an angel burning the incense which symbolises prayer, and casting its fire onto the earth. This shows that God will answer the prayers of "all the saints" who have called for justice on the earth.

(ii) Incense also symbolises Jesus' prayers of intercession making atonement for us. We can therefore be certain that God distinguishes between the righteous and the unrighteous, i.e. between those who are forgiven and those who are not yet forgiven.

(iii) He also makes this distinction in hope that the unrighteous will repent as we see graphically demonstrated in the ten plagues on Egypt during the Exodus. We need to keep these literal plagues in mind because they recur in Revelation in metaphorical form.

(iv) The first three were the Nile turning to blood, vast numbers of frogs, and the dust producing lice. The next three, the dog-flies, the death of livestock, and boils only afflicted the Egyptians and their beasts.

(v) The seventh plague, i.e. the hail-storm, struck the whole land of Egypt except Goshen where the Hebrew slaves lived. It was also avoided by every Egyptian who believed Moses' warning and took shelter. The eighth plague, however, was the swarm of locusts that stripped all surviving vegetation.

(vi) We see then the first eight manifested in the natural elements of water, earth, and air but the last two were undoubtedly supernatural - the three days of "thick darkness" and the targeted slaying of the first-born.

(vii) God's intention in the plagues was to reveal to the whole world not only the disastrous outcome of our living in opposition to Him and His way, but also the freedom we can find in Jesus.

8
The First Trumpet
Signs on the Earth

When the disciples asked Jesus "what will be the sign of Your coming, and of the end of the age?" (Matt 24:3), He replied that there will not be one but many, in the heavens, on the earth, and in the sea:

> 25. "There will be *signs in sun and moon and stars, and on the earth* dismay among nations, in perplexity at the *roaring of the sea and the waves,*
> 26. men fainting from fear and the *expectation* of the things which are coming upon the world; for the powers of the heavens will be shaken.
> 27. *"Then* they will see THE SON OF MAN COMING IN A CLOUD with power and great glory. (Luke 21:25-27*)

The disciples would have been familiar with His quotation from Daniel 7:13 (capitals in v. 27) as a Messianic prophecy, as were Caiaphas and the Sanhedrin when they convicted Him of blasphemy (Matt 26:63-66). However, it is very easy for us to miss the significance of these three verses - as I will show, Jesus was predicting what John sees in his vision of the seven trumpets.

Earth, Sea, and Sky

Looking at v. 25, these signs will be:

(i) "in sun and moon and stars"
(ii) "on the earth"
(iii) and in "the sea"

Back in 7

In other words, they will be in the three areas that God gave mankind to rule when He commissioned Adam and Eve, saying:

> "Be fruitful and multiply; fill the earth and subdue it; have dominion over *the fish of the sea*, over *the birds of the air*, and over *every living thing* that moves *on the earth*." (Gen 1:28*)

He repeated this commission to Noah and his family, saying:

> 1. ..."Be fruitful and multiply, and fill the *earth*.
> 2. "The fear of you and the terror of you will be on every beast of the earth and on every bird of *the sky*; with everything that creeps on *the ground*, and all the fish of the sea, into your hand they are given. (Gen 9:1-2*)

The first four trumpets are therefore to draw our attention to what we are doing to the earth, sea, and sky (Luke 21:25). 'The air' (Gen 1:28) or 'the sky' (Gen 9:2) is in Hebrew *shamayim* and refers to the earth's atmosphere where 'every bird' flies,[141] so we need to consider what we are doing to the atmosphere.

The 5th Trumpet is to draw our attention to one outcome of the first four, mankind's "fear and expectation of the things coming upon the world" (Luke 21:26) while the sixth sounds the alarm at what we are doing directly to mankind.

It was not until I was completing this book that I realised the significance of there being six - as I covered in Book 3,[142] *six is the number of man*. And, as I will show, the six trumpets

---

[141] God also "called the expanse, heaven" (Gen 1:8), i.e. the space between the clouds ("waters above") and the sea ("waters below") (Gen 1:6-7). This provides the context for Paul's reference to 'the third heaven' (2 Cor 12:2) as Paradise (v. 4), the presence of God: the first heaven is the earth's atmosphere; the second heaven is the place of the sun, moon, and stars (Ps 8:3), i.e. the rest of the created material universe.

[142] *Gotta Serve Somebody*, pp. 138-142.

have been sounding over the last fifty to one hundred years which means we should be expecting the seventh, Jesus' return for Judgement Day (Luke 21:27).

You Be the Judge

What follows is necessarily subjective. I am spelling out the world's situation as I see it regarding each of the trumpets; you decide for yourself if I am matching the texts and today's situation correctly.

I will just add three common-sense caveats:

(i) In the Scriptures, 'one third' is an approximate term.

When Daniel sees three out of ten horns being subdued by the spirit of antichrist (Dan 7:20 & 24), his audience would not have thought he meant 30%. Similarly, John's audience would not be looking for 'a third' to be exactly 33.33%.

When Jesus spoke of the seeds yielding crops, He used obviously approximate figures:

> "Other seeds fell into the good soil, and as they grew up and increased, they yielded a crop and produced thirty, sixty, and a hundredfold."
> (Mark 4:8*. Also 4:20 and Matt 13:8, 13:23)

We do not have to have exact figures for each trumpet but 30% is close enough.

(ii) Moving goal-posts.

Today we can almost count trees and sea-life and measure quantities of fresh and seawater using satellite observations and super-computers. However, how can we calculate 'a third of mankind' (Rev 9:18) when the world's population is forever changing? In the 16th century, there were only half a billion people; in 1800, we reached 1 billion; in 1927, we reached 2 billion; in 1974, 4 billion; now in 2023, we are 8 billion. That is an 800% increase in just the last 200 years.

However, God still expects us to see this sign and recognise its significance so let us get on with it as best we can.

(iii) Data can be boring and/or completely reversed.

I want to be thorough but reading lots of figures can be tedious. Having worked as a logistics analyst in the oil and shipping industry for fifteen years from 1982 to 1997, I also know how data and forecasts often need to be revised or even completely reversed. As Mark Twain observed:

> Figures often beguile me, particularly when I have the arranging of them myself; in which case the remark attributed to Disraeli would often apply with justice and force: "There are three kinds of lies: lies, damned lies, and statistics."[143]

What would Mr Twain have made of today's internet where we can find data to prove almost anything? We need to proceed carefully and prayerfully.

The First Trumpet – the Earth

> 6. And the seven angels who had the seven trumpets prepared themselves to sound them.
> 7. The first sounded, and there came hail and fire, mixed with blood, and they were thrown to the earth; and a third of the earth was burned up, and a third of the trees were burned up, and all the green grass was burned up.
> (Rev 8:6-7*)

As mentioned earlier, I used to fear that God was about to

---

[143] Mark Twain, *Chapters from My Autobiography*, published in the North American Review between September 1906 and December 1907.

do terrible things to the earth – to *us* – but my perspective was changed by Jacques Cousteau's observation that mercury poisoning is killing "a third of the fish of the sea". Making the connection to the 2nd Trumpet, I suddenly realised that we are doing it to ourselves because this mercury is a by-product of coal-fired power generation and mining. I then understood the trumpets sounding are warning us to watch what we are doing.

What then is this 'hail and fire, mixed with blood' that is 'thrown to the earth'?

The usual meaning of fire in this context is lightning, as in the seventh plague on Egypt:

> ...thunder and hail, and *fire ran down to the earth*... fire flashing continually in the midst of the hail... [which] shattered every tree of the field. (Ex 9:23-25*)

The lightning plague in Egypt 'shattered every tree' in Egypt. In John's vision, however, the hail and fire is 'mixed with blood' and only 'a third of the trees' are affected, being 'burned up' rather than 'shattered'.

Dealing firstly with the blood, is this literal or metaphorical?

Literal blood falling from the sky is extremely unlikely but 'blood' was a common metaphor in Biblical days to describe bloodshed,[144] murder,[145] guilt,[146] or death.[147] For example:

> ...when they resisted and blasphemed, [Paul] shook out his garments and said to them, *"Your blood be on your own heads!* I am clean. From now on I will go to the Gentiles." (Acts 18:6*)

Paul meant they would be held fully responsible for their own deaths on the Day. Blood being 'thrown to the earth' at

---

144 The injury or killing of people. E.g. 1 Sam 25:33, 1 Chron 28:3.
145 E.g. 2 Sam 16:7, Isa 5:7, Acts 5:28.
146 E.g. Matt 27:6, 25, Acts 5:28.
147 E.g. Matt 26:28; Mark 14:24.

the 1st Trumpet therefore reveals that God will be holding us responsible for what we have done to each other; it is mixed with hail and fire because it is somehow in response to the prayers of the saints (Rev 8:3-5). We will look at this properly in Book 7, *Kingdom Come: Justice for All.*

So what are we doing to the earth's trees and grass today?

Burning Trees

Under the wholly appropriate heading of 'Modern-Day Plague', *National Geographic* reported in 2022:

> Deforestation is clearing Earth's forests on a massive scale, often resulting in damage to the quality of the land. Forests still cover about 30 percent of the world's land area, but swaths half the size of England are lost each year. The world's rain forests could completely vanish in a hundred years at the current rate of deforestation.
> The biggest driver of deforestation is agriculture. Farmers cut forests to provide more room for planting crops or grazing livestock. Often, small farmers will clear a few acres by cutting down trees and burning them in a process known as slash and burn agriculture.[148]

The terms 'small farmers' and 'a few acres' can be misleading because they 'slash and burn' trees on a vast scale. In 2007, a UN report estimated that:

> Subsistence farming is responsible for 48% of deforestation; commercial agriculture is responsible for 32%; logging is responsible for 14%, and fuel wood removals make up 5%.[149]

In the Amazonian rainforest, however, the biggest factor has been large-scale agriculture:

---

148   https://www.nationalgeographic.com/environment/global-warming/deforestation, 24 Nov 2018.
149   http://unfccc.int/files/essential_background/background_publications_htmlpdf/application/pdf/pub_07_financial_flows.pdf, p. 81. 20 Mar 2024.

Since 1978 over 750,000 square kilometers (289,000 square miles) of Amazon rainforest have been destroyed across Brazil, Peru, Colombia, Bolivia, Venezuela, Suriname, Guyana, and French Guiana... For most of human history, deforestation in the Amazon was primarily the product of subsistence farmers who cut down trees to produce crops for their families and local consumption. But in the later part of the 20th century, that began to change, with an increasing proportion of deforestation driven by industrial activities and large-scale agriculture. By the 2000s more than three-quarters of forest clearing in the Amazon was for cattle-ranching.[150]

A 2009 Greenpeace report concluded:

> The cattle sector in the Brazilian Amazon is responsible for 14% of the world's annual deforestation. This makes it the world's largest driver of deforestation, responsible for more forest loss than the total deforestation in any country outside Brazil except Indonesia.[151]

In Indonesia, Greenpeace's 2017 report on palm oil concludes:

> The situation is critical for Indonesia's forests. The country has lost 31 million hectares of forest – an area almost the size of Germany – since 1990.[152]

One popular science website, LiveScience, reported in 2022:

> The world has lost about 10% of its tropical tree cover since 2000, and nearly 47,000 square miles (121,000 square kilometers) were destroyed in 2019 alone...[153]

---

150 https://rainforests.mongabay.com/amazon/amazon_destruction.html, 24 Nov, 2018.
151 www.greenpeace.org/archive-international/en/publications/reports/slaughtering-the-amazon, 24 Nov, 2018.
152 www.greenpeace.org/archive-international/en/press/releases/2017/Indonesias-forests-still-under-threat-from-palm-oil-industry-new-research-shows-/, 24 Nov, 2018.
153 www.livescience.com/27692-deforestation.html, 13 Mar, 2023.

Wildfires

Wildfires are a natural phenomenon, usually caused by lightning strikes or occasionally by volcanic eruptions:

> Between 2019 and 2021, immense wildfires burned down more than 1 million hectares of land in Siberia, killed nearly 3 billion animals in southeastern Australia, and took hundreds of buildings down across the US state of California.[154]

However, we humans have increased their frequency in three ways:

(i) Accident, arson, & losing control

Between 2000 and 2017, the US Forest Service reported on some 100,000 wildfires in North America:

> Nearly 85 percent of wildland fires in the United States are caused by humans. Human-caused fires result from campfires left unattended, the burning of debris, equipment use and malfunctions, negligently discarded cigarettes, and intentional acts of arson.[155]

They can also come from losing control of fires lit to clear land for farming, hunting, or regeneration of food plants.

(ii) Planting of exotics

We have also increased the intensity of wildfires by mass plantings of conifers instead of leaf trees and by introducing more inflammable species such as eucalyptus into the USA and the Middle East, or gamba grass into Australia.

(iii) Defective fire-management

Our fire-management practices have sometimes been counterproductive. Recent fatal wildfires in California may

---

154 https://earth.org/what-causes-wildfires, 25 Dec, 2022.
155 https://www.nps.gov/articles/wildfire-causes-and-evaluation.htm, 25 Dec, 2022.

have been due to a lack of planned and controlled burn-offs which remove slash and undergrowth, significantly lessening the damage of wildfires. Historically, fires ignited by lightning and Native Americans[156] were frequent and of low to moderate intensity. In 2007, it was reported that:

> A meta-analysis found that 17 times more land burned annually in California before 1800 compared to recent decades [1,800,000 hectares/year compared to 102,000 hectares/year].[157]

Today's fires can be vastly more damaging.

In Australia in the summer of 2019-2020, bushfires burned 18,000,000 hectares (18,000 sq km);[158] as I write, Canada's wildfires have already burned 2,700,000 hectares (2,700 sq km) which is more than 10 times the average over the last ten years.[159]

Overview

NASA's Ames Research Center has created a 'spatially continuous map of forest tree density at a global scale' and estimates:

> ...the global number of trees is approximately 3.04 trillion... Based on our projected tree densities, we estimate that over 15 billion trees are cut down each year, and the global number of trees has fallen by approximately 46% since the start of human civilization.[160]

The U.N.'s Food & Agriculture Organization (FAO) estimates:

> About half of the world's tropical forests have been

---

156   https://karuktribeclimatechangeprojects.com/chapter-2-fire-exclusion-and-changing-patterns-of-fire-behavior, 22 Feb, 2024.
157   www.sciencedirect.com/science/article/pii/S0378112707004379, 13 June, 2023.
158   www.unep.org/news-and-stories/story/ten-impacts-australian-bushfires, 13 June, 2023.
159   https://fortune.com/2023/06/01/canada-wildfires-climate-change, 13 June, 2023.
160   www.ncbi.nlm.nih.gov/pubmed/26331545, 24 Nov 2018.

cleared... 18 million acres (7.3 million hectares) of forest are lost each year...[161]

Scientists working with Botanic Gardens Conservation International (BGCI) which represents botanic gardens in over 100 countries are also giving us an uncannily specific warning:

> Over 100 tree species are already extinct in the wild, and with billions of trees being destroyed each year, *a third* of species face extinction.[162]

God is not sending angels with chainsaws to slash and burn the earth's trees – we are doing it. The 1st Trumpet's hail and fire is a metaphor for the vast storm of destruction that we have created.

Despite our losing this war, our response should be to still keep planting trees wherever we live. If we do not own our own land, we can work with or encourage city councils to increase plantings in nearby parks and reserves. We can also support non-profit organisations such as OneTreePlanted which has 'planted over 135,578,777 trees in 82 countries across the globe since 2014'.[163]

"All the Green Grass"

According to the *Encyclopaedia Britannica*, 'grasslands are one of the most widespread of all the major vegetation types of the world' and occupy the environmental midpoint between forests and deserts. Their article comments:

> This is so, however, only because human manipulation of the land has significantly altered the natural vegetation, creating artificial grasslands of cereal crops, pastures,

---

161 Or 7,300 sq. km. www.livescience.com/27692-deforestation.html, 24 Nov 2018.
162 www.sciencealert.com/scientists-studying-earths-trees-issue-stark-warning-to-humanity, 10 Feb, 2023. Emphasis added.
163 https://onetreeplanted.org/pages/faq, 18 Mar, 2024.

and other areas that require some form of repetitious, unnatural disturbance such as cultivation, heavy grazing, burning, or mowing to persist.[164]

The Global Environment Facility report that:

> Land degradation is one of the world's most pressing environmental problems and it will worsen without rapid remedial action. Globally, about 25 percent of the total land area has been degraded... Scientists recently warned that *24 billion tons* of fertile soil was being lost per year, largely due to unsustainable agriculture practices. If this trend continues, 95 percent of the Earth's land areas could become degraded by 2050.[165]

The UN's Food and Agriculture Organisation (FAO) agrees:

> Desertification has emerged as one of the most pressing global environmental challenges facing the world today. Drylands occupy 41% of the earth's land area and are home to more than 2 billion people, 90% of whom live in developing countries...[166]

Accordingly, FAO's Action Against Desertification (AAD) in Africa has been working with more than 20 countries to create the Great Green Wall, 'a great mosaic of green and productive landscapes across North Africa, the Sahel and the Horn' comprising '780 million hectares of arid and semi-arid land around the Sahara'.[167] Their aim is to restore 10 million hectares p.a.

China, meanwhile, faces the threat of the Gobi Desert, the fastest moving desert on earth, which is increasing at a rate

---

164 www.britannica.com/science/grassland, 18 Mar, 2024.
165 www.thegef.org/what-we-do/topics/land-degradation, 18 Mar, 2024. Emphasis added.
166 *Gender in Agriculture* Sourcebook, p. 454. www.fao.org/3/aj288e/aj288e.pdf, 15 Mar, 2024.
167 www.fao.org/in-action/action-against-desertification/overview/desertification-and-land-degradation/en, 18 mar, 2024.

of 3,370 sq. km (1,300 sq. miles) annually.[168] In 2016, *The New York Times* reported:

> Nearly 20 percent of China is desert, and drought across the northern region is getting worse. One recent estimate said China had 21,000 square miles more desert than what existed in 1975.[169]

There is also the depletion of groundwater globally:

> New data from NASA's… satellites show that many of the world's biggest aquifers are being sucked dry at a rate far greater than they are being replenished… Roughly *a third* of the world's 37 largest aquifers are under stress…[170]

Worst affected is India where 54% of 4,000 measured wells are declining[171] with China not far behind:

> Groundwater is used to irrigate more than 40% of China's farmland… Already, water is scarce for two-thirds of China's 660 cities… In southern and southeastern China, groundwater is now laden with heavy metals and other pollutants… 90% of groundwater is polluted, 60% of it seriously so.[172]

Grass is shallow-rooted so it can dry up in a sustained drought whereas the deeper-rooted shrubs and trees can survive for long periods. When John says 'all the green grass', therefore, he may be referring to a world-wide drought. Some grass must survive, however, because the locusts of the

---

168 www.nytimes.com/interactive/2016/10/24/world/asia/living-in-chinas-expanding-deserts.html?_r=0, 24 Nov 2018.
169 Ibid.
170 www.npr.org/sections/thetwo-way/2015/06/17/415206378/nasa-satellites-show-worlds-thirst-for-groundwater, 18 Mar, 2024. Emphasis added.
171 www.wri.org/insights/nasa-satellite-data-help-show-where-groundwater-and-where-it-isnt, 8 Mar, 2024.
172 'China faces up to groundwater crisis', www.nature.com/articles/466308a, 18 Mar, 2024.

5th Trumpet are commanded 'not to hurt the grass of the earth' (Rev 9:4).

Nevertheless, when it comes to land degradation and misuse, it is not God who is responsible but us. We must change what we are doing to stop it happening but, human nature being what it is, I doubt we will.

As we pray on these issues, God's answer is not always to intervene but to leave us facing the consequences of going our own way: this is the metaphorical blood mixed with the hail and fire. Accordingly, it seems to me we are hearing the 1st Trumpet today - what do you think?

'The Wrath of God'

Obviously, all vegetation was created for us to enjoy its beauty and fruit (Gen 2:9), to build our homes, and to fuel our fires for heat and light (we can easily forget that in Biblical times, their nights were lit by olive oil lamps). However, we have abused that trust and John hears at the 7th Trumpet that:

> "...*Your wrath came,* and the time came... to destroy those who *destroy the earth.*" (Rev 11:18*)

In Chapter 1, I showed how the 7th Trumpet is Judgement Day when God's wrath is finally poured out. However, the Scriptures also refer to times before then when His wrath is expressed in a way that we may not expect, when He actually refuses to act or intervene. Consider Paul's explanation to the Romans:

> For the wrath of God is revealed from heaven against all ungodliness and unrighteousness of men who suppress the truth in unrighteousness (Rom 1:18*)

How is it 'revealed from heaven'? By His giving us over to our own ideas and the desires of our own hearts. Paul went on to explain the behaviour of their idolatrous fellow-citizens in Rome:

> 22. Professing to be wise, they became fools,
> 23. and exchanged the glory of the incorruptible God for an image in the form of corruptible man and of birds and four-footed animals and crawling creatures.
> 24. Therefore *God gave them over in the lusts of their hearts to impurity*, so that their bodies would be dishonored among them… (Rom 1:22-24*)

Ignoring the Creator leads us to ignore how we are created and designed to function sexually:[173]

> 25. For they exchanged the truth of God for a lie, and worshiped and served the creature rather than the Creator, who is blessed forever. Amen.

---

[173] This is not to disparage anyone with gender dysphoria and dysfunction due to genetic, biological, environmental, and/or cultural factors due to the Fall. Jesus taught that "there are eunuchs who were born that way from their mother's womb; and there are eunuchs who were made eunuchs by men; and there are also eunuchs who made themselves eunuchs for the sake of the kingdom of heaven" (Matt 19:12), i.e. some are born with sexual disabilities, some are brutalised, and some freely choose how they live. According to the Mayo Clinic and the US National Library of Medicine, those with no choice include: 1 in 500-1,000 boys (0.1-0.2%) born with an extra copy of the X chromosome (Klinefelter Syndrome); 1 in 1,500-2000 of all babies (0.05-0.07%) born with ambiguous genitalia (Hermaphroditism or Intersex); 1 in 5-6,000 girls (0.02%) have an undeveloped vagina or uterus (Vaginal Agenesis); 1 in 5,000 girls (0.02%) are born with XY chromosomes, female genitalia but also testes and 90% lack a uterus (Androgen Insensitivity Syndrome or Testicular Feminisation Syndrome) – also 1 in 500 sports stars (0.2%) which led to the International Olympics Committee dropping sex-testing for women in 2004; 1 in 5,000-10,000 girls (0.01-0.02%) are born with ambiguous external genitalia and infertility (Congenital Adrenal Hyperplasia) while 1 in 66 girls (1.5%) face Late Onset Adrenal Hyperplasia and develop masculine characteristics and become infertile [https://medlineplus.gov/genetics/condition, 24 Nov, 2023]. Every one of these children "born that way" is always to be loved, accepted, and supported as they discover for themselves how to respond. Those who have been "made that way by men" include not only those physically mutilated but also those who have been traumatised as children (many of the lesbians I have known had been molested by adult relatives or neighbours). Lastly, those "who made themselves eunuchs for the sake of the kingdom of heaven" have chosen to be celibate and include, obviously, Jesus Himself, Paul, and Barnabas. See also Chapter 19, Sexual Delusion.

> 26. *For this reason God gave them over to degrading passions;* for their women exchanged the natural function for that which is unnatural… (Rom 1:25-26*)

'God gave them over' means He refused to intervene. Their punishment, 'the due penalty' (v. 27), was to suffer the dishonourable consequences of their wrongdoing:

> 27. and in the same way also the men abandoned the natural function of the woman and burned in their desire toward one another, men with men committing indecent acts and *receiving in their own persons the due penalty of their error.*
> 28. And just as they did not see fit to acknowledge God any longer, *God gave them over to a depraved mind,* to do those things which are not proper. (Rom 1:27-28*)

'The wrath of God is revealed' (v. 18) when He lets us have what we want and our punishment is that He does not rescue us from the consequences until we turn back.

On the other hand, His love is very often revealed by His intervening to discipline us. We are urged to remember the exhortation of Proverbs 3:11-12:

> 5. …the exhortation which is addressed to you as sons, "MY SON, DO NOT REGARD LIGHTLY THE DISCIPLINE OF THE LORD, NOR FAINT WHEN YOU ARE REPROVED BY HIM;
> 6. FOR THOSE WHOM THE LORD LOVES HE DISCIPLINES, AND HE SCOURGES EVERY SON WHOM HE RECEIVES."
> 7. It is for discipline that you endure; God deals with you as with sons; for what son is there whom his father does not discipline?
> 8. But *if you are without discipline,*… then you are *illegitimate children* and not sons. (Heb 12:5-8*)

'Do not regard lightly' means we should appreciate His discipline. As painful as it may be at times, His discipline actually proves He loves us *because* He is intervening in our lives. This is far preferable to His wrath which includes leaving us to face the outcome of our own decisions.

The 1st Trumpet then is to warn us of the consequences of our sinfulness on the earth and that God is angry about it but He will not intervene until the 7th.

Summary

(i) Jesus told the disciples asking for 'the sign of Your coming' that there would be many, and in all three areas of man's dominion: the earth, sea, and sky.

(ii) The seven trumpets are "signs of the times" in each of these areas, the first alarm/proximity alert being the destruction of a third of the trees on earth and 'all the grass'.

(iii) We have already reached and passed that amount of destruction of the trees, NASA estimating the global number of trees has fallen by 46% and BGCI reporting that 'a third of species face extinction' today. Losing 'all the grass' may yet be due to a severe widespread drought.

(iv) God is letting us face the global consequences of our greed and short-sightedness but we can still beautify our own areas of influence.

9

The Second Trumpet
Signs in the Sea

Next, we are supposed to look at what is happening in the sea:

> 8. The second angel sounded, and something like *a great mountain burning* with fire was thrown into the sea; and *a third of the sea* became blood,
> 9. and *a third* of the creatures which were in the sea and had life, died; and a third of the ships were destroyed. (Rev 8:8-9*)

Is it just mercury poisoning threatening "a third of the fish of the sea"? How is that 'something like a great mountain burning with fire' (v. 8), or is that literal?

A Great Burning Mountain

Today, it certainly looks like a literal asteroid striking the earth, killing sea-life and sinking ships but would that not be localised? Even if it could kill so much marine life from one catastrophic splashdown, could it affect shipping on the other side of the globe?

On the metaphorical side, John's 1st century Jewish audience would have had three historic Jewish metaphors to add to the mix.

(i) Mt Horeb/Sinai

Moses described Mt Sinai/Horeb as "burning with fire" (Deut 5:23, 9:15) as did the writer of Hebrews (Heb 12:18). Was John using that as metaphor?

(ii) An immovable, intractable problem

A "great mountain" was a also metaphor for a seemingly unresolvable problem:

> "What are you, O *great mountain*? Before Zerubbabel you will become a plain; and he will bring forth the top stone with shouts of 'Grace, grace to it!'" (Zech 4:7*)

In Zerubbabel's time, it had seemed impossible that his puny community of returnees from the Babylonian exile could rebuild Solomon's Temple but, thanks to Haggai and Zechariah's prophesying and the decrees of three Medo-Persian emperors (Ezra 6:14), he did "bring forth the top stone". Israel's immovable, intractable problem was resolved.

Jesus also used this metaphor but He added that the mountain can be "cast into the sea" if only we will trust in Him:

> "Truly I say to you, whoever says to this *mountain*, 'Be taken up and *cast into the sea*,' and does not doubt in his heart, but *believes* that what he says is going to happen, it will be granted him." (Mar 11:23*)

The Greek verb for "cast" is *ballo*, 'to throw, propel'[174] and that is the verb John uses in Revelation 8:8 - his burning mountain does not fall into the sea but is *thrown* there.

(iii) The Babylonian Empire

Thirdly, Jeremiah prophesied the downfall of the Babylonian Empire in strikingly similar terms to John's:

> "Behold, I am against you, O *destroying mountain*,
> Who destroys the whole earth," declares the LORD,
> "And I will stretch out My hand against you,

---

[174] Kittel, Gerhard & Friedrich, Gerhard, *Theological Dictionary of the New Testament*, abridged, Grand Rapids, MI; William B Eerdmans Pub, 1985, p. 91.

> And roll you down from the crags,
> And I will make you a *burnt out mountain*." (Jer 51:25*)

From being an active and "destroying mountain", the great Babylonian Empire became an extinct volcano.

Which of these three metaphors did John mean? Well, what do we see regarding marine-life, ships, and empires?

Marine-Life

Tragically, mercury-poisoning is only one of several man-made threats - we also have overfished and trashed our oceans to an astonishing extent.

(i) Overfishing

Today, fish-farming provides half of the world's seafood, with China producing 58%, followed by Indonesia, India, and Vietnam. However, this can obscure the fact that:

> Almost 90 percent of global marine fish stocks are now fully exploited or overfished...the demand for fish is twice the estimated supply of sustainably caught wild fish... According to FAO [the UN's Food and Agriculture Organization], the proportion of overfished stocks has been increasing over the last four decades...[175]

The annual world catch grew steadily from 30 million tonnes in 1950 to its peak of 130 million tonnes in 1997.[176] Since then catches have plateaued or declined, even though fishing practices have become more industrialised and efficient. Included in these figures is the appalling annual waste of 5-10 million tonnes due to bycatch:

---

[175] Explanation inserted. https://datatopics.worldbank.org/sdgatlas/archive/2017/SDG-14-life-below-water.html, 13 Mar, 2023.
[176] Ibid.

> ...large amounts of unwanted sea animals are captured during the fishing for a particular species and then are discarded as waste, causing the unnecessary loss of billions of fish and sea creatures.[177]

International regulating for sustainability has definitely helped but...:

> Illegal fishing... accounts for around 20 percent of the global catch... even if the most drastic measures to reduce fishing were implemented globally, it would still take up to 20 years for the overexploited stocks to recover and for global fisheries to be sustainable.[178]

What of sea-life other than fish? In 2015, the World Wildlife Fund (WWF) reported:

> Over just 40 years there has been a decrease recorded in marine species of 39%.[179]

In 2019, this startling summation appeared:

> Over *one-third* of marine mammals and nearly one-third of sharks, shark relatives, and reef-forming corals are threatened with extinction, according to a new report released today on the state of global biodiversity.[180]

The highlighting of the 'one-third' here is mine.

---

177 https://earth.org/facts-overfishing, 13 Mar, 2023.
178 https://datatopics.worldbank.org/sdgatlas/archive/2017/SDG-14-life-below-water.html, 13 Mar, 2023.
179 www.fishforward.eu/sl/facts-figures/#_ftn4, 13 Mar, 2023.
180 Lauren Kubiack, www.nrdc.org/experts/lauren-kubiak/marine-biodiversity-dangerous-decline-finds-new-report, 13 Mar, 2023. She explains: 'The Global Assessment Report on Biodiversity and Ecosystem Services, written by an intergovernmental body of biological and ecological experts representing 50 countries, lays out the dire situation for species richness across the globe. The most comprehensive assessment on the state of nature since 2005, the report finds that between half a million and one million species are threatened with extinction globally, and extinction rates have accelerated sharply in the past century.'

(ii) Trash

In February 2015, *National Geographic* reported:

> Scientists have come up with a new way to measure ocean trash - and the numbers are even worse than thought. In 2010, eight million tons of plastic trash ended up in the ocean from coastal countries—far more than the total that has been measured floating on the surface in the ocean's garbage patches. That's the bad news. The even worse news is that the tonnage is on target to increase tenfold in the next decade unless the world finds a way to improve how garbage is collected and managed.[181]

Vast islands of floating plastic have been formed by rotating ocean currents called gyres. In 1997, Captain Charles Moore sailed though one and wrote:

> ...as I gazed from the deck at the surface of what ought to have been a pristine ocean, I was confronted, as far as the eye could see, with the sight of plastic. It seemed unbelievable, but I never found a clear spot. In the week it took to cross the subtropical high, no matter what time of day I looked, plastic debris was floating everywhere: bottles, bottle caps, wrappers, fragments.[182]

Now called the Great Pacific Garbage Patch, it is estimated to have a 1,000,000 sq. km (386,000 sq. mile) 'heart', surrounded by a 3.6 million sq. km (1.4 million sq. mile) outer periphery. Others insist it is much smaller[183] but similar vortexes have formed in the Atlantic and Indian Oceans and the North Sea and the effects on marine birds and animals are disastrous:

---

[181] http://news.nationalgeographic.com/news/2015/02/150212-ocean-debris-plastic-garbage-patches-science, 28 Aug, 2015.
[182] https://education.nationalgeographic.org/resource/great-pacific-garbage-patch, 13 Mar, 2023.
[183] www.americanthinker.com/blog/2015/12/the_great_pacific_garbage_patch_myth.html, 26 Nov, 2018.

...loggerhead sea turtles often mistake plastic bags for jellies, their favorite food. Albatrosses mistake plastic resin pellets for fish eggs and feed them to chicks, which die of starvation or ruptured organs. Seals and other marine mammals are especially at risk. They can get entangled in abandoned plastic fishing nets, which are being discarded more often because of their low cost. Seals and other mammals often drown in these forgotten nets—a phenomenon known as "ghost fishing."[184]

Is God doing this to us?

About 80% of the debris in the Great Pacific Garbage Patch comes from land-based activities in North America and Asia… The remaining 20%… comes from boaters, offshore oil rigs, and large cargo ships that dump or lose debris directly into the water. The majority of this debris—about 79,000 tons—is fishing nets. More unusual items, such as computer monitors and LEGOs, come from dropped shipping containers.[185]

Why is it accumulating?

...plastics make up the majority of marine debris [because] plastic's durability, low cost, and malleability mean that it's being used in more and more consumer and industrial products [and] plastic goods do not biodegrade but instead break down into smaller pieces.

In the ocean, the sun breaks down these plastics into tinier and tinier pieces, a process known as photo-degradation. Scientists have collected up to 750,000 bits of microplastic in a single square kilometer of the Great Pacific Garbage Patch—that's about 1.9 million bits per square mile. Most of this debris comes from plastic bags, bottle caps, plastic water bottles, and Styrofoam cups.[186]

---

184   www.nationalgeographic.org/encyclopedia/great-pacific-garbage-patch, 26 Nov, 2018.
185   Ibid.
186   Ibid.

It is becoming possible to collect and remove floating debris but most of it does not stay afloat:

> Oceanographers and ecologists recently discovered that about 70% of marine debris actually sinks to the bottom of the ocean.[187]

While some micro-plastic may become simply part of the landscape, much enters the food chain where 'ingestion may lead to loss of nutrition, internal injury, intestinal blockage, starvation, and even death'.[188]

Marine biologists in Antarctica report that:

> We found microfibres, fibres that probably come from synthetic clothing, in every sample we took… in the air, the snow, the seawater and sediment in Antarctica… They were in 60% of krill [which are] food for penguins, whales, seals - they're at the heart of the Antarctic ecosystem.[189]

Ships Sinking

What destroys ships?

> …and a third of the ships were destroyed. (Rev 8: 9)

In peacetime, all ships are vulnerable to disastrous weather conditions, faulty design, crew error, and any combination of these. Consider the RMS *Titanic*. In 1912, the *Titanic* was the largest ship in the world and thought to be unsinkable but sank in calm seas with massive loss of life (1,517 dead, 706 survivors) due to faulty design, too few lifeboats, and human error.

In wartime, men deliberately sink ships and in the last 100

---

187   Ibid.
188   https://marinedebris.noaa.gov/discover-issue/impacts, 26 Nov, 2018.
189   www.9news.com.au/world/microplastics-plastic-pollution-antarctica-dying-everyday-human-activities-fueling-decline-expert-says-exclusive/0512077c-6f7f-4a44-a6fd-6adba963d266, 20 Mar, 2024.

hundred years, we have sunk well over a third.

At the beginning of the 20th century, the Battle of Tsushima between Russia and Japan ended with over two-thirds of the Russian Pacific fleet destroyed.[190]

In World War I, German U-boats sank over 6,000 Allied and neutral ships.

However, World War II brought about the single, largest loss of shipping in a relatively short period of time that the world has ever witnessed. In just the Battle of the Atlantic, the Germans sank 5,151 merchant ships[191] and 175 Allied warships[192] while losing 442 U-boats and 47 surface warships.[193]

Overall, British and Dominion[194] Navies lost 278 of their 885 ships in service (31%). They sank 827 ships and 780 U-boats of the German fleet while the Germans scuttled over 200 U-boats to avoid capture in 1945. After the war, the victorious Allies scuttled another 174 U-boats in Operation Deadlight to completely destroy the Kriegsmarine, i.e. German War Navy (100%). The Allies also sank 56 ships and 85 submarines of the Italian fleet (54%[195]) and 208 ships and 127 submarines of the Japanese Navy's total[196] of 645 ships (52%).[197]

---

190   All eleven battleships, five of nine cruisers, six of its nine destroyers, and five of six auxiliary vessels. The Japanese lost only three torpedo boats, leading them to believe they could overcome the American Pacific Fleet at Pearl Harbor in 1939 (Willmott, H. P., *The Last Century of Sea Power: From Port Arthur to Chanak, 1894–1922*, Volume 1, 2009. Indiana University Press).

191   Nathan Miller, *War at Sea - A Naval History of World War II* (New York, Scribner, 1995) and John Terraine, *Business in Great Waters: The U-Boat Wars, 1916-1945* (London: Leo Cooper, 1989), as quoted on website www.usmm.org/battleatlantic.html, 12 Mar, 2023.

192   Ibid.

193   Ibid.

194   Australian, Canadian, Indian, and New Zealand Navies. Many Dominion officers and men served in and sometimes commanded Royal Navy ships.

195   www.naval-history.net/WW2CampaignsItalianNavy.htm, 13 Mar, 2023.

196   www.naval-history.net/WW2aBritishLosses10tables.htm, 12 Mar, 2023.

197   https://worldwarwings.com/this-map-of-all-sunken-japanese-ships-during-wwii-is-absolutely-mind-blowing, 12 Mar, 2023.

The US Navy lost 695 ships,[198] having begun with just 350[199] and built another 1,200,[200] so so that was 44%.

Neutrality was no defence. Norway's Nortraship was the world's largest shipping company with a fleet of 1,081 and lost 570 (53%).[201]

After the war, the Greek merchant navy which had lost 245 of their 404 ships (61%) were able to buy some 500 Liberty ships[202] but thousands of warships and Liberty ships were simply decommissioned and scrapped. The World of Warships website summarises:

> There were 105,127 ships participated in WW2… 36,387 ships were destroyed at the end of the war.[203]

That was another 35%, over a third, *after the war.*

We have therefore seen well over 'a third of the ships… destroyed' (Rev 8:9) over those few years.

An Empire Ending

At the exact same time, we saw the end of a great empire.

I initially wondered if John's 'great mountain burning with fire' was the direct cause of the carnage in the sea, but what would happen to any blazing mountain thrown into the depths of the ocean? It would actually be extinguished, just as the Babylonian Empire was. Remember, God described the Babylonian Empire as a "destroying mountain who

---

198 www.usmm.org/navylossww2.html, 12 Mar, 2023.
199 Allan Ferguson Westcott et al, *American Sea Power Since 1775*, Chicago; J.B. Lippincott Company, ISBN 1399958712, p. 343.
200 www.ibiblio.org/hyperwar/USN/USNatWar/USN-King-B.html, 13 Mar, 2023.
201 https://warsailors.com/freefleet/index.html, 13 Mar, 2023.
202 Liberty ships were a class of cargo ship mass-produced in the USA under the Emergency Shipbuilding Act to carry about 10,000 tonnes. https://cosmosphilly.com/the-battle-of-the-atlantic-the-gruesome-tale-the-numbers-tell-of-triumph-and-tragedy, 12 Mar, 2023.
203 https://warship.info/how-many-navy-ships-were-produced-during-world-war-ii, 26 Dec, 2022.

destroys the whole earth" that He would make "a burnt out mountain" (Jer 51:15), i.e. an extinct volcano.

In World War II a vast empire was extinguished. Consider what happened to not just one but three nationalist empires which had joined forces - the Axis Powers.

This alliance between Hitler's Germany, Mussolini's Italy, and Hirohito's Japan began in 1936 and was joined by Hungary, Romania, and Slovakia in 1940, and by Bulgaria, Yugoslavia, and Croatia in 1941.

By then, Hitler's juggernaut had rolled through Austria, Czechoslovakia, Poland, Denmark, Norway, Belgium, the Netherlands, Luxembourg, France, Yugoslavia, Greece, Estonia, Latvia, and Lithuania, i.e. all of Western Europe.

The Italians had taken Tunisia, Libya, western Egypt, Ethiopia, Somalia, and British Somaliland, i.e. half of North and East Africa, as well as Albania to their east.

The Japanese had conquered Korea, Mongolia, North China, and Taiwan, and French Indochina (today's Vietnam, Cambodia, and Laos) and were about to take Thailand, Burma, British Malaya, Singapore, the Philippines, the Dutch East Indies (today's Indonesia), and Papua-New Guinea, i.e. all of South East Asia.

England was facing imminent invasion, having just lost the Battle of France in June 1940 with 66,500 of their soldiers dead or in prison camps.[204] The Battle of Britain had begun and by October, the Royal Air Force was on the verge of collapse and London was facing nightly bombing raids by up to five hundred German planes.[205]

Meanwhile, the USA was bound by US law to stay neutral and Stalin's USSR had signed a peace treaty with Hitler in

---

204 Sebag-Montefiore, Hugh. *Dunkirk: Fight to the Last Man,* New York: Viking, 2006, p. 506.
205 Other cities targeted were Liverpool, Birmingham, Sheffield, Manchester, Coventry, Southampton, Plymouth, Portsmouth, Bristol, Newcastle upon Tyne, and Hull in England, Swansea in Wales, Belfast in Northern Ireland, and Clydeside in Scotland.

1939 and taken half of Poland.

In 1941, the war seemed lost but by 1945, everything had turned around. The three great Axis Powers led by three antichrist regimes[206] had been defeated by nominally Christian nations with many genuine Christian citizens who earnestly and publicly prayed for "this mountain" to be "taken up and cast into the sea" (Mark 11:23). These events are so extraordinary that I detail all of this on our website,[207] noting how WWII also led to the breaking up of the victorious British Empire as well as the colonial empires of the Portuguese, Spanish, Dutch, French, Belgians, and Russians.

So is John's 'great mountain burning with fire' literal or metaphorical?

There may one day be a literal asteroid that strikes the earth. If so, we will have to wait for that to happen. However, I believe we have already seen this vision fulfilled metaphorically with the extinguishing of the empire of the Axis Powers. If so, we have already heard the 2nd Trumpet.

What do you think?

Summary

(i) We are supposed to look at man's dominion over the sea - *when we see* a third of the marine-life dead, a third of our ships destroyed, and a blazing mountain thrown into the sea and extinguished, *we are to recognise* the 2nd Trumpet's sounding.

(ii) Over the last 40 years, overfishing, mercury-poisoning, and polluting plastics have vastly depleted stocks, caused a 39% decrease in marine species, and today one-third of marine mammals, sharks, and reef-

---

206 Details in *Slouching Towards Bethlehem*, pp. 125-135.
207 Article *The 2nd Trumpet: The End of Empires*, www.emmausroad.org.nz, 8 Apr, 2024.

forming corals face extinction. We have killed 'a third of the creatures which were in the sea and had life'.

(iii) In World War II, at least a third and sometimes up to half of the warring nations' navies and merchant ships were sunk while another third were scrapped afterwards. We have destroyed 'a third of the ships'.

(iv) Also in World War II, we metaphorically extinguished the burning mountain of the Axis Powers of Germany, Italy, and Japan, and their allies.

(v) Only two of these three signs are related but all are man-made and have occurred in the last 80 years.

10
The Third & Fourth Trumpets
Signs in the Water & Air

10. The third angel sounded, and a great star fell from heaven, burning like a torch, and it fell on *a third of the rivers and on the springs of waters.*
11. The name of the star is called Wormwood; and *a third of the waters* became wormwood, and many men died from the waters, because they were made bitter. (Rev 8:10-11*)

Wormword

Wormword is the bitter herb *artemisia absinthium*[208] and its Ukrainian name is *chernobyl* (lit. black herb). Accordingly, when the nuclear plant in Chernobyl over-heated and burned for ten days in 1986, many believed this fulfilled the 3rd Trumpet. In the town centre, they erected the Wormwood Star Memorial Complex, featuring a statue called the Monument of the Third Angel. Twenty-nine people died from acute radiation-poisoning after the disaster, with hundreds more falling sick.[209]

Appalling as this was, however, it did not affect a third of the earth's rivers and springs.

What then does John mean? Who exactly is polluting all of our freshwater, angels or us? What is the "great star, burning like a torch"?

---

208 This herb is prized for its aroma, flavour, and purported health benefits and is used to make vermouth, that being the French pronunciation of the German word 'wermut' for wormwood. It also has a notorious reputation from its use in absinthe, a French liqueur with 70% alcohol and favoured by 19th century artists including Vincent Van Gogh and later, Pablo Picasso. www.healthline.com/nutrition/what-is-wormwood, 9 Mar, 2023.
209 www.atlasobscura.com/places/angel-monument-chernobyl, 9 Mar, 2023.

We begin as usual with the question, is this literal or metaphorical?

If it is a literal asteroid, terrifying and unavoidable, could a single rock affect 'a third' of all freshwater on the earth? Or is it a metaphor for the natural consequences all over the earth of our behaviour? In other words, is it one event or many?

One way to resolve this is to look at rivers and springs all over the earth today and consider what is happening.

Fig (vi) Bible illustration 1909

'A Third of the Waters'

Let us begin with India's holiest river:

> The Ganges River Pollution is now at such a high level that the amount of toxins, chemicals and other dangerous bacteria found in the river are now almost 3000 times over the limit suggested by the WHO as 'safe'. The river directly and indirectly affects the largest population of any river in the world with… more than 420 million people who rely on it for food, water, bathing and agriculture. And that is not to mention the tens of millions of pilgrims who venture to India's most holy of rivers each year to bathe and worship.[210]

Consider the Volga, Europe's longest river. In 2017, *The Times* summarised a Kremlin report admitting:

---

210 www.all-about-india.com/Ganges-River-Pollution.html#sthash.K4aLMQWB.dpuf, 28 Aug, 2015.

Graeme Carlé

> Pollution in parts of the Volga, the longest river in Europe, has reached a critical level.... A government report said that billions of cubic yards of waste, including oil byproducts, pesticides and heavy metals, were being dumped in the river every year by factories and cities along its banks. The situation has been made worse by an estimated 3,000 oil tankers, cargo and passenger ships that have sunk... and been abandoned by the authorities.[211]

The Volga supplies 20% of Russia's fish but 90% suffer mutations and 'less than 5 per cent of the river's water is believed to be safe to drink.'[212]

How about the Danube, 'the world's most international river'?

> After barely surviving decades of heavy pollution by industries in the communist era, the ecological status of the Danube river has dramatically improved. But threats from new sources of pollution are looming on the world's most international river, which tracks almost 1,800 miles through 10 countries and four capitals... One of the newer pollution threats is microplastics, which can affect fish and fish larvae that confuse the particles with food sources. A study in Austria last year discovered that 40 tonnes of microplastics, pieces of plastic 5mm or smaller in diameter, are being transported each year through the country's stretch of the river alone. It found that littering, wind carry and ineffective waste management are key contributors as larger plastic particles in the environment breakdown into smaller microplastics.[213]

Another crisis is antibiotic pollution. In 2019, one massive study across the world including the Seine, Thames, Mekong,

---

211 www.thetimes.co.uk/article/volga-river-being-poisoned-by-pollution-8606ljzlv, 10 Feb, 2023.
212 Ibid.
213 www.theguardian.com/sustainable-business/2016/nov/13/danube-looming-pollution-threats-worlds-most-international-river-microplastics-fertiliser, 26 Dec, 2022.

Tiber, and Danube spotlighted:

> ...the role played by waterways in the strengthening antibiotic resistance of environmental bacteria, which poses a significant threat to public health, researchers tested more than 700 sites in 72 different countries around the world to determine the concentration of 14 commonly-used antibiotics. [They found that] 65% of the monitored sites had antibiotics in them, with a concentration sometimes exceeding, like in the case of Bangladesh, safe levels by up to 300 times.[214]

Consider South America. Their Amazon River is the world's largest river system and in 2018, the World Wildlife Fund reported:

> The mercury pollution crisis in the Amazon is unfortunately both invisible and largely ignored despite growing evidence of the dangers it poses for people and wildlife across the river system... The Amazon is estimated to have the richest biodiversity in the world. However, mercury pollution is threatening its wildlife, putting iconic predators such as jaguars and river dolphins as well as fish that are critical to the food security of indigenous, rural and urban communities at risk... One study cited in the report found that 81 per cent of carnivorous fish had detectable levels of mercury, while another showed that 26 per cent of river dolphins had mercury levels above the recommended World Health Organization level for people.[215]

Who is causing this, mankind or the angel blowing the alarm?

> The main source of mercury pollution in the Amazon is artisanal and small-scale gold mining, which accounts for 15 per cent of the gold extracted from the region.

---

214   https://kafkadesk.org/2019/05/30/danube-is-most-polluted-river-in-europe-shows-new-global-study, 26 Dec, 2022.
215   wwf.panda.org/wwf_news/?338470/Toxic-mercury-poisoning-the-Amazon, 9 Mar, 2023.

> Mercury is used in the gold purification process – contributing around 71 per cent of all mercury emissions each year.

The report adds a significant global warning:

> Around the world, freshwater species populations have suffered the greatest decline since 1970 according to WWF's recent Living Planet Report – a catastrophic 83 per cent fall on average.[216]

How about lakes? Consider Lake Baikal, famed for the purest water on the planet and holding 20% of its unfrozen freshwater, more than all of America's Great Lakes combined. In 2015, *The Siberian Times* reported:

> One of the wonders of the world, Baikal is Russia's jewel, but it is now facing severe pollution, according to stark new warnings. Worryingly, its famously drinkable water is drinkable no more, say scientists, at least in the southern part of the lake, in an area covering around 30% of its area. It is regarded as unsafe for animals to drink, never mind humans, warned a report this week on UlanMedia, which stated Baikal 'does not meet sanitary and epidemiological requirements'.[217]

In other words, a third is undrinkable.

In my own country of Aotearoa-New Zealand, we have always prided ourselves on the purity of our environment but a recent report by our Ministry of Environment concludes that:

> 46% of all our lakes larger than 1 hectare (1,758 lakes) have poor or very poor health… Only 2% of those lakes rated good or very good… [218] In 2017, 76% of known indigenous freshwater fish species (39 of 51) were

---

216 Ibid.
217 https://siberiantimes.com/ecology/casestudy/news/n0494-pollution-crisis-in-lake-baikal, 26 Dec, 2022.
218 https://environment.govt.nz/assets/publications/our-freshwater-2023.pdf, p. 6. 24 Apr, 2023.

threatened with extinction... 63% of freshwater fish species have a decreasing population trend...[219]

"A Great Star"?

This devastation is obviously literal so how does it fit with the metaphor of a fallen star?

> ...a great star fell from heaven, burning like a torch... The name of the star is called Wormwood. (Rev 9:10-11*)

We have to consider *four* metaphors that John's 1st century Jewish audience would have already known.

(i) A fallen star

As we will see in the next chapter, John uses this metaphor to describe a fallen angel:

> Then the fifth angel sounded, and I saw a star from heaven which had fallen to the earth; and the key of the bottomless pit was given to him. (Rev 9:1*)

This 'angel of the abyss' (v. 5) is 'king' of the locust plague and he is given 'the key of the bottomless pit' (v. 1) to release the demonic locusts from there onto the earth.

Isaiah also used this metaphor to describe the fall of Satan from his role as Adam and Eve's guardian angel in the Garden.[220]

> "How you have *fallen from heaven*,
> O *star* of the morning, son of the dawn!
> You have been cut down to the earth..." (Isa 14:12*)

Centuries later, Jesus spoke of "watching Satan fall from heaven like lightning" (Luke 10:18) as he lost his dominion[221]

---

219 Ibid. p. 23.
220 See my earlier book *Because of the Angels: Unveiling 1 Corinthians 11:2-16*, Wellington; Emmaus Road Publishing, 1998.
221 Acts 26:18, Colossians 1:13.

over every individual who believed the message of the seventy.

However, Isaiah's prophecy had another layer to it because he was not only describing Satan's past but also predicting the downfall of the all-too human king Belshazzar and the Babylonian Empire (Isa 14:4) at the hands of Darius the Mede (Dan 5:30-31), as covered in Book 5.[222]

We see then a fallen star can mean both a fallen angel and a wicked emperor and his empire.

A third use of the metaphor is by Daniel in predicting Antiochus Epiphanes' killing of righteous Jews:

> "[he] caused... some of the stars to fall to the earth, and... trampled them down" (Dan 8:10).

The stars here symbolise the children of Abraham (Gen 15:5), Isaac (Gen 26:4), and Jacob, as Joseph saw in his dream (Gen 37:9-10) and as John saw in Revelation 12 (Rev 12:4);[223] their fall is not their fault but Satan's killing of righteous descendants of Abraham, Isaac, and Jacob.

Revelation 9:1 is further complicated by John's seeing 'a *great* star'.

Before we can deduce which meaning he intended, we need to be clear about the next three metaphors.

(ii) 'Burning like a torch'

This refers to the light the great star produces rather than its heat, and Isaiah used this metaphor too:

> "Behold, all you who kindle a fire,
> Who encircle yourselves with firebrands,
> Walk in *the light of your fire*
> And among the *brands you have set ablaze*.
> This you will have from My hand:
> You will lie down in torment. (Isa 50:11*)

---

222   *Threshing Hour*, pp. 110-113.
223   See *Dancing in the Dragon's Jaws*, pp. 12-13.

The light we kindle for ourselves, i.e. our own reasoning, can never match God's revelation so it can never bring us the peace He offers us. The great fallen star is offering light 'like a torch' but, as I will show, it is a false light.

(iii) '...called Wormwood'

This name may seem unusual to us today but it was very familiar to John's Jewish audience as a metaphor for bitterness. Jeremiah spoke of God feeding "wormwood and poisoned water" to Israel when He sent them into exile in Babylon (Jer 9:13-15, 23:15) and he wrote of his own overwhelming experience of this time:

> He has filled me with bitterness,
> He has made me *drunk with wormwood*. (Lam 3:15*)
>
> Remember my affliction and my wandering,
> The *wormwood and bitterness*. (Lam 3:19*)

Amos denounced Israel's unjust rulers who "turn justice into wormwood" (Amos 5:7) by overcharging the poor (v. 11), who have "turned justice into poison and the fruit of righteousness into wormwood" (Amos 6:12).

Accordingly, John's prediction that the whole world will drink 'wormwood' because we have polluted our own water supplies would have been easily understood and seen as appropriate by his Jewish audience.

However, they would also have known that wormwood is the fruit of turning away from God, i.e. apostasy. The children of Israel grew up hearing about it in their synagogues in God's warning to every generation (Deut 29:14-15):

> "...so that there will not be among you a man or woman, or family or tribe, whose heart turns away today from the LORD... that there will not be among you *a root bearing poisonous fruit and wormwood*." (Deut 29:18*)

They were taught that anyone turning away from the Lord becomes like a plant offering "poisonous fruit" with the bitter aftertaste of "wormwood" for all who eat it, that in betraying God, they begin to betray others.

The writer of Hebrews passes this warning on to Christians:

> 15. See to it that no one comes short of the grace of God; that no *root of bitterness* springing up causes trouble, and by it *many be defiled...* (Heb 12:15*)

In context, the writer had been urging believers to welcome God's loving discipline (Heb 12:5-14) and he goes on to apply the metaphor to anyone who chooses instead the pleasures of the world:

> 16. ...that there be no immoral or godless person like Esau, who sold his own birthright for a single meal.
> 17. For you know that even afterwards, when he desired to inherit the blessing, he was rejected, for he found no place for repentance, though he sought for it with tears. (Heb 12:16-17*)

Esau's apostasy also ended in grief for his parents (Gen 26:34-35) and his descendants, the Edomites, became an enemy nation to Israel (Num 20:14-21).

This then brings us to the betrayal in adultery.

(iv) The adulteress

We now come to the last and most important piece of this jigsaw puzzle we are assembling. Three thousand years ago, Solomon warned his son that the apparent sweetness of adultery can end in much bitterness:

> 3. ...the lips of an adulteress drip *honey*
> And smoother than oil is her speech;
> 4. *But in the end she is bitter as wormwood,*

>   Sharp as a two-edged sword.
> 5. Her feet go down to death… (Prov 5:3-5*)

In Book 5,[224] I showed how Solomon developed this generic adulteress into a personification of foolishness (Prov 9:13-18), contrasting her with the personification of wisdom (Prov 9:1-6), and that these two women ultimately manifest as the two great women of Revelation, Babylon the Great and the New Jerusalem.

There John reveals that New Jerusalem is the Bride of Christ (Rev 19:7, 21:2), the spiritual body made up of all who love and happily submit to Jesus as the Bridegroom, contrasting her with Babylon the Prostitute (Rev 17:1, 19:2), the spiritual body made up of all who will submit to virtually anyone or anything other than Him.

I showed that Babylon the Great is also called 'the world', the world who seduces mankind to love her and 'all that is in the world, the lust of the flesh and the lust of the eyes and the boastful pride of life' (1 John 2:16), to be 'lovers of self, lovers of money… lovers of pleasure rather than lovers of God' (1 Tim 3:2 & 4). She is the archetype of both foolishness and adultery.

Accordingly, James speaks of this love of the world as adultery:

> You adulteresses, do you not know that friendship with *the world* is hostility toward God? Therefore whoever wishes to be a friend of the world makes himself an enemy of God. (Jas 4:4*)

---

224 *Threshing Hour*, pp. 123-124.

Babylon the Great Star

As Solomon says, the lips of the ultimate Adulteress do 'drip honey... but in the end she is as bitter as wormwood'.

She also fulfils the other two metaphors - Babylon the Great is indeed 'a great star' which has fallen and 'burning *like* a torch' but issuing a false light. As I showed in Book 5[225] she is in her last 'hour' and about to be destroyed by the ten horns on the seventh head of the beast (Rev 17:16), i.e. the 'principality and power' of 'all the nations' combining to attack Israel for the last time in the Battle of Har-Magedon or, as it is commonly known, Armageddon.

John's vision therefore illustrates what we can already see to be true: it has been our love of self, money, and pleasure which has led fallen mankind away from the love of God, each other, and our environment; failing in our stewardship, we are now facing the consequences of our greed and short-sightedness in polluting the freshwater of the earth.

It seems obvious to me we are hearing the 3rd Trumpet's warning regarding 'a third of the waters'. I also believe the 'great star... called Wormwood' is Babylon the Great, i.e. the personification of 'the world', inhabited and loved by everyone who will not submit to Jesus, whose lips 'drip honey' but whose end will indeed be 'as bitter as wormwood'.

But what do you think?

The Fourth Trumpet – the Air

What about the darkening of the sun, moon and stars? Surely that can't be our fault, can it?

> 12. The fourth angel sounded, and *a third of the sun and a third of the moon and a third of the stars were struck, so that a third of them* would be darkened and the day would not shine for a *third* of it, and the *night* in the same way. (Rev 8:12*)

---

225   Ibid, pp. 185-192.

Almost twenty years ago in 2005, the BBC was reporting on the sun dimming since the 1950s:

> We are all seeing rather less of the Sun, according to scientists who have been looking at five decades of sunlight measurements. They have reached the disturbing conclusion that the amount of solar energy reaching the Earth's surface has been gradually falling. The effect was first spotted by Gerry Stanhill, an English scientist working in Israel. Comparing Israeli sunlight records from the 1950s with current ones, Dr Stanhill was astonished to find a large fall in solar radiation. "There was a staggering 22% drop in the sunlight, and that really amazed me." Intrigued, he searched records from all around the world, and found the same story almost everywhere he looked. Sunlight was falling by 10% over the USA, nearly 30% in parts of the former Soviet Union, and even by 16% in parts of the British Isles.[226]

Obviously, location matters - 22% in Israel, 10% in the USA, 30% in Russia - but consider the big picture:

> Although the effect varied greatly from place to place, overall the decline amounted to one to two per cent globally every decade between the 1950s and the 1990s. Dr Stanhill called it "global dimming", but his research, published in 2001, met a sceptical response from other scientists. It was only recently, when his conclusions were confirmed by Australian scientists using a completely different method to estimate solar radiation, that climate scientists at last woke up to the reality of global dimming.[227]

And the cause?

---

226   http://news.bbc.co.uk/2/hi/science/nature/4171591.stm, 8 June, 2023.
227   Ibid.

(i) Air pollution

The BBC report concluded:

> Dimming appears to be caused by air pollution. Burning coal, oil and wood, whether in cars, power stations or cooking fires, produces not only invisible carbon dioxide - the principal greenhouse gas responsible for global warming - but also tiny airborne particles of soot, ash, sulphur compounds and other pollutants. This visible air pollution reflects sunlight back into space, preventing it reaching the surface.
>
> But the pollution also changes the optical properties of clouds. Because the particles seed the formation of water droplets, polluted clouds contain a larger number of droplets than unpolluted clouds. Recent research shows that this makes them more reflective than they would otherwise be, again reflecting the Sun's rays back into space.[228]

Of course, this affects the world's rainfall as the report continues:

> Scientists are now worried that dimming, by shielding the oceans from the full power of the Sun, may be disrupting the pattern of the world's rainfall. There are suggestions that dimming was behind the droughts in sub-Saharan Africa which claimed hundreds of thousands of lives in the 1970s and 80s.
>
> There are disturbing hints the same thing may be happening today in Asia, home to half the world's population. "My main concern is global dimming is also having a detrimental impact on the Asian monsoon," says Professor Veerhabhadran Ramanathan, professor of climate and atmospheric sciences at the University of California, San Diego. "We are talking about billions of people."[229]

---

228 Ibid.
229 Ibid.

Since 2005, there has been some "global brightening" as the USA and Europe have significantly reduced air pollution but not in Asia:

> The brightening tendency also seems to level off at sites in Japan. In China there is some indication for a renewed dimming, after the stabilization in the 1990s. A continuation of the long-lasting dimming is also noted at the sites in India. Overall, the available data suggest continuation of the brightening beyond the year 2000 at numerous locations, yet less pronounced and coherent than during the 1990s, with more regions with no clear changes or declines.[230]

(ii) Light pollution

We have also created light pollution, the glow produced by artificial lighting which has increased exponentially over the last one hundred years due to population growth, new technologies, and the vast growth of our towns and cities. This is rapidly reducing the number of stars visible to the naked eye, as *Science* recently reported:

> Citizen scientists report global rapid reductions in the visibility of stars from 2011 to 2022.[231]

The pleasure of star-gazing is severely threatened, as *The Guardian* commented:

> In some locations where 250 stars are visible, it is estimated that only 100 will be visible in 18 years' time. "If these trends continue, eventually it will be very difficult to see anything at all in the sky, even the

---

[230] *Journal of Geophysical Research: Atmospheres*, 16 May, 2009, 'Global Dimming and Brightening: An Update Beyond 2000', Martin Wild, Barbara Trüssel, Atsumu Ohmura, Charles N. Long, Gert König-Langlo, Ellsworth G. Dutton, Anatoly Tsvetkov. https://agupubs.onlinelibrary.wiley.com/doi/10.1029/2008JD011382, 24 Nov, 2023.
[231] www.science.org/doi/10.1126/science.abq7781, 8 June, 2023.

brightest constellations…," said Dr Christopher Kyba, of the German Research Centre for Geoscience and first author of the research.[232]

This is projecting a 60% decrease and it is not caused by angels but, unwittingly, by us.

Summary

(i) The 3rd Trumpet signals 'a great star' called Wormwood, 'burning like a torch' and falling from heaven onto a third of the Earth's freshwater, turning it poisonous and bitter.

(ii) This could be another literal asteroid-strike but we have already polluted over a third of our freshwater with all-too literal toxins, chemicals, pesticides, antibiotics, and micro-plastics so we have to consider how this could be a metaphor.

(iii) John's 1st century Jewish audience would have been very familiar with metaphorical falling stars referring to fallen angels and wicked emperors and their empires, as well as the metaphors of burning torches, the bitter taste of wormwood, and the outcome of adultery.

(iv) I therefore believe John's vision of the great fallen star with its false light and bitter outcome is describing the effect of Babylon the Great, i.e. the world whose love of self, money, and pleasure rather than God, which has already led us to destroy a third of our freshwater.

(v) The 4th Trumpet is to alert us to the darkening of a third of the sun, moon, and stars and this is already occurring due to global air pollution and light pollution.

---

[232] www.theguardian.com/commentisfree/2023/jan/24/as-a-girl-i-was-thrilled-by-the-night-sky-must-my-son-grow-up-without-seeing-the-milky-way?CMP=share_btn_link, 8 June, 2023.

11
The Fifth Trumpet
The First Woe

After the 4th Trumpet is sounded, John hears an introduction to the last three:

> Then I looked, and I heard an eagle flying in mid-heaven, saying with a loud voice, *"Woe, woe, woe to those who dwell on the earth*, because of the remaining blasts of the trumpet of the three angels who are about to sound!" (Rev 8:13*)

Each of these last three trumpet alarms is then described as a 'woe' (Rev 9:12, 11:14), changing the focus from what we are doing to the earth, sea, fresh water, and the skies to what is happening to mankind.

The Three 'Woes'

'Woe' means 'affliction, bitter grief, distress'.[233] The Hebrew prophets often used it as a denunciation, as did Jesus:

> 20. Then He began to denounce the cities in which most of His miracles were done, because they did not repent. 21. "Woe to you, Chorazin! Woe to you, Bethsaida! For if the miracles had occurred in Tyre and Sidon which occurred in you, they would have repented long ago..." (Matt 11:20-21)

> 13. "But woe to you, scribes and Pharisees, hypocrites, because you shut off the kingdom of heaven from people..." (Matt 23:13)

---

[233] *Concise Oxford Dictionary*, p. 1238. The Hebrew *hoy* is 'a prolonged form of "Oh!"' (Strongs H1945); the Greek *ouai* is 'a primary exclamation of grief' like 'alas' (Strongs G3759).

Remember, these denunciations were warnings, urging the hearers to turn back from their mind-set and behaviour, and some Pharisees did so (Acts 15:5, 23:9).

Why an eagle or vulture?[234] Eagles and vultures soar the heights, circling and waiting to swoop on their prey (Job 39:27, Isa 40:31) or to feed on carcases (Matt 24:28) so their flight is ominous. This pronouncement of the three woes is therefore to warn that what is about to follow will cause much sorrow but the third will only be a woe for unbelievers because the third is the return of Jesus!

The first woe/5th Trumpet needs close and careful consideration by every believer because, like the preceding four trumpets, I believe it is already on us - we just need to recognise what is already happening around us. However, it takes quite some explaining because it uses images and metaphors that were familiar to John's audience but very unfamiliar to us. In the next three chapters, I will therefore cover how the four traditional perspectives explain it, then what John's 1st century audience would have already known, before offering my own view and leaving you to judge for yourself which it is.

The Mystery of the Locusts

The first four trumpets warn us of the natural consequences of our greed and/or foolishness in the natural realm but the fifth warns of a supernatural plague:

> 1. Then the fifth angel sounded, and I saw a star from heaven which had fallen to the earth; and the key of the bottomless pit was given to him.
> 2. He opened the bottomless pit, and smoke went up out of the pit, like the smoke of a great furnace; and the sun

---

[234] The *KJV* translators had the woes pronounced by an angel, based on the *Textus Receptus* having the Greek, *aggelos*. However, the older manuscripts have *aetos*, eagle or vulture.

and the air were darkened by the smoke of the pit.
3. Then out of the smoke came *locusts* upon the earth
(Rev 9:1-3)

These are not your usual locusts:

> 7. The appearance of the locusts was like horses prepared for battle; and on their heads appeared to be crowns like gold, and their faces were like the faces of men.
> 8. They had hair like the hair of women, and their teeth were like the teeth of lions.
> 9. They had breastplates like breastplates of iron; and the sound of their wings was like the sound of chariots, of many horses rushing to battle.
> 10. They have tails like scorpions, and stings; and in their tails is their power to hurt men for five months. (Rev 9:7-10)

As noted in Chapter 1, the four traditional ways of interpreting Revelation offer us very different fulfilments in different times.

Preterists

Preterists take the metaphorical approach. Believing that much of Revelation was fulfilled in the 1st century by the Romans destroying Jerusalem in 70 AD, they rightly note that:

> Locusts are an ancient Canaanite and Biblical metaphor for an invading foreign/Gentile army... [in] Judges 6:5, 7:12; Jeremiah 51:14, 27; and Nahum 3:15.[235]

They therefore believe John's vision of locusts was a metaphor for the Roman legions and that Apollyon was their general Titus, who later became Emperor of Rome.[236] They also quote the Babylonian Talmud:

---

[235] https://revelationrevolution.org/revelation-9-a-preterist-commentary-who-is-apollyon, 30 Dec, 2018.
[236] Ibid.

> The destruction of Jerusalem came through a *Kamza* [locust] and a *Bar Kamza* [son of a locust].[237]

The 'five months' of the locusts (Rev 9:10), they believe, is literal and refers to the siege of Jerusalem:

> For five months... Titus' army induced famine and plague in the closed quarters of the city before finally breaking through the last fortifications and putting thousands of people out of their misery. This five month interval... is also the same five month time frame in which locusts typically appear in Israel.[238]

However, Josephus recorded that Jerusalem was besieged for five months and twenty-two days[239] which is closer to six months.

Historicists

Historicists also take the metaphorical approach with some seeing the locust plague as the emergence of Roman Catholicism but others, Islam.

(i) Roman Catholicism

Protestant theologians, newly distanced from their Catholic roots, took a dim view of them. For example, Matthew Henry's 17th century *Complete Commentary* notes that some saw the star fallen from heaven as Pope Boniface I who deposed his rival, Pope Eulalius, in 418 AD. This would mean the locusts emerged in the 5th Century and are:

> ...all the rout and rabble of antichristian [religious] orders, [sent] to promote superstition, idolatry, error, and cruelty.[240]

---

237 Ibid.
238 Ibid.
239 In *The Wars of the Jews,* Josephus recorded Titus's siege began on 14th Nisan during Passover (*Wars*, 5.3.1; 5.13.7) and ended on 8th Elul (*Wars*, 6.10.1), i.e. the 1st and 6th months.
240 www.biblestudytools.com/commentaries/matthew-henry-complete/

In this view, the scorpion-like sting is heresy:

> The hurt they were to do… was not a bodily, but a spiritual hurt… it should not be a persecution, but a secret poison and infection in their souls, which should rob them of their purity, and afterwards of their peace. Heresy is a poison in the soul, working slowly and secretly, but will be bitterness in the end.[241]

The five months would be a metaphor for:

> …a certain season, and but a short season, though how short we cannot tell. Gospel-seasons have their limits, and times of seduction are limited too… it would be very sharp, insomuch that those who were made to feel the malignity of this poison in their consciences would be weary of their lives…[242]

As for the locusts' appearance, Matthew Henry lists seven details:

> These locusts were… equipped for their work like horses prepared to battle. (1.) They pretended to great authority, and seemed to be assured of victory: They had crowns like gold on their heads; it was not a true, but a counterfeit authority. (2.) They had the show of wisdom and sagacity, the faces of men, though the spirit of devils. (3.) They had all the allurements of seeming beauty, to ensnare and defile the minds of men - hair like women; their way of worship was very gaudy and ornamental. (4.) Though they appeared with the tenderness of women, they had the teeth of lions, were really cruel creatures.
> (5.) They had the defence and protection of earthly powers - breastplates of iron. (6.) They made a mighty noise in the world; they flew about from one country to another, and the noise of their motion was like that of an

---

revelation/9.html, 12 Dec, 2018.
241   Ibid.
242   Ibid.

army with chariots and horses. (7.) Though at first they soothed and flattered men with a fair appearance, there was a sting in their tails; the cup of their abominations contained that which, though luscious at first, would at length bite like a serpent and sting like an adder.[243]

Many therefore see the Catholic Church as fulfilling these criteria from the 5th century.

(ii) Islam

Other Historicists see the locusts as emerging in the 7th century, following the teachings of Muhammad. The Muslims had invaded Spain from North Africa so, as one commentary explains:

> The beast, which had previously been believed to represent the Roman Empire, now became the Caliphate, and Babylon was no longer Rome, but Córdoba... Many Christian expositors, including Martin Luther, the great Reformer; Sir Isaac Newton, the famous scientist; and the historian, Edward Gibbon; have seen in the fifth and sixth trumpets the rise and progress of Islam...[244]

John Calvin and John Wesley also believed this. As for the locusts' appearance:

> The cavalry was a prominent feature of the Arabian and Turkish military. Their horsemen wore turbans over long hair, "as the hair of women." They came with the strength and rapacity of "lions," and were seemingly unstoppable, pictured by the "breastplates of iron." The locust "wings," like the leopard wings of Daniel 7, represent speed.[245]

In this view, the 'five months' are 150 years:

---

243 Ibid.
244 https://amazingdiscoveries.org/S-deception-angels-abyss-Revelation-9-commentary, 12 Dec, 2018.
245 Ibid.

The "locusts" are given power to "torment" like the sting of a "scorpion" for 5 months, or 150 literal years. Starting in 1299 at the Battle of Bapheum the Turkish Muslims began a persistent assault on the eastern Roman Empire. In 1449, after 150 years of conflict, the Eastern Roman, or Byzantine, Empire became a vassal state, subordinate to the Ottoman Empire… During this time period the Byzantine Empire was "tormented" by the Ottoman Empire but not yet destroyed.[246]

Futurists

Some Futurists take the locusts to be a metaphor for helicopter gunships or drones, described as a 1st century observer might see them, while others see them as literal, i.e. living creatures, so we need to consider both options:

(i) Helicopter gunships or drones

This perspective takes John's description of the locusts - 'on their heads appeared to be crowns like gold and their faces were like the faces of men… hair like the hair of women' (Rev 9:7-8) - to be describing 'the sun's light reflecting off the top of the whirling propeller' while the pilots' faces can be seen looking through the Perspex windscreens.[247]

Others cite the recent technological development of drone swarms, even named appropriately:

> The US navy recently demonstrated its Low-Cost UAV Swarming Technology (LOCUST) program by putting 30 drones flying together in perfect formation. These drones are launched from a special tube in less than a minute to create a vicious swarm designed to overwhelm an adversary autonomously.
>
> What makes the swarm unique is that any hostile aircraft,

---

246 Ibid.
247 www.21stcenturyrevelations.com/my-2nd-interpretation-pictographic-relationships, 30 Dec, 2022.

manned or unmanned, can be brought down by a single missile, but a swarm can take multiple hits and keep going. The drones are self-reconfiguring so that if one drone gets taken out, the others autonomously change their behavior to complete the mission.[248]

I will be interested to hear how the drones will avoid killing anyone or any plants while discerning unbelievers from believers to torment only unbelievers. After all, John wrote that the locusts…:

> …were told not to hurt the grass of the earth, nor any green thing, nor any tree, but only the men who do not have the seal of God on their foreheads. And they were not permitted to kill anyone, but to torment for five months… (Rev 9:4-5*)

(ii) Living creatures

Tim LaHaye and Jerry B. Jenkins take the literal approach, as illustrated in their best-selling series of *Left Behind* novels:

> From out of the smoke came flying creatures - hideous, ugly, brown and black and yellow monsters. Swarming like locusts, they looked like miniature horses five or six inches long with tails like those of scorpions… The four horselike legs supported a horse-shaped body consisting of a two-part abdomen.[249]

In their book, however, the 'five months' of the plague becomes ten months:

> During the ensuing five months, the demon locusts attacked anyone who did not have the seal of God on his or her forehead. And for five months after that, those among the last bitten still suffered.[250]

---

248 www.prophecynewswatch.com/article.cfm?recent_news_id=580, 30 Dec, 2022.
249 LaHaye, Tim & Jenkins, Jerry B., *Apollyon: The Destroyer is Unleashed*, Wheaton, Ill; Tyndale Publishing House, 1999, pp. 305 & 316-317.
250 Ibid, p. 327.

Idealists

Lastly, the Idealists see them as literal demons. As William Hendriksen explains:

> Here are demons, robbing men of all light... their king... is Destroyer... The entire symbolic picture emphasizes this one idea: terror and destruction, for that is Satan's work![251]

He does not comment on any of their identifying features or the five months duration.

So which of these four views is correct?

Well, consider the context of their timing: the preceding four trumpets have all been sounding for the last 50-100 years (as has the 6th Trumpet, as I will show). This rules out the Preterist and Historicist interpretations, leaving only the Futurist and Idealist views as still possible.

However, we still need to catch up with what John's original audience would have already known - after all, they could face locusts, scorpions, and demons in their daily lives. Then we can look more closely at how they would have understood John's description.

John's Audience

Plagues of locusts were well-known in the ancient Middle East but are not so common today due to insecticides, careful surveillance, and intervention.

(i) Desert locusts

Locusts are a species of short-horned grasshopper, native to the Middle East, North Africa, and West India, and usually solitary, harmless, and edible. However, in certain conditions

---

[251] William Hendriksen, *More than Conquerors: An Interpretation of the Book of Revelation*, Grand Rapids, MI; Baker Book House, 1986, p. 122.

they swarm, multiplying rapidly, and take to the sky. Unusually heavy rains can foster swarms swelling to billions of locusts, spread out over thousands of square kilometres in densities up to 150 million per square kilometre (390 million per square mile), and devouring vegetation wherever they settle. Migrating with the wind, they can travel up 150 kms (93 miles) in a day.[252]

When the prophet Joel described their devastating effect in ancient Israel, he likened them to an invading nation[253] and marauding lions:

> 4. What the gnawing locust has left, the swarming locust has eaten;
> And what the swarming locust has left, the creeping locust has eaten;
> And what the creeping locust has left, the stripping locust has eaten…
> 6. *For a nation has invaded* my land,
> Mighty and without number;
> Its teeth are the teeth of a lion,
> And it has the fangs of a lioness. (Joel 1:4 & 6*)

This metaphorical army devoured all vegetation:

> 7. It has made my vine a waste
> And my fig tree splinters.
> It has stripped them bare and cast them away;
> Their branches have become white. (Joel 1:7)

---

[252] https://edrmc.gov.et/preparing-for-disaster/desert-locust, 29 Dec, 2022. In 2003, one plague in West Africa spread from Mauritania, Mali, Niger, and Sudan up into Egypt, Jordan, and Israel, causing an estimated US$2.5 billion damage to crops. While individual locusts live only three to five months, this plague kept regenerating and lasted two years (www.fao.org/in-action/countries-take-responsibility-for-regional-desert-locust-control/en, 11 Dec, 2018). In 2020, a swarm in Kenya was 60 kms (37 miles) long and 40 kms (25 miles) wide https://nypost.com/2020/01/24/climate-change-behind-africas-worst-locust-invasion-in-decades, 29 Dec, 2022.

[253] Some try to reverse the metaphor, believing that Joel's locust plague referred to the Assyrian or Babylonian invasions or both, but I do not.

Israel lost their olives (Joel 1:10), wheat and barley (v. 11), grapes, figs, pomegranates, dates, and apples (v.12); their livestock lost their pastures (v. 18).

Joel identified it as a divine warning:

> 15. Alas for the day! For the day of the LORD is near,
> And it will come as destruction from the Almighty.
> 16. Has not food been cut off before our eyes,
> Gladness and joy from the house of our God? (Joel 1:15-16)

The only solution was to call out to God:

> 12. "Yet even now," declares the LORD,
> "Return to Me with all your heart,
> And with fasting, weeping and mourning…
> 32. "And it will come about that whoever calls on the name of the LORD will be delivered" (Joel 2:12 & 32)

God promised to deliver them with east and west winds that blew the pests into the seas (2:20), just as He had with the locust plague at the time of the exodus from Egypt (Ex 10:19). He would also restore all their crops (Joel 2:19 & 22) and pastures (2:22).

John's 1st century Jewish audience would have understood all of this and recognised that the 5th Trumpet was proclaiming another exodus, this time from the old, corrupt world as described in Book 5,[254] and that "the day of the LORD is near" (Joel 1:15).

(ii) Demonic locusts

The locusts John sees, however, emerge from the 'bottomless pit' (Rev 9:2). As noted in Books 1, 2, and 4, the abyss (Greek, *abyssos*, lit. bottomless) symbolised the place of the dead (Rom 10:7, Rev 20:13) and of evil spirits (Luke 8:31,

---

254 *Threshing Hour.*

Rev 9:11)[255] and of Revelation 13's first beast (Rev 11:7).[256] These locusts are therefore demonic.

Desert locusts harm no one directly, devouring only vegetation; John's demonic locusts are commanded to avoid vegetation and target mankind - but not all mankind:

> They were told not to hurt the grass of the earth, nor any green thing, nor any tree, but only the men who do not have the *seal of God on their foreheads*. (Rev 9:4*)

John had earlier seen 144,000 men receiving the seal of God on their foreheads (Rev 7:1-8). As we saw in Book 3,[257] their seven identifying features reveal their number of 12 x 12 x 1,000 is a metaphor based on Jesus' commissioning of His twelve apostles:

(a) He sent the Twelve to evangelise Israel (Matt 10:5-6) for the literal three and a half years of His earthly ministry.[258]

(b) He has been sending the metaphorical number of '144,000' apostles to evangelise 'every nation and all tribes and peoples and tongues' (Rev 7:9) for the metaphorical three and a half years of "the times of the Gentiles", i.e. the last 2,000 years.[259]

I also showed in Book 3[260] that every one of us can have four metaphorical marks of God's ownership on our foreheads by simply:

---

255 *Dancing in the Dragon's Jaws*, pp. 36-37; *Slouching Towards Bethlehem*, p. 21.
256 *Silencing the Witnesses*, pp. 219-221.
257 *Gotta Serve Somebody*, pp. 159-174.
258 This was the first half of Messiah's Week which is also known as Daniel's 70th Week, as I show in *Dancing in the Dragon's Jaws*, pp. 102-106.
259 This was the second half of Messiah's Week, as I show in *Dancing in the Dragon's Jaws*, pp. 113-148.
260 *Gotta Serve Somebody*, pp. 49-69.

(a) Trusting in Jesus as our Passover lamb and cleaning out all malice and wickedness from our hearts

(b) Honouring and obeying Him as the First-born Son of God

(c) Loving God with all our heart, soul, mind, and strength

(d) Avoiding deception, especially false prophets

We see then that before these locusts are released, God has safeguarded His messengers and His people from the locusts' power:

> 3. …power was given them, as the scorpions of the earth have power.
> 5. And they were not permitted to kill anyone, but to torment for five months; and their torment was like the torment of a scorpion when it stings a man.
> 6. And in those days men will seek death and will not find it; they will long to die, and death flees from them.
> (Rev 9:3, 5-6)

What would the 'power' of earthly scorpions have meant to John's 1st century audience?

(iii) Middle-Eastern scorpions

Of the 2,807 scorpion species known today, only twenty-five have a sting potentially fatal to humans but three of the most toxic are Middle Eastern,[261] and therefore familiar to John and his hearers. Today, the annual number of scorpion stings world-wide is estimated to be 1.2 million causing

---

[261] The Deathstalker (*Leiurus quinquestriatus*, Lat. five-striped smooth-tail), the Yellow Fat-Tailed (*Androctonus australis*, Lat. southern man-killer), and the Arabian Fat-tailed (*Androctonus crassicauda*, Lat. man-killer fat-tailed). Rein, J. O. 2017. *The Scorpion Files*. Trondheim: Norwegian University of Science and Technology. www.ntnu.no/ub/scorpion-files, 10 Jan, 2023.

3,250 deaths, a fatality rate of only 0.27%.²⁶² This low rate is partially due to modern medicine's anti-venom but, remarkably, it is also due to the scorpions themselves. They have two kinds of venom and they choose which to inject and in what amount: one kind is to kill prey and the other, called pre-venom, is for stunning or warning. Pre-venom being easier to make, scorpions use it more often and reserve the more toxic venom for victims they want to eat.²⁶³

Either way, however, the effects of a scorpion's sting can be intense pain, numbness, tingling, and swelling, followed by excessive sweating, agitation, heart-palpitations, blurred vision, and slurred speech.

Their King

John sees the locusts released from the abyss by 'a star from heaven which had fallen to the earth' (Rev 9:1), a fallen angel who rules them:

> They have as king over them, the angel of the abyss; his name in Hebrew is Abaddon, and in the Greek he has the name Apollyon. (Rev 9:11)

Whereas desert locusts famously have no king (Prov 30:27), these demonic locusts do. His Greek name Apollyon means 'destroyer' and some scholars today think the locust king could be the Emperor Domitian who was reigning when John was writing.²⁶⁴

---

262   Chippaux, J.-P. & Goyffon M., *Epidemiology of Scorpionism: A Global Appraisal*, Acta Tropica, Vol 107, Issue 2, pp. 71-79 (www.sciencedirect.com/journal/acta-tropica/vol/107/issue/2, 10 Dec, 2018).
263   www.pnas.org/content/100/3/922, 10 Dec, 2018.
264   For example, the *Anchor Bible Dictionary*: 'the name Apollo (Gk *Apollon*) was often linked in ancient Greek writings with the verb apollymi or apollyo, "destroy"… The locust was an emblem of this god, who poisoned his victims, and the name "Apollyon" may be used allusively in Revelation to attack the pagan god and so indirectly the Roman emperor Domitian, who liked to be regarded as Apollo incarnate.'

However, his name would have been readily understood by John's 1st century audience as a metaphor. For those speaking Hebrew, Abaddon was a common synonym for Sheol, the place of destruction and the realm of the dead.[265] We saw a similar use of personification in Chapter 4 where the 4th Seal personifies Death as riding a pale horse, followed by a personification of Hades, the place of the dead (Rev 6:8). We see it again in Psalm 49 regarding the death of the wicked:

> As sheep they are appointed for Sheol;
> *Death* shall be their *shepherd*...
> And their form shall be for Sheol *to consume*
> So that they have no habitation. (Psa 49:14*)

Death 'shepherds' them into Sheol, or the grave, which is personified into 'consuming' them as their bodies turn into dust.

We see then in this vision the locusts' king is a personification of Destruction/Sheol/Hades[266] and, as in David's Psalm 23, casts a great shadow over the earth:

> He opened the bottomless pit, and smoke went up out of the pit, like the smoke of a great furnace; and the sun and the air were *darkened* by the smoke of the pit. (Rev 9:2*)

And out of this darkness emerge the locusts.

Let us summarise what we know so far.

---

265 E.g. Job 26:6, 28:8; Psalm 88:11; Proverbs 15:11, 27:20.
266 Hades is the Greek translation of the Hebrew Sheol, the place of the dead.

Summary

(i) The last three trumpets are "woes" to mankind but the last is the return of Jesus to judge the world which will be wonderful, ending the reign of evil and vindicating the saints.

(ii) The 5th Trumpet/first woe is a mysterious plague of locusts which look terrifying and can sting like scorpions. However, they have three restraints on them: they cannot harm believers; they cannot kill anyone; and their time is limited to five months.

(iii) Historically, most commentators have believed they are humans, whether Roman soldiers destroying Jerusalem in 70 AD (as Preterists believe), or Roman Catholic clergy spreading heresy from the 4th century until today, or Muslim warriors spreading Islam from the 7th century until today (as Historicists believe).

(iv) Futurists believe they are yet to appear, either as man-made 21st century technological weapons of war such as helicopter gunships and/or drones, or as hellish flying creatures.

(v) Others believe they are demons. I do too but, as I will show, these locusts are not to be feared by believers, can be redemptive for unbelievers, and their stings can be nullified.

(vi) John's 1st century Jewish audience would have readily recognised all of the metaphors he used to describe these demons including a plague of locusts being like an invading army, eating like lions, stinging like scorpions, and released and ruled by Destruction from Sheol/Hades.

12
A Plague
To Redeem?

To put the 5th Trumpet in Biblical context, consider the purpose of the locust plague God sent to ancient Egypt - it was not only to liberate the Hebrew slaves and punish their captors but also to reveal their God, our God, to every nation:

> 14. "For this time I will send all My plagues on you and your servants and your people, *so that you may know* that there is no one like Me in all the earth.
> 15. "For if by now I had put forth My hand and struck you and your people with pestilence, you would then have been cut off from the earth.
> 16. "But, indeed, for this reason *I have allowed you to remain*, in order to show you My power and in order *to proclaim My name through all the earth.*" (Ex 9:14-16*)

As we saw in Chapter 7, the locusts were the eighth of the ten plagues. However, by the seventh, the unprecedented hailstorm, some of the Egyptians had begun to believe Moses' prophecies:

> 20. The one among *the servants of Pharaoh who feared the word* of the LORD made his servants and his livestock flee into the houses;
> 21. but he who paid no regard to the word of the LORD left his servants and his livestock in the field. (Ex 9:20-21*)

When the Hebrew slaves were finally allowed to leave after the tenth plague, 'a mixed multitude' of free Egyptians and slaves of other nationalities joined them:

> 37. Now the sons of Israel journeyed from Rameses to Succoth...
> 38. A mixed multitude also went up with them, along with flocks and herds, a very large number of livestock.
> (Exo 12:37-38*)

This multitude had been convinced by Moses that the plagues were sent to redeem not only Israel but anyone, enslaved or free, who repented and believed 'the word of the Lord' (Ex 9:20).

So what or who are the locusts that John saw? After all, we are supposed to identify them from their description and their assignment. We just have to look more carefully.

Armoured *Horses?*

> 7. The appearance of the locusts was *like horses* prepared for battle...
> 9. They had *breastplates like breastplates of iron*; and the sound of their wings was like *the sound of chariots*, of many horses rushing to battle... (Rev 9:7-9*)

As we saw in the last chapter, three of the four traditional interpretations see the locusts as a metaphor for literal men in literal armour: the Preterists believe they were Roman legionaries; the Historicists believe they were either Catholic clergy being defended by the Pope's armies, or the Arabian and Turkish military enforcing Islam; some Futurists believe they will be soldiers inside helicopter gunships or controlling drones.

However, as you can see in v. 9, John says the horse-like flying *locusts* have breastplates like iron breastplates - he does not mention any men riding them. Accordingly, some Futurists like Tim LaHaye and Jerry Jenkins are expecting a whole new species of literal locusts while the Idealists see them as being demons.

Everyone agrees, though, that they *look like* armoured war horses. Today we even have graphic artists depicting them as having only four legs but John does not say "winged horses" - he says "locusts" (Rev 9:3 & 7) so, as usual, we have to ask what would the Jewish disciples in John's intended original audience have understood?

Joel's Locusts

Firstly, they would have recognised that he begins his description exactly as their prophet Joel[267] had centuries earlier described a swarm of ordinary desert locusts:

> 4. Their appearance is like the appearance of horses;
> And like war horses, so they run.
> 5. With a noise as of chariots
> They leap on the tops of the mountains,
> Like the crackling of a flame of fire consuming the stubble,
> Like a mighty people arranged for battle. (Joel 2:4-5*)

Joel's locusts were not literally armoured four-legged horses but six-legged flying insects. While their exoskeleton *looks* like the 'breastplates of iron' that John describes (Rev 9:9), their 'armour' is easily pierced by anyone eating them.

They are also very nutritious,[268] John the Baptist famously living on them and wild honey (Matt 3:4, Mark 1:6). More recently, in 2013, under the witty headline, 'Eating locusts: the crunchy, kosher snack taking Israel by *swarm*', the BBC reported:

---

[267] The Book of Joel was obviously well-known with Peter and Paul also quoting him (Acts 2:17-21, Rom 10:13).

[268] 'In many African, Middle Eastern and Asian countries, locusts are considered a delicacy and eaten in abundance. Locusts are an excellent source of protein and contain a variety of fatty acids and minerals. Although not considered palatable by most Americans, locusts are an important food source in many other countries.' www.livestrong.com/article/549444-the-nutritional-value-of-locusts, 30 Dec, 2022.

Locust is the only insect which is considered kosher. Specific extracts in the Torah state that four types of desert locust - the red, the yellow, the spotted grey, and the white - can be eaten [Lev 11:22]. As with fish, there are no rules surrounding their ritual slaughter, making them a particularly versatile ingredient for culinary connoisseurs, like chef Moshe Basson, founder and owner of the famous Eucalyptus restaurant in Jerusalem, and a specialist in reviving ancient Biblical foods.[269]

Chef Basson happily shares his recipes:

For the uninitiated, he recommends serving them crunchy - an effect that is best achieved as follows: Drop them into a boiling broth, clean them off, and roll in a mixture of flour, coriander seeds, garlic and chilli powder. Then deep-fry them. Pan-frying is another good option, and they are "crunchy, tasty and sweet", says Basson, when mixed with caramel and sprinkled into meringue.[270]

John's Locusts

John's locusts in Revelation, however, have other features:

7. ...and on their heads appeared to be *crowns* like gold, and their *faces* were like the faces of *men*.
8. They had *hair* like the hair of *women*, and their *teeth* were like the teeth of *lions*...
10. They have *tails* like *scorpions*, and stings...
(Rev 9:7-10*)

What are we to make of their crowns, faces, hair, teeth, tails, and stings?

---

269   www.bbc.com/news/magazine-21847517, 31 Dec, 2022.
270   Ibid.

(i) 'Crowns like gold'

Desert locusts are also called 'short-horned grasshoppers' because they are 'characterised by short, heavy antennae'.[271] In their swarming phase, their bodies change colour from green and tan to gold and black so their 'crowns' look 'like gold'. However, John adds that these demonic locusts are 'given power' (Rev 9:3) which is also denoted by crowns (Rev 13:1).[272]

(ii) 'Faces like the faces of men'

These are not literally human faces but look 'like' human faces, signifying an intelligence. This is similar to Daniel's eleventh horn having human-like facial features - 'eyes and a mouth uttering great boasts' (Dan 7:20). As I showed in Book 2,[273] Daniel was looking at the demonic spirit of antichrist; here John is looking at demons like locusts.

(iii) 'Hair like the hair of women'

Some link this simile to Jeremiah's describing locusts as 'bristly' (Jer 51:27) because the Hebrew adjective, *samar*, means 'shaggy'[274] but this refers to the bristles on their legs (photo on p. 186). Others[275] refer to an Arabic proverb comparing their antennae to the hair of girls but I cannot find it.

As for significance, as strange as this may seem initially, it can be to make them 'attractive and seductive'.[276] In Song of Solomon, the bridegroom delights in his bride's beautiful hair (Song 4:1, 6:4-5) and, as noted earlier, Historicist

---

271 www.britannica.com/animal/short-horned-grasshopper, 31 Dec, 2022.
272 Grk, *stephanos* - 'a badge of royalty, a prize in the public games, or a symbol of honour generally' (Strongs G4735).
273 *Slouching Towards Bethlehem*, pp. 69-73.
274 Strongs, H5569.
275 E.g. https://biblehub.com/commentaries/alford/revelation/9.htm, 1 Jan, 2023.
276 William MacDonald, *Believer's Bible Commentary*, ed. Arthur Farstad, Thomas Nelson Publishers, Nashville, 1995.

commentator Matthew Henry thought that the locust vision was to predict the Catholic clergy's being seductive:

> They had all the allurements of seeming beauty, to ensnare and defile the minds of men - hair like women... Though they appeared with the tenderness of women, they had the teeth of lions, were really cruel creatures.[277]

Jesus did tell us to watch for wolves concealing themselves under sheep's clothing - can these demonic locusts fool us into accepting their temptations? We will consider this in Chapter 14 - *Dangers & Antidotes*.

(iv) 'Teeth like the teeth of lions'

As mentioned earlier, John's description is quoting Joel's description, not of a single locust but a swarm of locusts:

> Its teeth are the teeth of a lion,
> And it has the fangs of a lioness. (Joel 1:6)

So what did Joel mean?

Desert locusts are harmless, solitary individuals but when they swarm, they undergo a complete transformation and become voracious, devouring every kind of vegetation.[278] They are so different before and after transformation that until the 1920s, entomologists thought they were two different species:

> The insect changes colour from a leafy green to a drab tan or a striking yellow-and-black, suddenly becomes very social and is possessed of a voracious appetite. Aided by newly-developed muscles, it sweeps through distant geographies in large swarms and at great speed.[279]

---

[277] www.biblestudytools.com/commentaries/matthew-henry-complete/revelation/9.html, 12 Dec, 2018.
[278] Some 20 species of the 7,000 known grasshopper varieties can change themselves into gregarious types.
[279] www.telegraphindia.com/india/dr-solitarious-mr-gregarious-desert-locusts-grasshoppers/cid/1777088, 31 Dec, 2022.

Professor Parthiba Basu, the director of Calcutta University's Centre for Agroecology and Pollination Studies, reports:

> The change in physical appearance is in keeping with the change in personality. From being a near-invisible creature, almost lost in the surrounding green, the locust swarm takes on the character of a lynch mob...[feeding and breeding] voraciously.[280]

This metamorphosis from solitary to gregarious is caused by environmental conditions and an internal natural chemical, serotonin:

> When locusts are driven to congregate by environmental conditions, see and smell one another and touch and rub one another's hind legs, this leads to a serotonin surge.[281]

Unlike Joel's locusts, however, John's demonic locusts do not eat vegetation - they attack humans, not to kill or eat them but to torment them (Rev 9:5). We see then the lions' teeth and fangs are not literal but metaphorical, based on the feeding frenzy of swarming desert locusts.

(v) 'Tails like scorpions'

The locusts' hybridisation includes 'tails like scorpions, and stings' (Rev 9:10). Unlike literal scorpions, however, they are not permitted to kill, only to torment (Rev 9:5).

As Big As…?

Remember, to the Preterists, John's 'locusts' were Roman soldiers; to the Historicists, they were Catholic clergy, i.e. up to 2 metres tall; to the Futurists, they will be either helicopter gunships (Hal Lindsay), which are some 20 metres long, or

---

280 Ibid.
281 Ibid.

hellish creatures 'five or six inches long' (Tim LaHaye), i.e. 13-15 cms; the Idealists do not suggest a size.

John does not give us any measurements at all but since he calls them 'locusts' (Rev 9:3, 7) rather than 'truly enormous locusts' and he quotes Joel's description, I believe they are the usual size of desert locusts, i.e. 7 cm at maximum. Here is one's actual size:

Figure (vii) Desert locust (Schistocerca gregaria)

This is vastly smaller than a man or a helicopter, and half the size of the creatures of the *Left Behind* series.

To summarise then, John sees a swarm of demons that actually look like Joel's desert locusts, flying insects which are harmless and edible in their solitary phase but, when driven to swarm in their gregarious phase, become like an invading army and eat vegetation as voraciously as lions tearing their prey.

We should therefore set aside any apprehension about their appearance and focus on their assignment - why exactly are they being released?

Their Assignment

They are not going to eat anything or anyone, they are not lethal, and they are assigned only to unbelievers:

> 4. They were told not to hurt the grass of the earth, nor any green thing, nor any tree, but only the men who *do not have* the seal of God on their foreheads. (Rev 9:4*)

As I showed in Book 3,[282] every believer in Jesus (Rev 3:12, 22:4) has the 'seal of God on their foreheads' but we will look at this again in the next chapter as a reminder.

Significantly they cannot kill anyone:

> 5. They were not *permitted to kill* anyone, but to *torment for five months;* and their torment was like the torment of a scorpion when it stings a man. (Rev 9:5*)

This shows again the flaws in three of the four traditional interpretations in believing the locusts were armed men in past centuries:

(i) Preterism

John's locusts cannot be the Roman legionaries of 70 AD because Josephus records that half the Jews in Israel were killed in that siege and, as shown in Book 5,[283] the Romans ended up killing two-thirds of the Jewish population in the three Jewish-Roman Wars between 66 and 136 AD.

(ii) Historicism

Similarly, the locusts cannot be the Catholic clergy and armies from the 4th to the 18th centuries since 'they were told... to hurt... only' those *not* belonging to God (v. 4) - the Catholic Church today admits to killing millions[284]

---

[282] *Gotta Serve Somebody*, pp. 49-69.
[283] *Threshing Hour*, pp. 81-83.
[284] Ibid, pp. 174-176. Also *Slouching Towards Bethlehem*, pp. 60-63.

in the Albigensian/Cathar Crusade (1209-1229), the St Bartholomew's Day Massacre of Huguenots (1572), and the War of the Camisards (1702-1710). They specifically targeted men of God such as Jan Hus, killed in 1415, and reforming Bishops Latimer, Ridley, and Cranmer, burnt at the stake in Oxford in 1555 and 1556.

Neither can the locusts be the Arabian and Turkish jihadists from the 7th to the 20th centuries since they too have killed millions, tens of millions,[285] including one million Armenian Christians and 750,000 Orthodox Greek Christians between 1915 and 1917.

(iii) Futurism

Futurists who believe the locusts will be soldiers inside helicopter gunships or controlling drones need to explain how they will not be killing anyone and sting only unbelievers, literally or metaphorically.

This still leaves Futurists like Tim LaHaye and Jerry Jenkins who believe in literal, material locusts with a literal sting and, as they graphically portray in their series of novels, that there will be 'no remedy for the torture and agony'.[286] One of their characters, Hattie, is isolated in a basement for five months because no-one can bear 'her anguished screams at all hours of the day and night' and she becomes 'skeletal'.[287]

(iv) Idealism

Idealists, however, see the locusts as spiritual beings, i.e. demons, and I agree with them in this instance because John says they come out of the abyss and, as his 1st century Jewish audience well-knew, the abyss is where Satan (Rev 20:3) and demons live (Luke 8:31).[288]

---

285 *Slouching Towards Bethlehem*, pp. 159-164.
286 *Apollyon: The Destroyer is Unleashed*, p. 309.
287 Ibid, pp. 327-328. Also pp. 315-316.
288 Explained further in *Slouching Towards Bethlehem*, p. 21.

We now need to answer some important questions: is their sting literal or is it a metaphor for psychological pain? Does it really last five months, and is it incurable? When will the locusts be released?

Literal or Metaphorical Torment?

Looking again at John's description:

> 5. They were not permitted to kill anyone, but to torment [Grk, *basanizo*] for five months; and their torment [Grk, *basanismos*] was like the torment [Grk, *basanismos*] of a scorpion when it stings a man.
> 6. And in those days men will seek death and will not find it; they will long to die, and death flees from them.
> (Rev 9:5-6*)

Comparing the locusts' sting to that of a scorpion seems literal but does it make men immortal?

As you would expect, the Greek can be literal or metaphorical:

> The verb *basanizo* means literally to rub on the touchstone (*basanos*) or to test by means of the touchstone and then to test or make proof of anything... Figuratively, [it] refers to any severe distress, and so means to afflict, to harass, to vex, to torment...[289]

It is used elsewhere to describe a boat being 'battered' by waves (Matt 14:24), a woman 'in pain' to give birth (Rev 12:2), and the disciples 'straining' at the oars in a storm (Mark 6:48). More importantly for our purposes, it is used to describe Lot's torment when he lived in Sodom:

> ...for by what he saw and heard that righteous man, while living among them, felt his righteous soul tormented [Grk, *basanizo*] day after day by their lawless deeds (2 Pet 2:8)

---

[289] www.preceptaustin.org/2_peter_26-8, 8 July, 2023.

Lot's 'righteous soul' being tormented is obviously metaphorical - it is emotional or psychological torment. As I will show, the locusts' stings are already here and no, those stung will not somehow be immortal and unable to die. Job complained of his torment:

> 20. "Why is light given to him who suffers,
> And life to the bitter of soul,
> 21. *Who long for death, but there is none,*
> And dig for it more than for hidden treasures,
> 22. Who rejoice greatly,
> And exult when they find the grave?" (Job 3:20-22*)

Job's longing "for death but there is none" (v. 21) was not thwarted by his becoming immortal but by his own conviction against suicide, that only God should take life (Job 6:8-9).

We also see that Job's torment came initially from external circumstances - he had lost his ten children and all his possessions; his health had broken down and he was in terrible pain - but then he was tormented by his own fears and his friends falsely accusing him of wrongdoing.

To understand the locusts' metaphorical sting, therefore, we need to know what part we play in it and the difference between 'usual/normal' psychological torment and the locusts' temporary, seasonal psychological torment. We will look at this in the next chapter, establish why and how it lasts five months, and, of course, its antidote.

Summary

(i) The 5th Trumpet's plague of locusts parallels the plague God sent on Egypt to not only liberate the Hebrew slaves but also demonstrate His power to all and redeem anyone else who would trust His prophet Moses.

(ii) John's description of the locusts as armoured war-horses - sounding like chariots rushing to battle, and with teeth like lions - matches Joel's poetic description of a plague of ordinary desert locusts.

(iii) John's locusts, however, are demons released from the abyss to attack unbelievers. Their 'crowns like gold' signify a power, their 'faces like the faces of men' denote intelligence, their 'hair like the hair of women' signifies some allure, and they sting 'like scorpions' but they cannot kill, only torment for a season.

(iv) Their assignment and inability to kill rules out the metaphorical approach of the Preterists, Historicists, and some Futurists, leaving only the Futurists' literal insects and the Idealists' reading of literal demons and we have yet to establish which.

(v) Their sting, however, is metaphorical, psychological temporary torment which we will also consider next.

13
The Sting
Temporary Torment

To understand the locusts' season of torment, we need to see how it differs from usual, everyday torment so that we can find and administer the antidote for our unbelieving family and friends.

Contrary to the *Left Behind* scenario of Tim LaHaye and Jerry Jenkins, we do not and never will have to isolate anyone because we cannot bear their blood-curdling screams!

Usual Torment

We can feel tormented due to many external factors such as heart-breaking loss or death of a loved one. However, the Scriptures spell out three other causes of torment that every one of us can bring on ourselves at any time: the first is within every unbeliever and is the normal consequence of *being unforgiven by God*; the second and third causes can be in unbelievers and believers alike because we can all be *impatient with God*, and we can all be *unforgiving of each other*.

Let us look at each of these.

(i) Being unforgiven

This torment for unbelievers varies, of course, according to the state of our conscience and self-awareness but it is entirely self-imposed and I remember it all too well.

Before I came to Jesus on 22 August 1973, I had made a complete mess of my life, heart-broken from a failed romance, and plagued with memories and regrets that Transcendental Meditation and frequent use of marijuana and hashish could neither resolve nor relieve. At times suicidal, I restrained myself just in case my situation somehow turned around.

I sang along with The Beatles:

> I'm so tired, I haven't slept a wink
> I'm so tired, my mind is on the blink
> I wonder should I get up and fix myself a drink
> No, no, no...
>
> You'd say I'm putting you on
> But it's no joke, it's doing me harm
> You know I can't sleep, I can't stop my brain
> You know it's three weeks, I'm going insane!
> You know I'd give you everything I've got
> For a little peace of mind![290]

However, at the moment I surrendered control of my life to Jesus, an astonishing peace flooded my being (Phil 4:7). I suddenly realised I had been carrying a heavy load that I did not even know was there until it was gone. I still had all my problems to overcome but, with my sins forgiven and God leading me, I could at last address them one by one (Rom 8:23).

As David wrote:

> 1. How blessed is he whose transgression is forgiven,
> Whose sin is covered!
> 2. How blessed is the man to whom the LORD does not impute iniquity...
> 3. When I kept silent about my sin, my body wasted away
> Through my groaning all day long.
> 4. ...My vitality was drained away as with the fever heat of summer.
> 5. I acknowledged my sin to You,
> And my iniquity I did not hide;
> I said, "I will confess my transgressions to the LORD";
> And You forgave the guilt of my sin. (Psa 32:1-5)

---

290   https://genius.com/The-beatles-im-so-tired-lyrics, 2 Jan, 2023.

I later read Isaiah's perfect depiction of my previous state of mind:

> ...the wicked are like the tossing sea,
> For it cannot be quiet,
> And its waters toss up refuse and mud.
> "There is no peace," says my God, "for the wicked."
> (Isa 57:20-21*)

As noted above, this torment of unbelievers varies according to the state of our conscience and self-awareness but it is entirely self-imposed. The antidote is the same today as it was then: surrender to God *in Jesus Christ* and ask for His forgiveness.

(ii) Being impatient with God

In Isaiah's time, God warned Israel that sometimes they would have to wait for His revelation (Isa 50:10). If they did, He would lead them to peace but if they did not, He would let them walk in their own reasoning:

> Behold, all you who kindle a fire,
> Who encircle yourselves with firebrands,
> Walk in the light of your fire
> And among the brands you have set ablaze.
> *This you will have from My hand:*
> You will lie down *in torment.* (Isa 50:11*)

To 'lie down in torment' usually means we will be unable to sleep. In my own experience, before I turned to Jesus I lay awake, stewing on heart-breaking mistakes I had made, "what ifs" and "if only…"

This was all too often Israel's problem in the wilderness:

> They quickly forgot His works;
> They did not *wait for His counsel*,
> But craved intensely in the wilderness,
> And tempted God in the desert. (Psa 106:13-14*)

Again, the antidote is the same today as it was then: surrender to God and wait for Him to answer. He requires us to become patient because this changes and shapes our character (Gal 5:22) and only those who endure receive what He promises (Heb 6:12).

In the meantime, Jesus promises:

> 28. "Come to Me, all who are weary and heavy-laden, and I will give you rest.
> 29. "Take My yoke upon you and learn from Me, for I am gentle and humble in heart, and you will find rest for your souls.
> 30. "For My yoke is easy and My burden is light."
> (Matt 11:28-30*)

This particular torment then is our consequent regret at making wrong choices so it is self-imposed by believers and unbelievers alike and can be avoided and treated.

(iii) Being unforgiving of each other

The third cause or reason for our torment has the sting in the tail.

Jesus taught that we are to ask God to "forgive us our debts, *as we also have forgiven* our debtors" (Matt 6:12), adding a very stern warning:

> 14. "For if you forgive others for their transgressions, your heavenly Father will also forgive you.
> 15. "But if you do not forgive others, then your Father will not forgive your transgressions." (Matt 6:14-15)

To illustrate the point, He gave us the parable about the unforgiving servant:

> 34. "And his lord, moved with anger, handed him over to the torturers until he should repay all that was owed him.
> 35. *My heavenly Father will also do the same to you*, if each

of you does not forgive his brother from your heart."
(Matt 18:34-35*)

Our loving heavenly Father will "hand over" any unforgiving servants to "the torturers". The release from this is more complicated.

"The *Torturers*"?

So did Jesus mean this literally or metaphorically, and when was the Father to do this?

Traditional Catholic teaching is that He meant it literally and that this occurs after death to every individual at present in Purgatory[291] and will continue "until he should repay all" (v. 34).[292] Protestant theologian John Calvin agreed that Jesus meant it literally but only after Judgement Day, commenting:

> The Papists are very ridiculous in endeavoring to light the fire of purgatory by the word "until"; for it is certain that Christ here points out not temporal death, by which the judgment of God may be satisfied, but eternal death.[293]

However, I believe Jesus meant it both literally and metaphorically *before we die* - it has already been happening throughout the last 2,000 years but will come to a climax as the 5th Trumpet's tormenting locusts just before He returns.

---

[291] They define Purgatory as 'a place or condition of temporal punishment for those who, departing this life in God's grace, are not entirely free from venial faults, or have not fully paid the satisfaction due to their transgressions'. (www.catholic.com/encyclopedia/purgatory#i-catholic-doctrine, 15 July, 2023). I address both Catholic and Protestant views and offer a more satisfactory exposition in Book 7, *Kingdom Come: Justice for All*.

[292] The Catholic Church also openly used torture between the 12th and 19th centuries, Pope John Paul II confessing in 1998 that "the Inquisition belongs to a tormented phase in the history of the Church, which… Christians [should] examine in a spirit of sincerity and open-mindedness" (see *Threshing Hour*, pp. 169-176).

[293] Calvin's *Commentaries*. We will look properly at the Catholic teaching on Purgatory and Calvin's teaching on Hell in Book 7, *Kingdom Come: Justice for All*.

(i) Metaphorically

It is normal to be tormented by our own bitter memories and thoughts of our sins and mistakes. This can continue until we at last find the forgiveness of God and subsequent peace that Jesus promises and David sang about in Psalm 32.

In Isaiah's prophecy, God also described a torment "from My hand" (Isa 50:11) in His allowing us to face the painful consequences of not waiting for Him.

(ii) Literally

Jesus and John's 1st century Jewish audience would also have known that a thousand years earlier, their first king, King Saul, was handed over to a tormenting spirit:

> 14. Now the Spirit of the LORD departed from Saul, and *an evil spirit from the LORD terrorized him*. (1 Sam 16:14*)

This was openly identified by Saul's servants at the time and provided an opportunity for Israel's most famous king, King David in his youth, to come to his aid:

> 15. Saul's servants then said to him, "Behold now, *an evil spirit from God is terrorizing* you.
> 16. "Let our lord now command your servants who are before you. Let them seek a man who is a skillful player on the harp; and it shall come about when *the evil spirit from God* is on you, that he shall play the harp with his hand, and you will be well"…
> 23. So it came about whenever *the evil spirit from God* came to Saul, David would take the harp and play it with his hand; and Saul would be refreshed and be well, and the evil spirit would *depart from him*. (1 Sam 16:15-16, 23*)

1st century Jews would therefore have readily understood Jesus' teaching about what God will do to every unforgiving servant:

> 34. "And his lord, moved with anger, handed him over to the torturers [Grk, *basanistēs*] until he should repay all that was owed him.
> 35. "My heavenly Father will also *do the same to you*, if *each of you* does not forgive his brother from your heart." (Matt 18:34-35*)

The Greek for 'torturers', *basanistēs,* comes from the same root (*basanos*) as the verb *basanizo* and noun *basanismos* that John used to describe the assignment of the locusts.

Jesus and John were warning them, and us, that anyone who is unforgiving can be tormented by a *basanistēs*. From God. We need to look at why this is good and necessary.

'Five Months'?

What then are we to make of the locusts' 'five months'? Is this literal or metaphorical?

The *Left Behind* scenario quoted in Chapter 11 predicts literal, material locusts coming soon with a literal sting for a literal five months and inflicting literal 'torture and agony' to which there will be 'no remedy'[294] as well as another 'five months after that…[for] those among the last bitten'.[295]

However, I believe it is a metaphor, based on the desert locusts' usual five month season. John's demonic locusts being the 5th Trumpet means they are loosed only for a metaphorical 'season', i.e. an indeterminate period, prior to the Lord's return at the 7th Trumpet. As I will show, the length of time each victim suffers has to differ according to each individual's response.

This is consistent with the Lord's teaching on the torturers only having power over the unforgiving servant 'until he should repay all that' he owed (Matt 18:34). It is also consistent with Saul being tormented for unspecified periods

---

294 *Apollyon: The Destroyer is Unleashed*, p. 309.
295 Ibid, p. 327.

of time which could be ended or alleviated by David's ministry. Does this mean that Saul was an unforgiving servant? He certainly let his jealousy of David become murderous but, as we will see, his tormenting spirit came for other reasons.

Learning from Saul

Firstly, happily, we learn that there was an antidote - in Saul's affliction, it came from David's harp-playing:

> ...*whenever* the evil spirit from God came to Saul, David would take the harp and play it with his hand; and Saul would be refreshed and be well, and the evil spirit would *depart from him.* (1 Sam 16:23*)

Obviously, this relief was only temporary because David had to play 'whenever' the tormenting spirit afflicted Saul and Saul did not seem to learn how to make this permanent.

I had a similar experience just before I became a follower of Jesus. In my state of heart-broken atheism, I initially found some relief in empty churches for about nine months. Then on the afternoon of 22nd August, 1973, I sensed for the first time an extraordinary peace that surrounded some Jesus freaks, as we called them then. Several hours later, I finally surrendered control of my life to Jesus and 'the peace of God which surpasses all comprehension' (Phil 4:7) became a permanent state of mind for me.

Secondly, there was good reason for why 'the Spirit of God departed from' Saul and 'an evil spirit from the LORD terrorized him'. The Scriptures actually give us two reasons: he was impatient, disobeying God in offering the sacrifice that only priests could offer (1 Sam 13:9-14), and he turned to the occult (1 Sam 28:7-19) for guidance:

> So Saul died for his trespass which he committed against the LORD, *because* of the word of the LORD which he did not keep; and *also because* he asked counsel of a medium,

making inquiry of it, and did not inquire of the LORD. Therefore He killed him and turned the kingdom to David the son of Jesse. (1 Chron 10:13-14*)

God had tolerated Saul's appalling behaviour for forty years,[296] leaving him as king to demonstrate to all of Israel how foolish they had been[297] in rejecting God Himself as their King:

> "Then you will cry out in that day because of your king whom you have chosen for yourselves, but the LORD will *not answer* you in that day" (1 Sam 8:18*).

As for Saul, however, his impatience and disobedience eventually ended up in occultism, despite God showing him such forbearance and grace for those forty years. Throughout this time, he could have turned back to God and we are not told if he did in his last moments.

Learning from Paul

Paul wrote of trying to provoke repentance by handing professing Christians over to Satan:

> 4. In the name of our Lord Jesus, when you are assembled, and I with you in spirit, with the power of our Lord Jesus, 5. I have decided *to deliver* such a one *to Satan* for the destruction of his flesh, so that his spirit may be saved in the day of the Lord Jesus. (1 Cor 5:4-5*)

---

[296] Many do not realise that Saul's reign was God's punishment on Israel for "forty years" (Acts 13:21), repeating the wilderness punishment (Psa 95:9-11) of some four hundred years earlier. Saul's jealousy of David became murderous and he tried to kill the very man that God was using to alleviate his torment (1 Sam 18:6-12); it culminated in his massacring an entire village of priests, 'both men and women, children and infants; also oxen, donkeys, and sheep' (1 Sam 22:19), for unwittingly helping David. When the forty years was up, God allowed Saul to be wounded in battle by the Philistines, prompting him to kill himself (1 Sam 31:3-5).
[297] 1 Samuel 8:6-8, 12:16-18.

In this instance, a man was sleeping with his step-mother (1 Cor 5:1). Even so, Paul's response may seem extreme until you realise that 'the whole world [already] lies in the power of the evil one' (1 John 5:19).

'Delivering' or 'handing over' someone to Satan is merely recognising that they still belong to his dominion rather than God's. Paul wanted this man to come to his senses by seeing the whole community refusing to associate or even to eat with him *as a brother* (1 Cor 5:9-11).[298]

The goal was to bring about 'the destruction of his flesh' as the man repented of both his hypocrisy and his desires of 'the flesh' i.e. old nature. As Paul explained to the Romans:

> 12. So then, brethren, we are under obligation, not to the flesh, to live according to the flesh -
> 13. for if you are living according to the flesh, you must die; but if by the Spirit *you are putting to death the deeds of the body, you will live.* (Rom 8:12-13*)

All of this 'so that his spirit may be saved in the day of the Lord Jesus' (1 Cor 5:5).

When it worked as hoped, Paul urged the Corinthians to quickly welcome him back into fellowship (2 Cor 1:6-8).

Paul also wrote of handing Hymenaeus and Alexander 'over to Satan, *so that* they will be taught not to blaspheme' (1 Tim 1:20) - Hymenaeus had 'gone astray from the truth saying that the resurrection has already taken place and… upset the faith of some' (2 Tim 2:17) while Alexander 'vigorously opposed our teaching' (2 Tim 4:14) - but we do not know the outcome.

What then should we make of God handing over the whole unbelieving world to the torment of the demonic locusts? He wants the whole world to come to their senses and repent.

---

[298] They could, however, associate and eat with him if he stopped claiming to be a brother and was honest about his immorality (1 Cor 5:12-13), which is why Jesus could associate and eat with 'tax collectors and sinners' (Matt 9:10-13).

The 5th Trumpet reveals He is hoping this will happen right up to the last minute, like the thief on the cross who initially mocked Jesus (Matt 27:44, Mark 15:32) but finally changed his mind and was saved (Luke 23:39-43).

Summary

(i) The Scriptures tell us of three distinct causes of torment that we can bring on ourselves: being unforgiven by God, being impatient with God, and being unforgiving of each other.

(ii) The third cause includes our loving heavenly Father handing us over to 'torturers', i.e. tormenting spirits, until we have resolved the issue.

(iii) Saul experienced times of torment which David, a godly young man, could alleviate with his music. Seeing this obvious antidote, Saul could have turned back to God for permanent relief but we are not told if he did.

(iv) Paul gives us examples of professing Christians being handed over to Satan in order that they might repent and this proved successful in the case of the immoral man in Corinth.

14
Dangers
& Antidotes

I began Chapter 8 with Jesus' prediction of the "signs of the time" of His return in His last public discourse on the Temple Mount[299] as recorded in Luke Chapter 21:

> 25. "There will be signs in *sun and moon and stars*, and *on the earth* dismay among nations, in perplexity at the roaring of *the sea* and the waves… (Luke 21:25*)

Fear of the Signs

As I have shown, the first four trumpets are the signs "on the earth" (1st & 3rd Trumpets), and in "the sea" (2nd Trumpet), and in "sun and moon and stars" (4th Trumpet). Jesus goes on to explain this "dismay among the nations" and "perplexity" as:

> 26. men *fainting from fear* and *the expectation of the things which are coming upon the world*; for the powers of the heavens will be shaken. (Luke 21:26*)

This "fear and the expectation" of what is "coming upon the world" *is the 5th Trumpet.*

How long will it last? John says the demonic locusts will

---

[299] Matthew and Mark record that He explained more to the disciples in private on the Mount of Olives (Matt 24:1-44, Mark 13:1-7). They therefore heard of the imminent "abomination of desolation" (Matt 24:15-22, Mark 13:14-20) which I showed in Book 2 was His crucifixion in 30 AD (*Slouching Towards Bethlehem*, pp. 273-275). Luke, on the other hand, reports Jesus' prediction of the desolation of the Temple and Jerusalem (Luke 21:20-24) which came forty years later in 70 AD. Luke then records Jesus' prediction regarding His future return (Luke 21:25-36).

only be around for a season but it will climax in 'one hour' with 'the fear', fall, and 'torment' of Babylon the Great:

> And the kings of the earth... will weep and lament over her, standing at a distance because of *the fear of her torment* [Grk, *basanismos*], saying, 'Woe, woe, the great city, Babylon, the strong city! For in *one hour* your judgment has come.' (Rev 18:10* Also 18:15)

Until then, in fact today, the world is continually telling us that we have much to fear.

The Covid-19 pandemic has shaken us from any complacency that in our lifetime life will just go on as usual. I do not believe our government in New Zealand was malicious or part of a New World Order conspiracy but they violated freedom of conscience in mandating vaccinations without providing alternative ways forward - I believe in vaccinations but have friends who lost their jobs, homes, friends, and reputations. We also saw American BigTech and social media censoring unapproved perspectives and even true reports, violating freedom of speech. The startling capabilities of Artificial Intelligence are also causing many to fear what might go wrong.

Jesus warned that every one of us will need to guard our own hearts:

> 34. "Be on guard, so that your hearts will not be weighted down with dissipation and drunkenness and the worries of life, and that day will not come on you suddenly like a trap;
> 35. for it will come upon all those who dwell on the face of all the earth.
> 36. "But keep on the alert at all times, praying that you may have strength to escape all these things that are about to take place, and to stand before the Son of Man." (Luke 21:34-36)

The only lasting antidote to these fears is faith - we have to trust instead in what Jesus went on to say:

> 28. "But when these things begin to take place, *straighten up and lift up your heads*, because your redemption is drawing near." (Luke 21:28*)

Dissipation & Drunkenness

The world, however, is not listening to Jesus, often choosing "dissipation and drunkenness" (Luke 21:34) as is increasingly evident today.

The World Health Organisation (WHO) reports that worldwide, 3 million die every year due to alcohol abuse, i.e. 5.3% of all premature deaths, and that figure jumps to 13.5% for those aged 20-39 years.[300] Add to this the damage of '200 associated diseases and injury conditions, …a range of mental and behavioural disorders… and significant social and economic losses'[301] to individuals, their families, and our communities.

Other drugs causing devastation are summarised in the 2023 World Drug Report of the United Nations Office on Drugs and Crime (UNDOC):

> Cannabis continues to be the most used drug, with an estimated 219 million users (4.3% global adult population) in 2021… 36 million people had used amphetamines, 22 million had used cocaine and 20 million had used "ecstasy"-type substances in the past year… Opioids [make] the highest contribution to severe drug-related harm, including fatal overdoses… [used by] 60 million people in 2021, 31.5 million of whom used opiates (mainly heroin).[302]

---

300 www.who.int/news-room/fact-sheets/detail/alcohol, 24 Nov, 2023.
301 Ibid.
302 www.unodc.org/res/WDR-2023/WDR23_Exsum_fin_DP.pdf, p. 12, 24 Nov, 2023.

In the USA, pharmaceutical companies and doctors irresponsibly prescribing opioids, the availability of cheap heroin, fentanyl, methamphetamine, and xylazine in 2023 led to a new record of 112,000 deaths with no sign of abating.[303] On YouTube, heart-breaking videos of city streets in Philadelphia, Los Angeles, and Seattle show hundreds of addicts stumbling around like zombies.[304]

Meanwhile, 280 million otherwise healthy individuals worldwide have depressive disorders,[305] requiring vast quantities of antidepressants, while 'the prevalence of depression in the world rose from 17.2% in 2005 to 19.5% in 2015'.[306] That is, even before the Covid-19 pandemic, one fifth of the world was depressed!

Dangers Real & Imagined

Obviously we are supposed to be concerned about real dangers and, as suggested in Chapter 8, we should all do whatever we can to better steward the planet.

However, the locusts' torment will amplify what is true and inspire imaginary dangers so we have to discern which is which and apply the antidote as needed.

(i) Hot and Cold Wars

World War II (1939-1945) was terrifying for the world. For the first time in history, as I will cover in the 6th Trumpet, the whole world erupted into simultaneous warfare in Asia, Oceania, Europe, Africa, and the Americas with tens of millions killed and maimed and millions displaced.

---

303   www.opb.org/article/2023/12/28/fentanyl-crisis-addiction-overdose, 4 Apr, 2024.
304   E.g. www.youtube.com/watch?v=5I_Kq9HzQiE (3:39 mins), www.youtube.com/watch?v=F2X31j9MALc (2:56 mins), www.youtube.com/watch?v=IyBkJES4QyU (13:22 mins), accessed 24 Nov, 2023.
305   www.who.int/news-room/fact-sheets/detail/depression, 26 Nov, 2023.
306   www.sciencedirect.com/science/article/pii/S2666915321002298, *Introduction*, 24 Nov, 2023.

Afterwards though we moved from the fear of 'hot war'[307] to the fear of the Cold War, which was…:

> the open yet restricted rivalry that developed after World War II between the United States and the Soviet Union and their respective allies. The Cold War was waged on political, economic, and propaganda fronts and had only limited recourse to weapons. The term was first used by the English writer George Orwell in an article published in 1945 to refer to what he predicted would be a nuclear stalemate between "two or three monstrous super-states, each possessed of a weapon by which millions of people can be wiped out in a few seconds."[308]

This idea became known as the MAD Doctrine, i.e. Mutually Assured Destruction. Until the Berlin Wall fell in 1989, young couples in the West debated the ethics of bringing children into such a world.

(ii) Climate Change

Today, young couples debate the ethics of bringing children into Global Warming or Climate Change:

> Climate change harms mental wellbeing in a number of ways. From trauma and stress following disasters, to relationship damage caused by separation and displacement, the psychological effects of climate change can be enduring… As noted in a report by psychology professor Susan Clayton… "the ability to process information and make decisions without being disabled by extreme emotional responses is threatened by climate change".[309]

One 2020 survey of child psychiatrists in England showed

---

307 'Hot war' is open or actual fighting between warring parties.
308 www.britannica.com/event/Cold-War, 3 Jan, 2023.
309 www.bbc.com/future/article/20191010-how-to-beat-anxiety-about-climate-change-and-eco-awareness, 3 Jan, 2023.

that 57% are seeing children and young people distressed about the climate crisis and the state of the environment.[310] The Save the Children Fund report that:

> Every day the children we work with tell us that leaders are not doing enough to limit catastrophic climate change and that they need to see more action.[311]

(iii) Rising sea-levels

Over the last hundred years, the Intergovernmental Panel on Climate Change (IPCC) tell us:

> ...the average global sea level rose by 15–25 cm (6–10 in), or 1–2 mm per year. This rate accelerated to 4.62 mm per year for the decade 2013–2022.[312]

They see this as due to melting ice-sheets and glaciers and the expansion of warming seawater. The World Economic Forum (WEF) warn that 'over 410 million people are predicted to be at risk from rising sea levels by 2100'.[313]

Australian rock-group and climate activists Midnight Oil sing in *Rising Seas* that we should confess to our children that we have not acted in time to stop the seas rising, that as the earth's temperature rises and mankind denies it, "fever is gripping" and "nobody's listening!"[314]

Listening Uncritically

Despite Midnight Oil's fear that nobody is listening, vast numbers are, via ever-new forms of communication

---

310 www.theguardian.com/society/2021/oct/06/eco-anxiety-fear-of-environmental-doom-weighs-on-young-people, 4 Jan, 2023.
311 www.savethechildren.org/us/about-us/media-and-news/2021-press-releases/children-share-their-biggest-fears-about-climate-change, 4 Jan, 2023.
312 Special report, *The Ocean and Cryosphere in a Changing Climate,* 24 July, 2023.
313 www.weforum.org/agenda/2022/09/rising-sea-levels-global-threat, 24 July, 2023.
314 James Moginie, https://genius.com/Midnight-oil-rising-seas-lyrics, 24 July, 2023.

technology, but do they know how to process or examine what they are hearing?

(i) The Anxious Generation

Jonathan Haidt, a social psychologist studying adolescent mental health trends, reports that since 2010 there has been an alarming surge in rates of anxiety, depression, self-harm, and suicide throughout the Western world, with those born after 1995 hit hardest.[315]

In his book, *The Anxious Generation: How the Great Rewiring of Childhood is Causing an Epidemic of Mental Illness*, he shows that between 2010 and 2015, there was a calamitous decline in the "play-based childhood" and matching rise in "phone-based childhood". He attributes this use of smart-phones to social media, new high-speed internet, and unlimited data plans causing 'sleep deprivation, attention fragmentation, addiction, loneliness, social contagion, social comparison, and perfectionism', particularly among young women.[316]

(ii) TikTok Frenzies

TikTok is a Chinese video-hosting service which, in 2017, offered a free app which allows anyone to post self-made videos up to 10 minutes long. Within three years, it had been downloaded 2 billion times![317]

Initially touted as a site for 15-second, music videos, it has since become a major news source and promoter of rallies to any cause. A recent BBC report on Tiktok 'frenzies' highlighted four episodes which led to false murder accusations in the USA, widespread vandalism in schools

---

315 https://jonathanhaidt.com/anxious-generation, 4 Apr, 2024.
316 www.stern.nyu.edu/experience-stern/faculty-research/anxious-generation-how-great-rewiring-childhood-causing-epidemic-mental-illness, 4 Apr, 2024.
317 www.theverge.com/2020/4/29/21241788/tiktok-app-download-numbers-update-2-billion-users,0 Nov, 2023.

in the UK, and riots in France. The latter were due to the shooting of a 17-year-old Nahel M by a police officer who was later charged with homicide but, in the meantime:

> On TikTok, public videos using the hashtag [Nahel] racked up 850 million views. In one town, Viry-Châtillon, on the outskirts of Paris, videos showed a bus on fire and a ransacked newsagent… Jean-Marie Vilain, the mayor, said [it was] "incredible and dramatic" in… that the riots spread to "the provinces, in cities, in small towns where nothing is happening, where everything is fine" - as far afield as Provence and Guadeloupe. "Unfortunately, once the riots started, TikTok became a tool to show, here, this is what I'm capable of doing. Can you do better?"[318]

The report noted:

> Ex-staffers at TikTok liken these frenzies to "wildfires" and describe them as "dangerous", especially as the app's audience can be young and impressionable.[319]

In the USA, as I write (November, 2023), Osama bin Laden's 'Letter to America' has just gone viral on TikTok. American teenagers were thrilled to hear his justification for killing 3,000 civilians on 9 November, 2001, by flying civilian passenger planes into the World Trade Center and the Pentagon. *Time* magazine reports that one TikToker with 900,000 views proclaimed his or her 'truth':

> "Everything we learned about the Middle East, 9/11, and 'terrorism' was a lie."[320]

Before TikTok could remove the letter, videos with the hashtag #lettertoamerica had had over 14 million views.[321]

---

318 www.bbc.com/news/technology-66719572, 20 Nov, 2023.
319 Ibid.
320 https://time.com/6336280/osama-bin-laden-letter-to-america-tiktok, 20 Nov, 2023.
321 Ibid.

While we should consider why he did what he did, my concern is how was his Islamic jihadist perspective critiqued by these millions of viewers?

(iii) Doomscrolling

Today's fears and expectations have in turn led to doomscrolling or doomsurfing, i.e. excessively scrolling through bad news on social media. In her article *Doomscrolling is Slowly Eroding Your Mental Health,* journalist Angela Watercutter quotes Mesfin Bekalu of Harvard's T. H. Chan School of Public Health:

> "As humans we have a 'natural' tendency to pay more attention to negative news… Since the 1970s, we know of the 'mean world syndrome' [the belief that the world is a more dangerous place to live in than it actually is] as a result of long-term exposure to violence-related content on television…So, doomscrolling can lead to the same long-term effects on mental health…"[322]

Ms Watercutter explains the term:

> There's something else in the etymology, though. Particularly in the word *doom*. Originally, the word had connotations that related it to judgement day and the end of the world, but now it's just as likely to be associated with destruction or ruin. The act of doomscrolling, then, is to roll toward annihilation.[323]

She then adds a deeply insightful observation:

> Or to borrow a phrase from Joan Didion (writing during America's last traumatic, generation-defining year,

---

322 Article published 25 June 2020, www.wired.com/story/stop-doomscrolling. Accessed 13 Mar, 2023.
323 Ibid.

1968), it is an act of slouching toward quietus.[324] Taken biblically, it has a Revelation tone. Each swipe through the timeline marks the end of a day of reckoning - for the state of the world at large and for the person attached to each appendage doing the scrolling. Simultaneously, each person watches the demise of so much, while also slowly destroying themselves.[325]

Ms Watercutter concludes:

> Didion lifted "slouching towards Bethlehem" from W. B. Yeats' poem "The Second Coming," itself a reflection on the destruction caused by World War I written amidst the 1918 flu pandemic. It's only natural that the world's scrolling reflects those writers' apocryphal Apocalypse visions.[326]

Readers of Book 2 in this series, *Slouching Towards Bethlehem*, will know that I too took my title[327] from Yeats's poem but I applied it to the coming of the Antichrist rather than to Ms. Didion's drug-hazed dissolution of San Francisco in 1967. Her essay[328] then was "a devastating depiction of the aimless lives of the disaffected and incoherent young"[329] - I am saying that what we are seeing today is the sounding of Revelation's 5th Trumpet.

'Hair like Women'?

I noted in Chapter 12 that 'hair like women' can mean to make them attractive and seductive. What could possibly be alluring about all of this?

---

324   The final discharge or settlement of a duty or a debt.
325   Article published 25 June 2020, www.wired.com/story/stop-doomscrolling. Accessed 13 Mar, 2023.
326   Ibid.
327   *Slouching Towards Bethlehem*, pp. 2-3.
328   First published in *The Saturday Evening Post* on 23 Sept, 1967.
329   Jonathan Yardley, *In a Time of Posturing, Didion Dared Slouching*, The Washington Post, Dec 27, 2007.

Well, there is much fame, money, and apparent virtue to be gained by elevating these fears and expectations.

(i) Fame

US Vice President Al Gore's 2006 movie, *An Inconvenient Truth*, was a critical and commercial success, winning two Academy Awards for 'Best Documentary Feature' and 'Best Original Song'. In 2007, he was awarded the Nobel Peace Prize.

However, some of his predictions and/or projections were quickly ruled to have been alarmist and exaggerated[330] and, as the *Smithsonian Magazine* reported, while he 'seared the image of a polar bear paddling, paddling, paddling hopelessly in search of the vanished Arctic pack ice into minds around the world', his portrayal of their looming extinction is simply not true.[331] Polar bears have actually multiplied threefold since the 1960s, despite 600 a year being legally hunted by Canadian Inuits.[332]

He claimed the global sea levels could rise by "20 feet [6 m] in the near future" which would inundate major cities such as Beijing, Shanghai, Calcutta, San Francisco and Manhattan in New York City and entire low-lying countries such as The Netherlands and Bangladesh. However, as mentioned earlier, the UN's panel reports that over the last 100 years the seas rose by 15–25 cm (6–10 in), or 1–2 mm (0.0 in) per year, but 4.6 mm (0.2 in) per year for the decade 2013–2022.[333] The USA's National Oceanic and Atmospheric Administration (NOAA) agrees:

---

330   www.theguardian.com/environment/2007/oct/11/climatechange, 26 Feb, 2024.
331   *Smithsonian Magazine*, www.smithsonianmag.com/science-nature/doomed-beloved-polar-bear-dangerous-180969092, 26 Feb, 2024.
332   The current scientific consensus places the worldwide polar bear population between 20,000 and 25,000 animals. https://canadiangeographic.ca/articles/the-truth-about-polar-bears, 27 July, 2023.
333   Special report, *The Ocean and Cryosphere in a Changing Climate*, 24 July, 2023.

> Sea level along the US coastline is projected to rise, on average, 10-12 inches [25- 30 cm] in the next 30 years (2020-2050), which will be as much as... over the last 100 years (1920-2020).[334]

In 2009, VP Gore told the Copenhagen Climate Conference that there was:

> ...a 75% chance that the entire north polar ice cap, during some of the summer months, could be completely ice-free within the next five to seven years.[335]

However, while melting ice-caps are obviously deeply concerning, the data in 2024 are far less alarming. NASA's 2023 'Current State of Sea Ice Cover' stated:

> A satellite-based data record starting in late 1978 shows that indeed rapid changes have been occurring in the Arctic, where the ice coverage has been declining at a substantial rate. In contrast, in the Antarctic the sea ice coverage has been increasing although at a lesser rate than the decreases in the Arctic.[336]

Moreover, they record that the Arctic ice coverage has actually increased since 2012.[337]

Today, many young people want to become influencers like Greta Thunberg who rocketed to international fame as a deeply sincere 15 year old, addressing the 2018 UN Climate Change Conference and 2019 UN Climate Action Summit with her famous "How dare you!" reverberating around the world.

Time magazine named her as their youngest 'Person of the Year' in 2019 as well as one of the '100 Most Influential

---

[334] https://oceanservice.noaa.gov/hazards/sealevelrise/sealevelrise-tech-report.html, 26 Feb, 2024.
[335] Ibid.
[336] https://earth.gsfc.nasa.gov/cryo/data/current-state-sea-ice-cover, 28 July, 2023.
[337] Ibid.

People' in the world. *Forbes* likewise listed her as one of 'The World's 100 Most Powerful Women' in 2019, and she was nominated for the Nobel Peace Prize in 2019, 2020, 2021, 2022, and 2023.

(ii) Money

Scientific researchers have to compete for government funding and internationally, governments are funding climate-change promoters but not "deniers". Economist Stephen Moore notes:

> In America and around the globe governments have created a multi-billion dollar Climate Change Industrial Complex… According to a recent report by the U.S. Government Accountability Office, "Federal funding for climate change research, technology, international assistance, and adaptation has increased from $2.4 billion in 1993 to $11.6 billion in 2014, with an additional $26.1 billion for climate change programs and activities provided by the American Recovery and Reinvestment Act in 2009."[338]

He adds an ironic caveat:

> This doesn't mean that the planet isn't warming. But the tidal wave of funding does reveal a powerful financial motive for scientists to conclude that *the apocalypse is upon us*.[339]

(iii) Apparent virtue

On a personal and individual level, we all face the temptation of virtue signalling, trying to show others that we are good people by expressing opinions that will be acceptable to

---

338 www.heritage.org/environment/commentary/follow-the-climate-change-money, 28 July, 2023.
339 Ibid. Emphasis added.

them. The on-line *Cambridge Dictionary* puts it well:

> Virtue signalling is the popular modern habit of indicating that one has virtue merely by expressing disgust or favour for certain political ideas or cultural happenings.[340]

My Own View?

Obviously, if Climate Change and rising sea-levels are real and anthropogenic, i.e. caused by mankind, this would confirm my case that we are fully responsible for the first four trumpet-alarms sounding today.

However, I am not yet convinced either way.

In the 1970s, we were warned the data showed we were heading towards another Ice Age. Every year for that decade we faced headlines such as:

> 'Colder Winters Herald Dawn of New Ice Age – Scientists See Ice Age In the Future' (*The Washington Post*, 11 Jan, 1970)
> 'New Ice Age Coming – It's Already Getting Colder' (*L.A. Times*, 24 Oct, 1971)
> 'Science: Another Ice Age?' (*Time Magazine*, 3 Nov, 1972)
> 'Weather-watchers think another ice age may be on the way' (*The Christian Science Monitor*, 11 Dec, 1973)
> 'Another Ice Age?' (*Time Magazine*, 24 June, 1974)
> 'Climate Change: Chilling Possibilities' (*Science News*, 1 Mar, 1975)
> 'The Big Freeze' (*Time Magazine*, 31 Jan, 1977)
> 'Little Ice Age: Severe winters and cool summers ahead' (*Calgary Herald*, 10 Jan 10, 1978)
> 'New Ice Age Almost Upon Us?' (*The Christian Science Monitor*, 14 Nov, 1979)[341]

---

340 https://dictionary.cambridge.org/dictionary/english/virtue-signalling, 29 July, 2023.
341 https://climatechangedispatch.com/120-years-of-climate-scares-1970s-ice-age-scare, 29 July, 2023.

As noted earlier, I worked as a logistics analyst for fifteen years, using readily checked historical data to project future usage of every kind of fuel in New Zealand as well as imports and exports and the production of feedstocks from our oil and gas fields. Every week, I reported to our Ministry of Energy the state of our country and our expectations for the next 90 days.

Familiar with checking and analysing data and forecasting, I have been astonished at how some temperature data and reports have been manipulated to suit today's favoured narrative. However, it could still all be true so I leave it to you to judge for yourself what to believe. There is also no doubt whatsoever that we should all doing whatever we can to be better stewards of the planet God gave us to rule.

Returning to the locusts, their sting of fear of dangers real or imagined torments whoever allows themselves to be targeted. Happily, there is a very simple antidote.

The Antidote

Let us finish this chapter focussed on the antidote to the demonic locusts' torment - it is always well-directed faith. Faith in our heavenly Father's goodness and love for us all; faith in Jesus as "the Lamb of God who takes away the sins of the world!" (John 1:29); faith in the Holy Spirit to lead us into all truth (John 14:26, 16:12-13); and faith in His Scriptures for understanding what we see.

(i) The seal of God

Remember the locusts' specific assignment:

> They were told not to hurt the grass of the earth, nor any green thing, nor any tree, but only the men who do not have *the seal of God* on their foreheads. (Rev 9:4*)

As noted in Chapter 12 and Book 3,[342] all we need is this mark of God's ownership, i.e. His name metaphorically written on our forehead:

> "He who overcomes… *I will write on him the name of My God…*" (Rev 3:12*)

Overcoming means keeping our faith in Jesus whenever we are tested (1 John 5:4-5) and continuing to serve Him:

> His bond-servants will serve Him… and His name will be *on their foreheads.* (Rev 22:4*)

Faith is the antidote to fear. Many years ago, I heard a saying that, as corny as it may seem, has helped me:

> Fear is thinking on the worst and believing it to happen;
> Faith is thinking on the Word and believing it to happen.

We just need to find what the Scriptures say regarding any situation and trust them to be true.

I also spelled out in Book 3[343] that His ownership mark is not literal but metaphorical and seen in four essentials: in our trusting Jesus for forgiveness, living His way, loving our neighbours, and avoiding being misled, particularly by false prophets.

This means, of course, that anyone stung by the locusts can join us by surrendering to Jesus as Lord.

(ii) God's forgiveness

If we are still tormented by regrets and memories of our sins, we need to talk to Him:

> "Come now, and let us reason together," says the LORD

---

342 *Gotta Serve Somebody,* pp. 23-38.
343 Ibid, pp. 47-69.

> "Though your sins are as scarlet,
> They will be as white as snow;
> Though they are red like crimson,
> They will be like wool." (Isa 1:18)
> "I, even I, am the one who wipes out your transgressions for My own sake,
> And I will not remember your sins." (Isa 43:25)

John added that He really will forgive us:

> If we confess our sins, He is faithful and righteous to forgive us our sins and to cleanse us from all unrighteousness. (1 John 1:9)

We simply have to stick with Him:

> Now, little children, abide in Him, so that when He appears, we may have confidence and not shrink away from Him in shame at His coming. (1 John 2:28)

> There is no fear in love; but perfect love casts out fear, because fear involves punishment, and the one who fears is not perfected in love. (1 John 4:18)

(iii) Birth-pangs

In context, "that day" (v. 34) will be preceded by the "signs in sun and moon and stars…on the earth…the sea" and "men fainting from fear and the expectation of the things which are coming upon the world" (Luke 21:25-26).

As alert believers, however, we need have no fear of the locusts.

We should also have a very different perspective to the world's. Just before He was crucified, Jesus promised the disciples:

> 20. "Truly, truly, I say to you, that you will weep and lament, but the world will rejoice; you will grieve, but *your grief will be turned into joy.*" (John 16:20*)

He then used the vivid analogy of childbirth:

> 21. "Whenever a woman is in labor she has pain, because her hour has come; but when she gives birth to the child, she no longer remembers the anguish because of the joy that a child has been born into the world.
> 22. "Therefore you too have grief now; but *I will see you again*, and your heart *will rejoice*, and no one will take your joy away from you." (John 16:21-22*)

These first five trumpets are telling us that the 7th Trumpet is also about to sound, when we will see Him again and what an astonishing day that will be!

Summary

(i) The locusts introduce a season of psychological torment which differs from the usual torments of life such as heart-breaking grief due to death or loss. The Scriptures describe three other reasons for seasons of torment: being unforgiven by God; being impatient with God; and being unforgiving of each other.

(ii) Jesus taught that if we are unforgiving of each other, our heavenly Father will hand us over to 'the torturers' for a season. We see seasons of torment in the life of Saul which were alleviated by David's music and also in Paul's practice of 'handing over to Satan' immoral and blasphemous transgressors that they might learn and repent.

(iii) The 5th Trumpet alerts us to a season when God is handing over the whole world to the locusts' torment in hope that every unbeliever and any disobedient believer will look to Him for relief and salvation.

(iv) The locusts' sting is the 'fear… and the expectation of the things which are coming upon the world', i.e. the signs of the times on the earth, in the sea and in the heavens as identified by the first four trumpets, and by real and imagined fears of all kinds.

(v) The antidote every time is faith so while believers are protected from the locusts simply by 'abiding in Jesus', so too can any unbeliever who allows their regrets, memories, or fears to bring them to Him.

(vi) The world's anguish is like the pain of childbirth and will be quickly forgotten at the 7th Trumpet when we will see Him face to face!

15
The Sixth Trumpet
The Second Woe

After the 5th Trumpet's locusts, John comments:

> The first woe is past; behold, two woes are still coming after these things. (Rev 9:12)

The 6th Trumpet is therefore the second woe and like the first woe, directly impacts mankind. It also returns to the pattern of impacts on 'a third' seen in the first four trumpets when a third of the earth, a third of the seas, a third of the fresh water, and a third of the heavens are affected by mankind's greed, selfishness, and short-sighted behaviour. The 5th Trumpet alerts us to recognise a season of fear and torment for unbelievers at seeing these four signs of the times in hope that they will pray.

The 6th Trumpet warns of the time when a third of mankind are killed:

> 13. Then the sixth angel sounded, and I heard a voice…
> 14. …saying to the sixth angel who had the trumpet, "Release *the four angels* who are bound at the great river Euphrates."
> 15. And the four angels, who had been prepared for the hour and day and month and year, were released, so that they would kill *a third of mankind*.
> 16. The number of the armies of the horsemen was *two hundred million*; I heard the number of them.
> (Rev 9:13-16*)

When we see this, we are to recognise it as the 6th Trumpet sounding. We can also see that while the first four of these signs are mankind's impact on our dominion, the fifth and sixth are where we impact ourselves.

200 Million *"Horsemen"?*

When I first heard of this prediction in 1973, Hal Lindsay was proclaiming its imminent fulfilment, quoting China's claim that their People's Liberation Army was 200 million strong and backed up with H-bombs.[344] More recently, in 2008, David Jeremiah[345] was publicising a report by Colonel Larry Wortzel, retired director of the Strategic Studies Institute of the US Army War College:

> China's standing armed force of some 2.8 million active soldiers…1 million reservists… 15 million militia… and another 200 million males fit for military service available at any time.[346]

However, neither Mr Lindsay nor Dr Jeremiah commented on the Chinese soldiers being horsemen.

So are John's horsemen and horses literal or metaphorical?

If literal, could the Chinese produce 200 million warhorses, given that there are only 60 million horses on Earth today?[347] If the horses are metaphorical, however, they could be any means of transporting vast numbers of troops inland to the Euphrates including ships, planes, trains, and trucks, as well as armoured personnel carriers and tanks.

Their weaponry seems modern enough:

> 17. And this is how I saw in the vision… the heads of the horses are like the heads of lions; and out of their mouths

---

344 Hal Lindsay, with Carole C. Carlson, *The Late Great Planet Earth*, pp. 86-87.
345 David Jeremiah, *What in the World is Going On? 10 Prophetic Clues You Cannot Afford to Ignore,* Nashville, TN; Thomas Nelson, 2008, pp. 205-206.
346 https://nuke.fas.org/guide/china/doctrine/chinamil.htm, 5 Jan, 2023.
347 www.horsenation.com/2017/11/02/info-graph-global-horse-populations, 7 Dec, 2023.

proceed *fire and smoke and brimstone.*
18. A third of mankind was killed by these three plagues, by the fire and the smoke and the brimstone which proceeded out of their mouths. (Rev 9:17-18*)

Literal or Metaphorical Power?

So, are these 'three plagues… [of] the fire and the smoke and the brimstone' (v. 18) literal or metaphorical?

If literal, they could be exploding gunpowder as many have noted:

> The exact idea, whether that was intended or not, would be conveyed by the discharge of musketry or artillery. The fire, the smoke, and the sulphurous smell of such a discharge would correspond precisely with this language.[348]

How then do the four traditional views explain the horsemen and their plagues?

(i) Futurism

As just noted, Hal Lindsay and David Jeremiah were expecting Chinese armies; others focus on the literal gunpowder of the 20th century's helicopter gunships and/or 21st century drones.

However, Tim LaHaye and Jerry Jenkins teach the horsemen are soon-to-come demons with metaphorical/spiritual gunpowder:

> The 200 million in 9:16 are not humans but demons, doing things men cannot do. These "horsemen" have a supernatural effect on the earth… Creatures that are so awesome to look on, as we portrayed them in *Assassins*, that they actually frighten some people to death.[349]

---

348 *Barnes' Notes.* https://biblehub.com/commentaries/barnes/revelation/9.htm, 9 Jan, 2023.
349 *Are We Living in the End Times? Current Events Foretold in Scripture… And What They Mean*, Wheaton, Ill; Tyndale House Publishers, 1999, pp. 191-192.

They believe these demons will contribute to the killing of *half* of the world's population. In the words of one character in that novel:

> "After the Rapture... one-fourth of the remaining population... died from plague, war, and natural disaster. That left, of course, 75%. One third of 75% is 25%, so the current wave of death [from the horsemen demons] will leave only 50% of the people left behind at the Rapture."[350]

However, happily, as shown in Chapter 4, the first four seals do not predict a future in which "one-fourth" of the earth's population will die "from plague, war, and natural disaster". Instead, they reveal what we have *already seen* throughout the last 2,000 years, in what we consider "normal" life, that three-fourths die non-violently or of old age.

(ii) Historicism

Historicists can point to the invention of gunpowder in 9th century China.

They can also claim a fulfilment in the Greek Fire used in 7th century Byzantine flamethrowers. Credited to a Greek named Kallinikos who fled to Constantinople from Muslim-held Syria in 668 AD, Greek Fire was Christendom's most devastating weapon for the next eight centuries.

Its composition was a closely-guarded secret but one known ingredient was naphtha, possibly mixed with quicklime, sulphur, potassium nitrate, and resin which made it sticky; it was fired through bronze tubes using a syphon pump and a swivelling nozzle.[351]

Their emperor Leo VI (866-912 AD), called the Wise,

---

350 LaHaye, Tim & and Jenkins, Jerry, *Assassins (Assignment: Jerusalem, Target: Antichrist)*, Wheaton, Ill; Tyndale House Publishers, 1999, p. 174.
351 In 919 AD, the Chinese were also using siphon projector-pumps to spread the 'fierce fire oil' that could not be doused with water, as recorded by Lin Yu in *Wu-Yue Beishi*.

wrote a military treatise *Tactica* mentioning a hand-held flamethrower, the *cheirosiphon*,[352] which was used on land against siege machines, while their soldiers filled small terracotta pots to throw, like medieval hand-grenades or 'Molotov cocktails'.

The Byzantine navy sprayed it at enemy ships and historian Constantinos Karatolios writes of one intriguing feature:

> When in 1099 the Byzantines used Greek fire against the Pisans, according to writings of Anna Komnene,[353] they placed bronze and iron lions and the heads of other fearsome creatures on the prows of their ships, connected them with hoses or *siphonia* to pumps and shot Greek fire to drive off their enemies.[354]

This Byzantine use of 'bronze and iron lions' heads' on their fire-ships to squirt 'fire and smoke and brimstone' could therefore seem to support the Historicist literalist view. However, this was naval warfare - where were the 200 million horsemen? We will also come back to Greek Fire soon, because John's audience would have known of its being used by the Greeks, 1,000 years before the Byzantines' use.

(iii) Preterism

The Preterists, with their idea that the trumpets were all blown in 70 AD, when the Romans razed Jerusalem, read the 200 million horsemen as hyperbole symbolising the 60,000 Roman soldiers, only 6,000 of whom were horsemen,[355] and

---

352 Lit. hand syphon.
353 Anna Komnene (1083 – 1153) was a Byzantine princess and historian who wrote the *Alexiad*.
354 *Greek Fire and Its Contribution to Byzantine Might.* https://militaryhistorynow.com/2014/03/19/greek-fire-nine-little-known-facts-about-byzantines-secret-weapon, 11 Jan, 2023.
355 Flavius Josephus, *The Wars of the Jews*, 3.4.2. (*The Works of Flavius Josephus*. Translated by. William Whiston, A.M. Auburn and Buffalo. John E. Beardsley. 1895). www.perseus.tufts.edu/hopper/text?doc=J.+BJ+3.4.2, 9 Aug, 2023. Also Tacitus, *The Histories* 5.1.

supported by 16,000 non-combatants.³⁵⁶ They also note that Titus had earlier stationed the four legions at the Euphrates in 63 AD³⁵⁷ so their legates could be the four angels bound there (Rev 9:14).

They read 'the fire and the smoke and the brimstone' from the horses' mouths as a metaphor for God's judgement, based on the literal 'brimstone and fire from the LORD out of heaven' that 'rained on Sodom and Gomorrah' (Gen 19:24).

(iv) Idealism

Idealists also take the metaphorical approach but see the 6th Trumpet being fulfilled throughout the last 2,000 years. William Hendriksen, for example, writes:

> The sixth trumpet describes war; not one particular war is indicated but *all* wars, past, present and future. Yet we are convinced that the symbol refers especially to those most frightful wars that shall be waged toward the close of this dispensation... [which extends] from the first to the second coming... [of] our exalted Lord Jesus Christ.³⁵⁸

He further explains:

> It should be clear by this time that these are not ordinary horses. They clearly symbolize war engines and war tools of every description. All this terrible death-dealing war machinery...³⁵⁹

N.T. Wright likewise:

> ...with the fifth and sixth plagues - and again we should not think of them all as separate, distinct events, but as

---

356 www.revelationrevolution.org/revelation-9-a-preterist-commentary-who-is-apollyon, 8 Jan, 2023.
357 Ibid. They were the Legio V Macedonica, Legio X Fretensis, Legio XII Fulminata, and Legio XV Apollinaris.
358 William Hendriksen, *More than Conquerors*, pp. 122-123. Emphasis in original.
359 Ibid, p. 123.

different dimensions of the same terrible overall reality - [John] is warning his hearers that the plagues to come will, from one point of view, consist of foul, hellish, destructive forces, and, from another point of view, of massive, terrifying armies charging against defenceless people.[360]

So how does he explain the 200 million horsemen?

> ...in a sense, the sixth trumpet corresponds to the first seal: the rider on the white horse, going off to conquer, has become an army the size of the entire population of Britain three times over, or of two thirds of the population of the United States. It is as though John is systematically saying, 'Think of your worst nightmares; now double them; and then imagine them coming true all at once, together'.[361]

John's 1st Century Audience

As usual, to understand which view is correct or the most correct we have to ask, what would John's original listeners have understood - what would they have already known?

In quoting from Revelation 9 at the beginning of this chapter, I highlighted only the parts of verses referenced by the four perspectives. However, we need to consider the rest of the details such as the golden altar, its four horns, the four angels, and the Euphrates River in vv. 13-14:

> 13. Then the sixth angel sounded, and I heard a voice from *the four horns of the golden altar* which is before God,
> 14. one saying to the sixth angel who had the trumpet, "*Release the four angels* who are bound at *the great river Euphrates.*" (Rev 9:13-14*)

---

360 N.T. Wright, *Revelation for Everyone*, Louisville, KY; Westminster John Knox Press, 2011, p. 91.
361 Ibid.

John's 1st century Jewish audience would have readily recognised the significance of these details. They would also have recognised the number '200 million', the description and colours of the horsemen, and their weaponry.

(i) The golden altar's horns

This was Israel's incense altar and, as we saw in Chapter 7, burning incense symbolises prayer (Rev 8:3-4) and its fire being thrown to the earth (Rev 8:5) symbolises God answering the prayers of the saints.

The horns of the golden altar, however, were where the blood of the sin offering was to be placed to atone for sins (Lev 4:7, 18).[362] The voice coming from there signifies that there is no atonement being made - they are calling for justice instead and 'a third of mankind' would be killed (v. 15).

(ii) The release of the four angels

Ancient Israel had seen God releasing and restraining angels before.

In the 10th century BC, King David, Ornan the Jebusite, and Ornan's four sons saw God's destroying angel 'with his drawn sword in his hand stretched out over Jerusalem' (1 Chron 21:16, 20) which symbolised 'three days of... pestilence in the land' in which 70,000 died (1 Chron 21:12-14). David 'saw the angel who was striking down the people' (2 Sam 24:17) and when God commanded the angel to sheath his sword, the plague stopped (1 Chron 21:27, 2 Sam 24:16).

In the 6th century BC, Ezekiel saw six 'executioners' each holding 'a shattering weapon in his hand' coming to strike Jerusalem (Ezek 9:1-10) and they symbolised

---

362 The bronze altar also had four horns which were smeared with blood to atone for sins and, being in the outer court, were accessible to non-priests to grasp and appeal for mercy (1 Kin 1:50-51, 1 Kin 2:28).

Nebuchadnezzar's Babylonian army razing the city and Solomon's Temple.

Here, however, John sees four angels who had previously been restrained but are now being released to lead vast angelic and/or human armies against the whole world:

> 15. And the four angels, who had been prepared for the hour and day and month and year, were *released*, so that they would kill *a third of mankind*.
> 16. The number of the armies of the horsemen was two hundred million; I heard the number of them.
> (Rev 9:15-16*)

(iii) 'The great river Euphrates'

Why are the angels 'bound' (v. 14) and 'released' (v. 15) at the Euphrates River?

The Euphrates is indeed a great river. At 2,800 km (1,700 miles), it is the longest in Western Asia, flowing from two sources in Turkey through Syria and Iraq to the Persian Gulf, and the glory of the Assyrian (Isa 8:7) and Babylonian Empires (Jer 51:13).

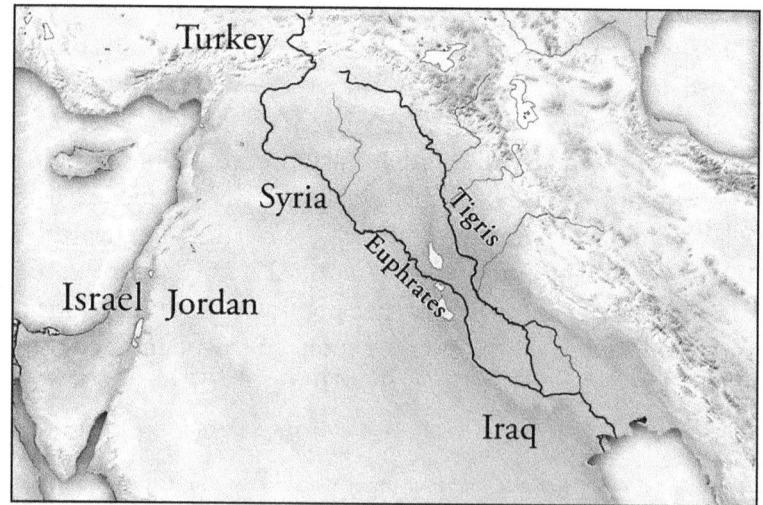

Fig (viii) The Euphrates River

Back in 7

John's Jewish audience would have immediately recognised it as the northern border of the land promised to Abraham (Gen 15:18, Deut 11:24), established by David (1 Chron 18:3), and maintained by Solomon (1 Chron 9:26). When the Assyrians crossed it in 722 BC, they enslaved the ten tribes of Israel's northern kingdom; when the Babylonians crossed it in 598 BC, they enslaved the southern kingdom of Judah.

In John's time, however, as everyone in John's audience knew, it was the eastern border of the Roman Empire with the Parthian Empire, and as we saw in Chapter 4 with the 1st Seal, the Parthians were the greatest threat there was to the Roman Empire at that time. Remember, at the Battle of Carrhae in 53 BC, the Parthians had defeated them in one of the most crushing defeats in Roman history.[363]

John's audience would therefore have understood that in the time of the 6th Trumpet, a vast and invincible army would be unleashed into Israel and the Roman Empire, and beyond.

(iv) In which direction?

As mentioned earlier, the Preterists believe the four angels could have been the Roman legates of the four legions that Titus had stationed at the Euphrates in 63 AD to guard against the Parthians invading the Empire from the east but then redeployed to capture Jerusalem.

However, the four horns of the altar and the four angels signify their armies will go forth to 'the four corners of the earth' (Isa 11:12), i.e. to the *north, south, east, and west* - after all, they are going to kill a third of mankind. They have been restrained, held back 'for the hour and day and month and year' (v. 15) with that hour arriving just before the 7th Trumpet of Jesus' return.

---

363 https://static.independent.co.uk/s3fs-public/thumbnails/image/2018/07/02/13/iraq-rivers-2-0.jpg, 12 Aug, 2023.

But what of the 200 million horsemen - are they literal or metaphorical, human or angelic?

The 200 Million

Actually, the number 'two hundred million' is the *NASB* translators[364] simplifying the Greek phrase 'twice ten thousand times ten thousand', as the *KJV*, *NIV* and *ESV* translate it.

This really matters when we have to judge whether this number is literal or metaphorical because to the Jews in John's original audience, 'ten thousand' was a common metaphor and they would have known its meaning.

For example, when the women of Israel celebrated David's prowess in battle even as a teenager, they sang:

> "Saul has slain his thousands,
> And David his *ten thousands*." (1 Sam 18:7*)

Saul was jealous, knowing the women meant that David would overcome countless numbers (1 Sam 18:8). Even King Achish in Gath (1 Sam 21:11) and the Philistine commanders on the battlefield understood their song (1 Sam 29:5).

When David became king, the people described him as "worth ten thousand of us" (2 Sam 18:3), meaning all of us.

When God rebuked Israel for ignoring "ten thousand precepts of My law" (Hos 8:12), had He forgotten that He had only given them 613 commands?

When the bride in Song of Solomon described her beloved as "outstanding among ten thousand" (Song 5:10), was she thinking literally, that when Man Number 10,001 came along he would be more outstanding? Obviously, she meant no matter how many there were, her beloved was the best!

---

364 Likewise the *NKJV* and N.T. Wright's *The Kingdom New Testament*.

Jesus uses the metaphor in describing the debt of the unforgiving servant as "ten thousand talents" (Matt 18:24) - 1 talent was worth more than 15 years' wages of a labourer so 10,000 talents would be 150,000 years!

Likewise when Paul said it was better to speak 'five words' in a known language than 'ten thousand' in an unknown tongue (1 Cor 14:19).

As for multiplying 'ten thousand' by thousands, consider how Isaac's bride Rebekah was blessed by her family:

> "May you, our sister, become *thousands* of *ten thousands*,
> And may your descendants possess the gate of those who hate them." (Gen 24:60*)

This figure of speech was well understood then.

Daniel took it even further, describing God's throne and:

> ...*ten thousand times ten thousand* standing before Him...
> (Dan 7:10*).

John saw this too:

> ...the number of them [angels] was myriads of myriads, and thousands of thousands (Rev 5:11)

Again, our translators have tried to help us by using more natural English expressions like 'myriads' but the Greek is literally 'ten thousand of ten thousand, and thousands of thousands'.

John's original audience would therefore have known he meant an innumerably vast multitude in Revelation 5:11 and they would have known this when, soon after, he described the 6th Trumpet's armies as 'twice ten thousand times ten thousand' (Rev 9:16, *NIV*). To paraphrase Tom Wright's phrase above, "Think of a vast number, multiply it by itself, and then double it!" i.e. 'massive, terrifying armies charging against defenceless people'.[365]

The number John hears is a metaphor for a vast multitude.

Graeme Carlé

Heads & Tails

Bizarrely, the weapons are not being held by the horsemen. Whereas the Seals' horsemen carry a bow (Rev 6:2) and a sword (Rev 6:4), here it is the horses that are weaponised:

> 17. ...the heads of *the horses* are like the heads of lions; and out of *their mouths* proceed fire and smoke and brimstone...
> 19. For the power of the horses is in *their mouths* and in *their tails*; for their tails are *like serpents and have heads*, and with them they do harm. (Rev 9:19*)

Leaving aside for a moment the 'fire and smoke and brimstone' from the horses' mouths, consider their tails.

(i) Tails 'like serpents'

This is *'twice ten thousand times ten thousand'* serpents doing harm.

The Scriptures speak of "the venom of serpents and the deadly poison of cobras" (Deut 32:33), also naming vipers and asps.[366] This was often used as a metaphor in ancient Israel with David,[367] John the Baptist,[368] Jesus[369] and Paul[370] using it to describe evil men speaking poisonous words. Jeremiah also described literal Babylonian horsemen, armed with 'bow and javelin' (Jer 50:42), metaphorically striking Israel like serpents and adders (Jer 8:16-17).

In Revelation, however, John turns this around - the snake-like tails on his metaphorical horsemen strike with literal poison, as I will show in Chapter 17.

---

[366] Job 20:16, Psalm 58:4, 91:13; Prov 23:32, Isaiah 11:8, Acts 28:3.
[367] Psalm 140:3.
[368] Matthew 3:7, Luke 3:7.
[369] Matthew 12:34, 23:33.
[370] Romans 3:13.

(ii) Heads 'like the heads of lions'

John's 1st century Jewish audience would have readily understood his description of the horses' heads being 'like the heads of lions' (Rev 9:17) to signify their ferocity: David's 'mighty men' had 'faces like the faces of lions' (1 Chron 12:8); Israel's false prophets and corrupt princes were 'roaring lions' (Ezek 22:25, Zeph 3:3). Peter wrote of Satan prowling around 'like a roaring lion' (1 Pet 5:8).

We will consider their 'fire and smoke and brimstone' in the next chapter.

Their Colours

> 17. And this is how I saw in the vision the horses and those who sat on them: *the riders* had breastplates *the color of fire and of hyacinth and of brimstone*… and out of their [the horses'] mouths proceed *fire and smoke and brimstone.* (Rev 9:17*)

'Brimstone' is the old name for sulphur so the *NIV* translates their breastplates as being 'fiery red, dark blue, and yellow as sulfur'. 'Hyacinth' today is a deep blue flower so some believe John is describing smoke; others, Historicists, see this as describing the armies of the Ottoman Empire: 'the colours the Turks commonly wore'.[371]

However, the *NASB* translators[372] have added in the words 'the color of' - the phrase in Greek reads literally 'breastplates *of* fire and of hyacinth and brimstone' as the *KJV* had it.[373] N.T. Wright confirms this in his *The Kingdom New Testament*:

> They had breastplates *made of fire*, sapphire, and sulphur…

---

[371] *Gill's Exposition of the Entire Bible.* https://biblehub.com/commentaries/gill/revelation/9.htm, 9 Jan, 2023.
[372] Also the *ESV, ISV,* and *NRSV.*
[373] Also the *ASV, ERV, Darby, Literal Standard Version, Berean Literal,* and *Young's Literal* translations.

He also uses 'sapphire' for the Greek, *huakinthinos*,[374] while others use 'jacinth'[375] to describe the beautiful blue of a gemstone.[376]

However, when sulphur burns, it burns with an electric blue flame.[377] I therefore take it that the riders' breastplates and their weapons are actually flames of fire, burning red, yellow, and blue. This would be consistent with what Elijah and Elisha saw:

> As they [Elijah and Elisha] were going along and talking, behold, there appeared *a chariot of fire* and *horses of fire* which separated the two of them. And Elijah went up by a whirlwind to heaven. (2 Kin 2:11*)

Also Elisha's servant, after the Lord 'opened the servant's eyes', saw that:

> ...the mountain was full of *horses and chariots of fire* all around Elisha. (2 Kin 6:17*)

The writer of Hebrews quotes Psalm 104:4 to explain:

> And of *the angels* He says, "WHO MAKES HIS ANGELS WINDS, AND HIS MINISTERS *A FLAME OF FIRE*." (Heb 1:7*)

John's horsemen and their horses are similarly aflame - he is simply giving a fuller description of the colours of the fire.

His Jewish audience would also have known, as the Preterists note, that this was God's weapon of destruction when He judged Sodom and Gomorrah:

> Then the LORD rained on Sodom and Gomorrah *brimstone and fire* from the LORD out of heaven (Gen 19:24*)

---

374 Also *ESV, Berean Study Bible, GNT, ISV, Darby.*
375 E.g. *KJV, KJV 2000, Literal Standard Version,* and *Young's.*
376 The eleventh gemstone in Revelation 21:20 is a similar Greek word, *huakinthos.*
377 www.smithsonianmag.com/science-nature/why-does-indonesian-volcano-burn-bright-blue-180949576, 24 Jan, 2023.

Jesus, Peter, and Jude reminded them of this (Luke 17:29, 2 Pet 2:6, Jude 7) and to this day, balls of sulphur of unique purity[378] can be found there.

This would suggest the horsemen and their weapons are God's destroying angels or demonic forces being allowed by Him to inflict just consequences of sin. However, as I will show next, their weaponry was actually familiar to John's audience from natural sources near the Euphrates River. Let us therefore leave deciding the identity of the horsemen until we have unpacked all the images John has given us.

Summary

(i) The 6th Trumpet is called the second woe because, like the 5th Trumpet, the first woe, it was predicting a time directly impacting mankind, when a third of mankind will be killed.

(ii) Attempts to explain the four angels leading 200 million fiery horsemen projecting fire and injecting poison as being fulfilled by the Romans sacking Jerusalem in 70 AD, or by the Byzantine fire-ships from the 7th century, or yet to be fulfilled by China, ignore most of the details John gives us. His 1st century Jewish audience, however, would have readily understood them.

(iii) The golden altar's four horns calling for the release of the four angels signified there was no longer any atonement and what follows is God's judgement by His non-intervention; they also signified the attack

---

[378] Naturally occurring sulphur rarely exceeds 40% purity but at Sodom and Gomorrah, the balls are 96-98% pure (https://biblearchaeology.org/research/patriarchal-era/2364-the-discovery-of-the-sin-cities-of-sodom-and-gomorrah, https://forums.carm.org/threads/sulfur-balls-brimstone-found-at-sodom-gomorrah.1004, 11 Aug, 2023).

would not be limited to the land of Israel and the Roman Empire but would extend to 'the four corners of the earth' and to 'all mankind', killing a third everywhere.

(iv) The number 'twice ten thousand times ten thousand' is not literal but a metaphor for vast numbers, actually innumerable horsemen of fire. Their appearance, fiery colours, and weapons suggest they are angelic/demonic but we have yet to identify their weaponry.

16
Fire & Brimstone
1st Century

As mentioned earlier, in the 7th century AD, the Byzantine Empire began using a remarkable weapon called Greek Fire which utilised fire and brimstone. For the next eight hundred years, their fire-ships repelled sea-borne Muslim invasion forces by setting ablaze their wooden ships.

However, John's 1st century audience would have known about Greek Fire long before this.

The Greeks & Romans

Five hundred years before John's vision, Greek historian Thucydides (c. 460-400 BC) wrote of Greek Fire being used in the Peloponnesian War, the war between Sparta and Athens (431-404 BC). He describes in detail how the Battle of Delium was won in 424 BC by Sparta's allies, the Boeotians, using a hollowed-out log and bellows to project 'burning coals and sulphur and pitch' against the city's fortifications.[379] The 'pitch' contained naphtha from the crude oil which welled up from the ground in Mesopotamia, today's Iraq and Iran, and contains sulphur.[380]

Strabo (64-24 AD) reports 'there is a spring of it near the Euphrates'[381] and that in 330 BC, Alexander the Great was fascinated by a lake of naphtha there at Ecbatana,[382] the

---
379 Thucydides, *History of the Peloponnesian War*, Book 4:100. Emphasis added.
380 'Sweeter' Middle Eastern crude oil has 2% sulphur while heavier 'sour' North American crude oil has 5%. www.britannica.com/science/petroleum/Nonhydrocarbon-content, 4 Oct, 2023.
381 *Geography*, XVI, I, 15.
382 Today's Hamadan in western Iran.

capital city of ancient Media and later, Parthia. He had some sprinkled along a street and 'when it was set on fire at one end the flame flashed in an instant to the other end'.³⁸³

Roman historian Pliny the Elder (23-79 AD) recorded that in the Third Mithridatic War (73–67 BC), the inhabitants of Samosata, also on the Euphrates:

> ...defended their walls against Lucullus [the Roman general, using a *flammable mud* from a nearby pool] and the soldiers were burned in their armour. It is even set on fire in water... [and] can be extinguished only by earth.³⁸⁴

The Greeks and Romans in John's 1st century audience would therefore have readily known about naphtha, its use in warfare against Greeks and Romans, and its sources by the Euphrates River.

The Jews

John's 1st century Jewish audience also had a long history with naphtha, recorded in the Apocrypha in the 2nd century BC. It described Nehemiah and some priests finding a thick flammable liquid in the 5th century BC and urged the readers to celebrate...:

> 18. ...*the festival of the fire* given when Nehemiah, who built the temple and the altar, offered sacrifices.
> 19. For when our ancestors were being led captive to Persia, the pious priests of that time took some of *the fire of the altar* and secretly hid it in the hollow of a dry cistern, where they took such precautions that the place was unknown to anyone.
> 20. But after many years had passed, when it pleased God, Nehemiah, having been commissioned by the king

---

383   J.R. Partington, *A History of Greek Fire and Gunpowder* (https://archive.org/details/historyofgreekfi00part/page/3).
384   *Natural History*, 2:108-109, emphasis added. www.perseus.tufts.edu/hopper/text?doc=Plin.%20Nat.%202.108&lang=original, 11 Feb, 2023.

of Persia, sent the descendants of the priests who had hidden the fire to get it. And when they reported to us that they had not found fire but only *a thick liquid*, he ordered them to dip it out and bring it. (2 Macc 1:19-20*, *NRSV*)

The preserved 'fire from the altar' (v. 19) had gone out but Nehemiah decided to experiment with the liquid found in its place:

> 21. When the materials for the sacrifices were presented, Nehemiah ordered the priests to sprinkle the liquid on the wood and on the things laid upon it.
> 22. When this had been done and some time had passed, and when the sun, which had been clouded over, shone out, a great fire blazed up, so that *all marveled*…
> 31. After the materials of the sacrifice had been consumed, Nehemiah ordered that the liquid that was left should be poured on large stones.
> 32. When this was done, a flame blazed up; but when the light from the altar shone back, it went out.
> (2 Macc 1:21-32*)

This Jewish historian believed this marvellous spontaneous fire (v. 22) was 'given' (v. 18) to rekindle the Temple's fire.

Artaxerxes, the Persian emperor, was similarly impressed but presumably attributed it to the Persian god of fire:

> 33. When this matter became known, and it was reported to the king of the Persians that, in the place where the exiled priests had hidden the fire, the liquid had appeared with which Nehemiah and his associates had burned the materials of the sacrifice,
> 34. the king investigated the matter, and *enclosed the place and made it sacred.* (2 Macc 1:19-34*)

The Persians called the liquid *naft*, i.e. petroleum, hence our naphtha, but Nehemiah celebrated its connection to the fire of the altar:

> Nehemiah and his associates called this "nephthar," which means purification, but by most people it is called naphtha. (2 Macc 1:36)

Although the Apocrypha is not inspired Scripture, it was widely read by the Jews in the 1st century AD. John's Jewish audience may therefore have associated the horsemen's fire with the purifying fire of the altar, the four horns of which call for them to be released.

The Mithridatic Wars (88-63 BC)

In addition to this general knowledge, John's audience in the seven churches, whether Greek, Roman, or Jewish, had a particular acquaintance with naphtha due to their more recent history and location in Asia Minor, today's Turkey/Turkiye.

Two hundred years before John wrote Revelation, Mithridates the Great, aka Mithridates VI Eupator (135-63 BC), was ruling over all of Asia Minor and he was one of the Roman Republic's most formidable opponents. He fought them in three wars using naphtha which not only still wells up near the Euphrates but also in the southern part of what was his kingdom, just below the seven cities of the seven churches. Pliny the Elder also recorded:

> [In] Lycia, the mountains of Hephæstius, when touched with a flaming torch, burn so violently, that even the stones in the river and the sand burn, while actually in the water: this fire is also increased by rain. If a person makes furrows in the ground with a stick which has been kindled at this fire, it is said that a stream of flame will follow it.[385]

Today, it is a tourist attraction called Yanartaş, Turkish for 'flaming stone'.

---

[385] *The Natural History*, 2:110. www.perseus.tufts.edu/hopper/text?doc=Plin.%20Nat.%202.110&lang=original, 11 Feb, 2023.

We see then that the Greeks, Romans, and Jews in Asia Minor all had very good local and historical reasons to know about Greek Fire and its use in battle.

The Seven Churches

How can we be sure that John's 1st century audience in the seven churches in the cities of 'Ephesus, Smyrna, Pergamum, Thyatira, Sardis, Philadelphia, and Laodicea' (Rev 1:11) would have known about this?

Consider the following.

Mithridates had ruled over *all seven cities* and had a residence in Pergamum.[386] This coin, struck while he was there, features the Monogram of Pergamum, i.e. the wreath of figs and grapes.

Fig (ix) Coin depicting Mithridates VI Eupator (135-63 BC)

Mithdridates was also famous for the massacre in 88 BC of 150,000[387] citizens of the Roman Republic throughout Pontus but notably in Pergamum and Ephesus. This massacre

---

386 Plutarch (46-119 AD), *The Life of Sulla*, 23.4. https://penelope.uchicago.edu/Thayer/E/Roman/Texts/Plutarch/Lives/Sulla*.html#ref43, 12 Feb, 2023.
387 Ibid, 24.4. Contemporary Greek historian, Memnon of Heraclea, estimated 80,000 (*History*, 22:9), www.attalus.org/translate/memnon2.html, 12 Feb, 2023.

is today referred to as the Ephesian Vespers[388] and, remember, John also lived in Ephesus.

Mithridates was finally defeated in 63 BC by Pompey the Great, the Roman general.

John and his 1st century Gentile audience would have known this as surely as we know our own nation's history but his Jewish audience had good reason to know even more - Pompey went on to conquer Israel that same year. Capturing Jerusalem, the Romans slew 12,000 including the priests while they were officiating at the altar.[389] Josephus adds:

> But there was nothing that affected the nation so much, in the calamities they were then under, as that their holy place, which had been hitherto seen by none, should be laid open to strangers; for Pompey, and those that were about him, went into the temple itself whither it was not lawful for any to enter but the high priest…[390]

Pompey left untouched the golden table, menorah, jars, bowls, and 2,000 talents of gold stored there and commanded the surviving priests 'to cleanse it, and to bring what offerings the law required to God'.[391]

These 1st century Jews would also have known of Mithridates because he was the grandson of Antiochus IV Epiphanes who had invaded Israel in 167 BC and set up "the abomination of desolation" in the Temple in Jerusalem.[392] He was also the son of Laodice VI after whose namesake the city of Laodicea (Rev 1:11) was named in 261 BC.

What then would John's 6th Trumpet vision have meant to his audience in the seven churches of Revelation?

---

388   'Vespers' is literally the time of evening prayer but is today used as a euphemism for a massacre, after the Sicilian Vespers 'ethnic cleaning' in 1282 when the Sicilians turned on their French overlords.
389   Josephus, *Wars of the Jews*, 1:7:5 - www.academia.edu/32013960/Complete_Works_of_Josephus_pdf, 13 Feb, 2023. Also in *Antiquities of the Jews*, 14.4.4.
390   Ibid. 1:7:6.
391   *Antiquities of the Jews*, 14.4.4.
392   The third instance, as described in *Slouching Towards Bethlehem*, pp. 270-273.

Both Jews and Gentiles, knowing about Greek Fire and the local Mithridatic Wars, would have understood that in due time, something like Greek Fire would be used in a new and devastatingly more mobile way by vast angelic and/or human armies related to the Euphrates.

Summary

(i) Greeks, Romans, and Jews in John's audience in 1st century AD Asia Minor would have known about Greek Fire.

(ii) The Greeks had a long history of its use in warfare from the 5th century BC; the Romans would have known of Mithridates the Great using this dread weapon to defeat them in Asia Minor in the 2nd century BC.

(iii) John's intended audience in the seven cities would have known about Mithridates because he had ruled over the seven cities of the seven churches, had a palace in Pergamum, massacred the Romans in Ephesus, and Laodicea was named after his mother's family.

(iv) John's Jewish audience had particular reason to know this history because Mithridates' notorious grandfather Antiochus IV Epiphanes had conquered Israel and desecrated the Holy of Holies in the Temple in Jerusalem. He had then been defeated by the Roman general Pompey who had also conquered Israel and entered the Holy of Holies.

(v) Now that we have caught up with what the disciples would have already known in the 1st century AD, we can properly consider the 6th Trumpet and its relevance for today.

17
The Horsemen *Today*

As we have just seen, John's 1st century audience, whether Roman, Greek, or Jewish, would have understood that the 6th Trumpet's fiery horsemen would one day have weaponry like Greek Fire but in a more devastating and mobile form.

The 20th century indeed saw the advent of flame-throwers that men could carry on their backs, developed for the trench warfare of World War I; by World War II, flame-throwers were also mounted on tanks. By 1944, the Americans were using napalm[393] bombs in incendiary attacks on Berlin and then on Japanese cities, to appalling effect. These were then used in the First Indochina War, the Algerian War, the Korean War, and the Vietnam War.

Flame-throwers and napalm can therefore be seen as a literal fulfilment of John's prophecy but what of the number?

> *A third of mankind* was killed by these three plagues, by the fire and the smoke and the brimstone which proceeded out of their mouths. (Rev 9:18*)

These literal weapons have not yet killed 'a third of mankind' so could John's also be metaphorical?

Literal and Metaphorical?

If the horsemen are 'the horses and chariots of fire' that Elijah, Elisha, and Elisha's servant saw, they are literally

---

[393] 'An incendiary mixture of gasoline or other petroleum fuel and a thickener or gel-forming agent', *The American Heritage® Dictionary of the English Language*, 5th Edition.

Back in 7

the angelic hosts/armies of God. However, as we saw earlier, David saw a destroying angel with a sword which symbolised a literal plague that killed thousands; Ezekiel saw six that symbolised the Babylonian armies which trampled Israel, razing Jerusalem and Solomon's Temple.

N.T. Wright's summation could therefore be correct that they are literal *and* metaphorical:

> ...the plagues to come will, from one point of view, consist of foul, hellish, destructive forces, and, from another point of view, of massive, terrifying armies charging against defenceless people.[394]

However, I believe there is more for us to see here.

So far I have established that the horsemen and their horses are metaphorical, the number 'twice ten thousand times ten thousand' is metaphorical, their breastplates are metaphorical, the lion-like heads and serpent-like tails of their horses are metaphorical. But how can 'the fire and the smoke and the brimstone' be metaphorical?

Greek Fire burned due to naphtha, i.e. crude oil; this provides a powerful metaphor for lethal firepower of every kind including the gunpowder used in bullets, artillery shells, mortars, high explosives, and bombs, as well as napalm and nuclear weapons. However, it also provides a metaphor for the *peaceful* use of naphtha with unintended consequences.

We saw this with the first four trumpets - mankind's peaceful and legitimate use of the earth, seas, freshwater, and atmosphere has, through our pride, greed, carelessness, and short-sightedness, led to us overusing, despoiling, and polluting every part of our dominion. It is therefore not surprising that we have done the same with naphtha.

---

394 N.T. Wright, *Revelation for Everyone*, p. 91.

Harnessing Fire

What makes our time unique in world history is that we have harnessed 'the power of fire and smoke and brimstone' to our daily household use. Yes, we now have devastating weapons but we also have internal combustion engines - it is, after all, fire igniting refined naphtha in our petrol-fuelled cars, motorcycles, and lawn mowers, diesel-fuelled tractors, trains, and trucks on land, ships at sea and submarines under the sea, as well as heavy oil-fuelled ships and jet-fuelled aeroplanes.

This harnessed fire and naphtha has given us unprecedented power and ability to roam the earth, sea, and sky - our God-given dominion - wherever and whenever we like. In the last one hundred years, this power has become an indispensable part of daily and family life - today there are on Earth 1.4 billion cars and 600 million motorcycles.[395]

However, as noted in Chapters 10 and 14 regarding the 3rd, 4th, and 5th Trumpets, the Intergovernmental Panel on Climate Change (IPCC) believes emissions from fossil fuels - coal, oil, and gas - are the dominant cause of global warming. It was estimated in 2018 that 89% of global CO_2 emissions came from fossil fuels and industry.[396]

Another unintended consequence has been a massive loss of human life through road accidents. In 2022, the World Health Organisation was reporting that 1.3 million are killed every year.[397] Looking back, one study estimated that by 1990 there were on average some 1.1 million people killed every year, rising to 1.3 million by 2019 and giving us a death toll of 30 million for those 29 years.[398] Some therefore put the

---

[395] www.riders-share.com/blog/article/number-motorcycles-world-top-countries, 23 May, 2024.
[396] www.clientearth.org/latest/latest-updates/stories/fossil-fuels-and-climate-change-the-facts, 25 Oct, 2023.
[397] www.who.int/news-room/fact-sheets/detail/road-traffic-injuries, 8 Oct, 2023.
[398] 250,000 in China, 212,000 in India, 44,000 in Brazil, and 41,000 in the USA. https://ourworldindata.org/grapher/deaths-from-road-injuries?tab=table, 3 Oct, 2023.

figure for the 20th century at 60 million![399]

Even with this appalling loss of life, we have not yet seen 'a third of mankind' killed but when this peaceful use of naphtha is used in deliberate killing, the death toll quadruples.

Deadlier Warfare

The Italo-Turkish War saw the first use of aeroplanes dropping bombs on 1 November, 1911, when an Italian pilot dropped four small hand-grenades on Turkish troops in Libya. By the end of World War II, the British and American air forces had dropped an astonishing 3.4 million tons[400] of bombs on the Axis Powers. I have not yet found any figures for bombing by the Russian, German, Italian, and Japanese air forces but I assume they would be huge.

World War II also saw new strategies. In 1939, Hitler sparked the war with his blitzkrieg combination of dive-bombers, fast tanks, motorised and mechanised infantry to overwhelm Poland, and in 1944, introduced the world to guided missiles with V1 and V2 rocket attacks on London; in 1942, the Americans developed their own version of Greek Fire, napalm, to set ablaze civilian housing in Japan; in 1944, the Japanese enacted *Ten Go* (lit. Heavenly Operation) in which suicidal *kamikaze* pilots in the air were supplemented by suicide squads of piloted rockets, submarines, torpedoes, motor-boats, and divers.[401] The war ended in 1945 after the Americans dropped nuclear bombs on Hiroshima[402] and Nagasaki.[403]

During the Vietnam War (1955-1975), the Americans

---

399   https://web.archive.org/web/20150520222249 & www.visualnews.com/2013/03/19/visualizing-major-causes-of-death-in-the-20th-century, 8 Oct, 2023.
400   American measures. https://brilliantmaps.com/uk-us-bombs-ww2, 15 Jan, 2023.
401   *Slouching Towards Bethlehem*, pp. 136-141.
402   Hiroshima had a population of 255,000; 66,000 were killed and 69,000 injured. https://avalon.law.yale.edu/20th_century/mp10.asp, 15 Jan, 2023.
403   Nagasaki had a population of 195,000; 39,000 were killed and 25,000 injured. https://avalon.law.yale.edu/20th_century/mp10.asp, 15 Jan, 2023.

dropped another 4.5 million tons of bombs on Vietnam, Cambodia, and Laos.[404]

Throughout the 20th century, all sides developed machine guns, hand-grenades, mortars, artillery, and rockets to increase killing power as well as armoured personnel carriers and tanks to protect those using them. The 21st century saw Islamic terrorists using civilian aircraft in the September 11 attacks on New York and Washington DC to kill themselves and 3,000 civilians.

We also have developed intercontinental ballistic missiles (ICBMs), shorter range cruise missiles, and in 1995, rocket-launching drones such as the Predator with its aptly-named Hellfire missiles.

And what have we achieved with our new weapons and technology?

Satan's Century

By anyone's estimation, we have inflicted on ourselves a truly appalling death toll. In 1995, on the 50th anniversary of Auschwitz being liberated, the *New York Times* declared that 'at its worst, this has been Satan's century', adding:

> In no previous age have people shown so great an aptitude, and appetite, for killing millions of other people for reasons of race, religion or class.[405]

For the first time in human history we had two *world* wars.

While exact figures are obviously unobtainable,[406] it is

---

404   www.statista.com/statistics/1334783/vietnam-war-us-military-bombs-dropped, 15 Jan, 2023.
405   *Remembering Auschwitz*, www.nytimes.com/1995/01/26/opinion/remembering-auschwitz.html, 29 Aug, 2021.
406   In Book 2, *Slouching Towards Bethlehem*, I often referred to the research of Rudolph Rummel, Professor Emeritus of Political Science at Hawaii University, and his *Statistics of Democide: Genocide and Mass Murder Since 1900* (www.hawaii.edu/powerkills/NOTE5.HTM, 13 Jan, 2023). This time I have used Matthew White's *Historical Atlas of the 20th Century*, via his Necrometrics website which averages out figures from many historians.

estimated that in World War I, 8.5 million soldiers and 6.5 million civilians were killed;[407] in World War II, another 66 million were killed,[408] thus a total death toll of 81 million people!

Warfare erupted in all 'four corners of the earth' throughout the last hundred years, leading to immense death tolls and some conflicts were not so much wars as massacres. In Book 2,[409] I identified some massacres imposed by emperor-worship:[410]

(i) The Belgian plundering of the Congo (1886-1908) and killing of 8-10 million Congolese.[411]

(ii) The Turkish genocides (1914-1923) killing 3.5 million Armenians, Greeks, and Assyrians.[412]

(iii) The Japanese invasion of China (1937-1945) and killing of 13.25 million Chinese.[413]

(iv) Pol Pot's 'Killing Fields' (1975-1979) which swallowed up 1.7 million Cambodians.[414]

(v) Pakistan's 1971 'ethnic cleansing' of 3 million Hindus.[415]

Space does not allow me to give details of 20th century wars here but in the widespread carnage across every part of every continent except Antarctica, we have killed about 200 million people in our warfare over the last one hundred years.

We also need to add another 10%, due to the hundreds of

---

407   https://necrometrics.com/20c5m.htm#WW1, 14 Jan, 2023.
408   https://necrometrics.com/20c5m.htm#Second, 14 Jan, 2023.
409   *Slouching Towards Bethlehem*, pp. 125-141.
410   Ibid, pp. 103-124.
411   https://necrometrics.com/20c5m.htm#Congo, 14 Jan, 2023.
412   https://borgenproject.org/10-facts-about-the-greek-genocide/, 14 Jan, 2023.
413   R.J. Rummel, www.hawaii.edu/powerkills/CHINA.TAB6.2.GIF and 6.1.GIF, 28 Jul, 2011.
414   https://gsp.yale.edu/case-studies/cambodian-genocide-program, 14 Jan, 2023.
415   Koenraad Elst, *Decolonizing the Hindu Mind: Ideological Development of Hindu Revivalism*, New Delhi: Rupa, 2001, pp. 507-509.

thousands of gun deaths every year throughout the world due to drug cartels, gangs, criminals, and 'ordinary' citizen homicides and suicides. Studies of the years 1960 to 2019 show there have been over 16 million killed in those sixty years[416] so the total could be as high as 20 million in the last hundred years.

But again, as appalling as these figures are, this is still not 'a third of mankind'. We need to keep looking for this sign of the times.

Serpents as Tails

All of these deaths have been due to the power of explosion in weapons and internal combustion engines and it is easy for us to focus on the 'fire and smoke and brimstone' from the horses' mouths. But what of their 200 million tails?

> For *the power* of the horses is in their mouths *and in their tails*; for their tails are *like serpents* and have heads, and with them they do harm. (Rev 9:19*)

Like the horsemen and the horses, their serpent-like tails are 'fiery' and the Jews in John's audience would have been very familiar with this judgement of God from their nation's history. In the 15th century BC, the liberated Hebrew slaves had begun blaspheming, speaking against God and His provision of manna, and:

---

[416] One study (1990-2016) produced figures of 209,000 p.a. in 1990 rising to 251,000 p.a. in 2016 so in those three decades there were over 6 million gun deaths (https://jamanetwork.com/journals/jama/fullarticle/2698492, 30 Aug, 2023). A later study details over 250,000 p.a. in 2019. Of these, 71% were homicides, 21% suicides, and 8% were accidental; 66% were in just six countries: Brazil (49,436), the United States (37,038), Venezuela (28,515), Mexico (22,116), India (14,710), and Colombia (13,169) (https://worldpopulationreview.com/country-rankings/gun-deaths-by-country, 30 Aug, 2023). The World Health Organization's figure for 2019 was 475,000 but that was by any means of killing (https://apps.who.int/violence-info/homicide, 5 Oct, 2023). Another study says that the 1990s figures were 40% lower than the 1960s, 70s, and 80s (https://theconversation.com/homicide-is-declining-around-the-world-but-why-125365, 5 Oct, 2023) so those three decades would be another 10 million.

> The LORD sent *fiery serpents* among the people and they bit the people, so that many people of Israel died. (Num 21:6*)

God had also provided a remedy then. He told Moses to make a bronze replica of a serpent and to lift it up on a standard where everyone could see it and 'if a serpent bit any man, when he looked to the bronze serpent, he lived' (Num 21:9).

In the 1st century AD, Jesus taught that this event foreshadowed His crucifixion in the prelude to John 3:16, the most famous of all New Testament verses today, so Gentile disciples in John's audience would also have learned of this Jewish history.

John's vision of these 'twice ten thousand times ten thousand' horsemen with 'twice ten thousand times ten thousand' *serpents as tails* was therefore predicting an appalling outcome for the whole world. It also marks a major increase in severity from the 5th Trumpet's locusts' tails, where their 'tails like scorpions' (Rev 9:10) could only hurt and torment unbelievers for a season and not 'kill anyone' (Rev 9:5).

What then are we to make of the 'twice ten thousand times ten thousand' fiery serpents? When and where has mankind poisoned hundreds of millions?

'1 Billion Babies'

I am ashamed to confess that I have taken part in this.

As an atheist in 1972, I pressured my then fiancée to ignore her conscience and abort our baby but when I became a follower of Jesus in 1973, the Holy Spirit spoke into my heart through Isaiah 1:15, "Your hands are covered in blood". Stunned, I asked what He meant, and within moments I knew. I cried for and immediately received His forgiveness; soon after, I was able to confess my sin to my now ex-fiancée who had known intuitively what I had denied and David had prayed:

> For You formed my inward parts;
> You wove me in my mother's womb.
> I will give thanks to You, for I am fearfully and wonderfully made (Psa 139:13-14)

She had suffered great remorse[417] but she too had become a Christian and forgave me too. She had not known what to do so we prayed together, confessing everything to God and receiving in our hearts His assurance of forgiveness.

Jesus said, "Let him who is without sin, cast the first stone" (John 8:7) so I cannot condemn anyone. I just want to present the facts of what we are doing today so we can see and recognise this sign of the times.

N.B. This sign can only be seen and recognised by those who believe abortion is the killing of human beings in utero; those who do not believe this will remain unaware of this major sign even occurring.

(i) Legalised abortion

In 1920, Russia became the first country to legalise abortion and one hundred years later, it is widely considered normal.

---

[417] Singer Britney Spears writes in her memoir, *The Woman in Me*, of being pressured to abort her baby 20 years earlier: "To this day, it's one of the most agonizing things I have ever experienced in my life. If it had been left up to me alone, I never would have done it. And yet Justin was so sure that he didn't want to be a father." (https://people.com/britney-spears-justin-timberlake-pregnancy-abortion-exclusive-8362622, 19 Oct, 2023). In 2011, The British Journal of Psychiatry published an analysis by Priscilla K Coleman of 22 studies between 1995 and 2009 of 877,181 participants which concluded that women who have abortions are 81% more likely to experience subsequent mental health problems. In closing, she refers to a later study in 2010 by Canadian researchers Mota et al which found an increased risk of mood disorders (61%), social phobia (61%), suicide ideation (59%), and abuse of alcohol (261%), alcohol dependence (142%), drug misuse (313%), drug dependence (287%), and any substance abuse disorder (280%) (www.cambridge.org/core/journals/the-british-journal-of-psychiatry/article/abortion-and-mental-health-quantitative-synthesis-and-analysis-of-research-published-19952009/E8D556AAE1C1D2F0F8B060B28BEE6C3D#F1, 31 Jan, 2024).

With medical abortions, pills induce a miscarriage; surgical abortions use either suction devices or forceps to remove the baby from the womb. If the baby is 'viable', i.e. older than 23 or 24 weeks, he or she is usually poisoned with digoxin, potassium chloride, or lidocaine[418] in what is called 'induced fetal demise' or 'feticide':

> Inducing demise before induction terminations at near viable gestational ages to avoid signs of life at delivery is practiced widely.[419]

In plain English, 'inducing demise' means killing them in the womb 'to avoid signs of life' after they are born, to hide from the mother and any unwitting medical staff the reality of what is happening and to evade charges of homicide:

> …[to] avoid potential *emotional distress* or the possibility of resuscitation *or litigation* related to survival of a neonate [i.e. the baby][420]

Today, the World Health Organization proudly proclaims how legalisation has produced truly staggering results in 136 nations:

> Around *73 million* induced abortions take place worldwide *each year*. Six out of 10 (61%) of all unintended pregnancies, and 3 out of 10 (29%) of all pregnancies, end in induced abortion. Comprehensive abortion care is included in the list of *essential health care* services published by WHO in 2020.[421]

---

418 www.ncbi.nlm.nih.gov/pmc/articles/PMC7689273, 15 Feb, 2024.
419 https://societyfp.org/_documents/resources/InductionofFetalDemise.pdf, 11 Oct, 2023.
420 www.uptodate.com/contents/induced-fetal-demise#!, 11 Oct, 2023. Emphasis added.
421 www.who.int/news-room/fact-sheets/detail/abortion, 3 Oct, 2023. Emphasis added.

Under this 'essential health care', between 2010 and 2014 there was an estimated average of 56,000,000 abortions p.a.[422] (i.e. 280,000,000 babies); between 2015 to 2019, the average grew to 73,000,000 abortions p.a.[423] (i.e. 365,000,000 babies) where it has stayed (2020-2023, another 292,000,000 babies). In total, in just the last fourteen years we have killed 937,000,000 babies!

Four countries have led the way over the last one hundred years: China (336,000,000+), USSR (200,000,000+), India (100,000,000+), USA (62,000,000+).[424]

In a more careful analysis, in 2017, W. Robert Johnston and Thomas W. Jacobson published the results of their decades of research:

> The Abortion Worldwide Report is the first to systematically track reported abortions in 100 nations, territories and regions, from the year of authorization through 2015. The Report contains 4,915 country years of data, major findings, country abortion graphs showing the impact of authorization, world maps, and a policy table for 196 nations.[425]

They summarised their findings of the years 1920 to 2015 as '100 countries, 1 century, 1 billion babies'.[426]

To complete the hundred years from 1920 to 2019, if we add WHO's figures for 2016 to 2019 from 136 countries, the total would be 1,292,000,000 babies!

---

422   www.prb.org/wp-content/uploads/2021/03/2021-safe-engage-abortion-facts-and-figures-media-guide.pdf, p. 8, 3 Oct, 2023.
423   www.usnews.com/news/best-countries/articles/2022-03-28/global-abortion-rate-rebounds-to-90s-levels-study-finds, 3 Oct, 2023.
424   https://en.wikipedia.org/wiki/List_of_countries_by_abortion_statistics, 3 Oct, 2023.
425   www.frc.org/familypolicylecture/abortion-worldwide-report-100-countries-1-century-1-billion-babies, 3 Oct 2023.
426   Ibid.

(ii) Illegal abortions

The above figures are records of reported abortions but in countries where abortion is only partially legal, there are often more illegal abortions. In Brazil, for example, between 2015 and 2019 there were 1.8 million legal abortions p.a.[427] but Human Rights Watch report:

> An estimated one to four million illegal abortions occur in Brazil annually (2004).[428]

Likewise in Argentina: between 2015 and 2019 there were 368,000 legal abortions p.a.[429] but 500,000 illegal abortions.[430] And in Mexico, 1 million legal abortions p.a.[431] but 100,000 to 500,000 illegal abortions.[432] In Pakistan, 'almost all abortions take place illegally and in secret'[433] but it is estimated that there are 2.2 million p.a.[434] Similarly in the Philippines[435] where it is estimated there are 1.1 million p.a.[436]

Obviously, it is very hard to establish figures for illegal abortions and there may be some double-counting. However, given that these estimates by Human Rights Watch are for millions p.a., we have to add tens of millions, perhaps hundreds of millions to the totals for one hundred years.

From 1920 to 2019, this would mean 1.5 billion, and another 300 million since then.

---

427 www.guttmacher.org/regions/latin-america-caribbean/brazil, 12 Oct, 2023.
428 www.hrw.org/legacy/women/abortion/brazil.html, 12 Oct, 2023.
429 www.guttmacher.org/regions/latin-america-caribbean/argentina, 12 Oct, 2023.
430 www.hrw.org/legacy/women/abortion/argentina.html, 12 Oct, 2023.
431 www.guttmacher.org/regions/latin-america-caribbean/mexico, 12 Oct, 2023.
432 www.hrw.org/legacy/women/abortion/mexico.html, 12 Oct, 2023.
433 www.guttmacher.org/report/abortion-pakistan, 12 Oct, 2023.
434 www.guttmacher.org/regions/asia/pakistan, 12 Oct, 2023.
435 www.guttmacher.org/regions/asia/Philippines, 12 Oct, 2023.
436 www.thelancet.com/journals/lanwpc/article/PIIS2666-6065(22)00270-X/fulltext, 12 Oct, 2023.

Grim Totals

In 1759, an English bishop Beilby Porteous wrote:

> One Murder made a Villain,
> Millions a Hero. Princes were privileg'd
> To kill, and numbers sanctified the crime.[437]

Joseph Stalin killed 43 million during his reign and is still considered 'a Hero' by many Russians.[438] He was also quoted as responding to the Ukrainian famine he had caused:

> "If only one man dies of hunger, that is a tragedy. If millions die, that's only statistics."[439]

Mao Zedong is similarly 'a Hero' in China despite killing 45 million[440] and all in peacetime! Most of his and Stalin's victims died due to deliberate famines[441] but Stalin also ordered the cold-blooded shooting of 30,000 Ukrainian Kulaks in the 1932-1933 Holodomor,[442] 681,692 Russians in his Great Purge between 1937 and 1938,[443] and 15,131 Polish officers in the Katyn Forest in 1940.[444]

So, not counting the tens of millions who were starved to death, how many fellow-humans have we killed with modern

---

[437] *Death: A Poetical Essay,* J. Bentham Printer to Cambridge University for T & J. Merrill, Booksellers. Joseph Stalin is often quoted as saying, "If only one man dies of hunger, that is a tragedy. If millions die, that's only statistics." https://quoteinvestigator.com/2010/05/21/death-statistic/#f+358+1+2, 14 Aug, 2023.
[438] *Slouching Towards Bethlehem,* p. 123.
[439] 1947 January 30, *Washington Post,* Loose-Leaf Notebook by Leonard Lyons, Quote Page 9, Washington, D.C. (ProQuest).
[440] *Slouching Towards Bethlehem,* pp. 126-127.
[441] Mao had exported the grain to fund his nuclear ambitions.
[442] 'Kulak' means 'tight-fisted', so named because they resisted his collectivization of their small land holdings; 'Holodomor' is a combination of the Ukrainian words for 'starvation' and 'to inflict death'. www.history.com/news/ukrainian-famine-stalin, 17 Aug, 2023.
[443] Thurston, Robert W. *Life and Terror in Stalin's Russia, 1934-1941.* Yale University Press, 1998, p. 139.
[444] www.latimes.com/archives/la-xpm-1990-03-22-mn-1021-story.html, 17 Aug, 2023.

technology in the last 100 years?

By my reckoning here, we have killed some 2 billion individuals - every one of whom was made in the image and likeness of God, precious to Him and their families and friends - using 'the power of fire and smoke and brimstone' and 'medicinal' poison.

A Third of Mankind?

> 15. And the four angels, who had been prepared for the hour and day and month and year, were released, so that they would kill *a third of mankind*...
> 18. *A third of mankind* was killed by these three plagues, by the fire and the smoke and the brimstone which proceeded out of their mouths.
> 19. For the power of the horses is in *their mouths* and in *their tails*; for *their tails* are like serpents and have heads, and *with them they do harm*. (Rev 9:15 & 18*)

'A third of mankind' makes no distinction between believers and non-believers and many Christians perished in these wars and conflicts; it also makes no distinction between Jews and Gentiles. However, we have accurate figures for Jews.

(i) Jews

Between 1941 and 1945, Hitler and his allies killed a third of all the Jews on earth in the Holocaust. We know because the Jews set out to document and commemorate every death in their Holocaust museums and they estimate the toll as 5,820,960 out of a world-wide population 16,648,000,[445] i.e. 35%. Initially, many were suffocated in gas vans or shot in cold blood, especially in the Ukraine and Hungary but in 1942, the Nazis built six extermination camps in Poland which used gas chambers and Zyklon-B to kill 2.7 million in

---

445   *Dancing in the Dragon's Jaws*, p. 35.

that year alone.[446]

We therefore have reliable figures for the Jews but when it comes to Gentiles, we have many gaps in our records.

(ii) Gentiles

We also have a major problem in assessing this sign of the times because the world's population is not static - in the last 100 years, it has grown exponentially to reach 8 billion people today, as you can see here.

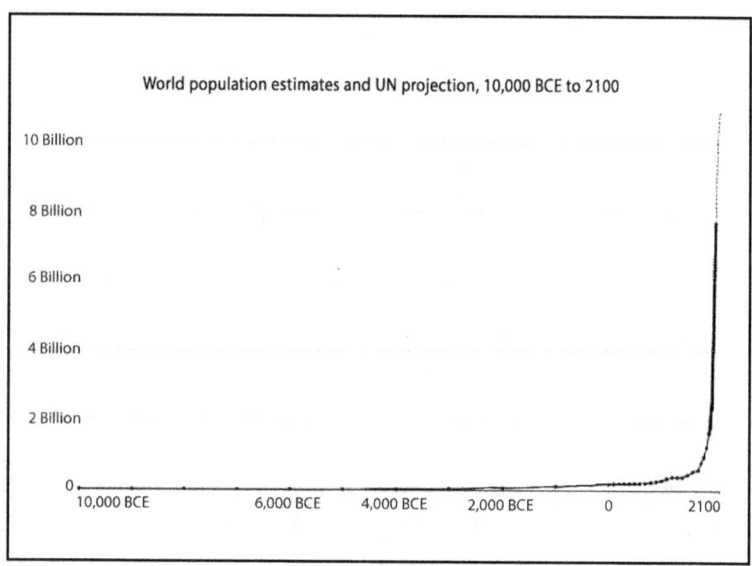

Fig (x) World population

In the 16th century, there were only half a billion people; in 1800, we reached 1 billion; in 1927, we reached 2 billion; in 1960, 3 billion; in 1974, 4 billion; in 1999, 6 billion; now in 2023, we are 8 billion.[447]

In other words, we took:

---

446 www.bbc.co.uk/newsround/16700249, 30 Oct, 2023.
447 www.worldometers.info/world-population/world-population-by-year, 20 Jan, 2023.

(i) 200 years to double from a half to 1 billion, i.e. to grow by half a billion

(ii) 127 years to double from 1 to 2 billion, i.e. by 1 billion

(iii) 47 years to double from 2 to 4 billion, i.e. by 2 billion;

(iv) 50 years to double from 2 to 4 billion, i.e. by 4 billion.

How then are we to recognise the sign of a third of Gentiles with an ever-moving target?

If we calculate from the beginning of World War I in 1914 when the population was 1.8 billion, a third would have been 600 million; from the beginning of World War II in 1939 when the population was 2.3 billion, a third would have been 767 million; from 1974 when the population was 4 billion, a third would have been 1.3 billion; from 1999 when the population was 6 billion, a third would have been 2 billion; in 2023, a third of 8 billion is 2.7 billion.

Further, our total population figures have to include the 2 billion we have killed, i.e. our population in 2023 would have been 10 billion and a third would be 3.3 billion.

Mathematicians can give us better figures but it seems to me that in the last one hundred years, we have killed 'a third of mankind' and the 6th Trumpet is sounding.

I leave it to you to judge for yourself.

Normal Life

Many of us have been taught that Jesus will come secretly in the Rapture to snatch away all Christians as portrayed in the *Left Behind* novels.[448] We were told this would save us from the catastrophic Armageddon of a fully nuclear World War III, followed by global starvation, which will kill 'a third of mankind'. This would mean another 3.5-4 billion people will have to die.

---

448   I will address that properly in Book 7, *Kingdom Come: Justice for All.*

However, consider Jesus' prediction about life on earth immediately before He returns at the 7th Trumpet:

> 26. "And just as it happened in the days of Noah, so it will be also *in the days of the Son of Man*:
> 27. they were *eating*, they were *drinking*, they were *marrying*, they were *being given in marriage*, until the day that Noah entered the ark, and the flood came and destroyed them all. (Luke 17:26-27*)

The world will not be in the throes of nuclear war or global starvation but living life as usual, eating, drinking, and marrying; they will be completely surprised by Jesus' return to judge the world.

And not just as "in the days of Noah" but also as "in the days of Lot" because Jesus continues:

> 28. "It was the same as happened in the days of Lot: they were *eating*, they were *drinking*, they were *buying*, they were *selling*, they were *planting*, they *were building*;
> 29. but on the day that Lot went out from Sodom it rained fire and brimstone from heaven and destroyed them all.
> 30. "It will be just the same on *the day that the Son of Man is revealed*. (Luke 17:28-30*)

Again, the whole world will be going about their normal daily lives, just as we are today: eating, drinking, buying and selling in the moment but also planning for the future, "planting and building" (v. 28).

Who would be doing this during or in the aftermath of a global nuclear war?

Unleashing Islam

There is also a spiritual aspect to the horsemen crossing the Euphrates:

> "Release the four angels who are bound at the great river Euphrates... The number of the armies of the horsemen was two hundred million..." (Rev 9:14 & 16)

Another unintended consequence of the 20th century's harnessing the power of naphtha from east of the Euphrates was the revitalizing of Islam which had lost all momentum under the 400 year-long caliphate of the decaying Ottoman Empire. The world's first oil well was drilled east of the Euphrates River in Azerbaijan in 1846[449] which led to the discovery and development of the vast oil fields also east of the Euphrates in today's Iran (1908), Iraq (1927), and Saudi Arabia, UAE, Qatar, and Kuwait (1938).

By the 1960s, these Muslim nations were supplying almost half the world's oil and, flush with petro-dollars, they set about educating the Muslim world and the immigrant populations of the Western world[450] into their various fundamentalist versions of Islam. As I showed in Book 2,[451] this is leading directly to the rise of the Antichrist and we will look at this further when we come to the 6th Bowl.

In the 1970s, Libya's Muammar Gaddafi and the Organization of Arab Petroleum Countries (OAPEC) increased the price of oil ten-fold, from US$3 a barrel to US$34,[452] and began funding and arming the Palestinian 'Black September' group and the Popular Front for the Liberation of Palestine (PLO) to fight Israel, as well as the Irish Republican Army (IRA) to fight Great Britain.[453]

---

449 Azerbaijan was at that time part of the USSR and considered to be Russian. America's first oil well was drilled in Pennsylvania in 1859.
450 In 2014, 45% of Britain's mosques and almost all the UK-based training of Islamic scholars were controlled by the Deobandi, an Islamic group funded by Saudi Arabia. Douglas Murray documents the outcome in *The Strange Death of Europe: Immigration, Identity, Islam* (Bloomsbury Continuum, London, 2018).
451 *Slouching Towards Bethlehem*, pp. 153-172, 245-257.
452 Kenyon, Paul, *Dictatorland: The Men Who Stole Africa*, London; Head of Zeus Ltd, 2019, p. 177-178.
453 Ibid, p. 172-173.

The Outcome?

I believe that John and his audience in the 1st century would have understood that the 6th Trumpet would be to alert the world to the significance of 'a third of mankind' being killed by mankind.

John then sees the tragic outcome of this vast death-toll:

> 20. The rest of mankind, who were not killed by these plagues, *did not repent* of the works of their hands, so as not to worship demons, and the idols of gold and of silver and of brass and of stone and of wood, which can neither see nor hear nor walk;
> 21. and they *did not repent* of their murders nor of their sorceries nor of their immorality nor of their thefts.
> (Rev 9:13-21*)

Refusing to learn their lessons, 'the world' and its loves will be just as Paul prophesied:

> 1. But realize this, that in the last days difficult times will come.
> 2. For men will be *lovers of self, lovers of money*, boastful, arrogant, revilers, disobedient to parents, ungrateful, unholy,
> 3. unloving, irreconcilable, malicious gossips, without self-control, brutal, haters of good,
> 4. treacherous, reckless, conceited, *lovers of pleasure* rather than *lovers of God*... (2 Tim 3:1-4*)

Some will pretend to be godly:

> 5. ...holding to a form of godliness, although they have denied its power. (2 Tim 3:5)

Not recognising the signs of the times, unwilling to learn from the Flood in the time of Noah nor the destruction of Sodom and Gomorrah in the time of Lot, they will continue to live as if nothing is happening around them, just as Jesus predicted (Luke 17:26-29).

Summary

(i) In John's vision of the 6th Trumpet, the fiery horsemen and their horses are metaphorical, the number 'twice ten thousand times ten thousand' is metaphorical, their breastplates are metaphorical, the lion-like heads and serpent-like tails of their horses are metaphorical, but their weapons are literal and metaphorical.

(ii) John's 1st century audience in Asia Minor may have thought the fire from the horses' mouths would be literal Greek Fire. However, in hindsight, we can see it is a metaphor based on naphtha, predicting a far greater use in literal weapons of war but also in peacetime's internal combustion engines which have enabled us to travel freely throughout our dominions of earth, sea, and sky.

(iii) They would also have understood the horses' tails being like serpents' heads means there would be 'twice ten thousand times ten thousand' injecting poison into humans, just as the fiery serpents killed Hebrews in the wilderness.

(iv) The 6th Trumpet was predicting a time when mankind would make extraordinary advances in weaponry, transportation, and medicine that we would use to kill 'a third of mankind'.

(v) We know that a third of the Jews were systematically targeted and killed in just five years and it looks like we have killed a third of all Gentiles in the last one hundred years so we should recognise this sign of the times.

(vi) Tragically even this has not been enough to alert all of us to our peril but anyone willing to listen can always repent, believe, and turn to our God for salvation.

18

The Seventh Trumpet
The Third Woe

Between the 6th and 7th Trumpets, John sees a very different angel with a book:

> 1. I saw another *strong angel* coming down out of heaven, clothed with a cloud; and the rainbow was upon his head, and his face was like the sun, and his feet like pillars of fire; 2. and he had in his hand *a little book* which was open. He placed his right foot on the sea and his left on the land. (Rev 10:1-2*)

This angel is enormous, straddling 'the sea' and 'the land' and crowned with a rainbow. Like the angel who led Israel through the wilderness (Ex 13:21), he is 'clothed with a cloud' and his feet are 'like pillars of fire' (v. 1). However, in Exodus, that angel is called 'the LORD',[454] i.e. He is a theophany, the visible manifestation of God Himself.

John had earlier seen a rainbow around the throne of God (Rev 4:2-3), as had Ezekiel (Ezek 1:28), and although the angel's face is as fearsome as the sun, there is reassurance in the rainbow:

> 16. "When the rainbow is in the cloud, then I will look upon it, to *remember the everlasting covenant* between God and every living creature of all flesh that is on the earth."
> 17. And God said to Noah, "This is *the sign* of the covenant which I have established between Me and all flesh that is on the earth." (Gen 9:16-17*)

---

[454] The NASB uses 'LORD' to translate the Hebrew YHWH, the 'I Am' name of God.

As noted in Book 4,[455] Noah's "everlasting covenant" was made with "all successive generations" (Gen 9:12) which includes us today. It not only reaffirmed the Adamic Covenant for mankind to rule and care for the earth (Gen 1:28, 9:1-3) but also to govern justly, treating every human being as sacred because we are made "in the image of God" (Gen 9:5-6).

The Angel of the LORD has two messages, the first declared to all of Creation and the second in the little book he was about to give to John, a small scroll[456] which has been left unsealed.

No More Delay

The first message is that the Creator of heaven and earth and sea has had enough:

> 5. Then the angel... lifted up his right hand to heaven,
> 6. and swore by Him who lives forever and ever, who *created heaven* and the things that are in it, *the earth* and the things that are in it, and *the sea* and the things that are in it, that *there will be delay no longer*,
> 7. but in the days of the voice of *the seventh angel*, when he is about to sound, then the mystery of God is *finished*, as He preached to His servants the prophets. (Rev 10:5-7*)

We have violated the Noahic Covenant in failing to take care of the dominion He gave us over heaven and earth and sea and each other - when Jesus returns, He will hold us accountable.

The angel is also declaring to the last generation that the 7th Trumpet will be the last, that it will be the end of 'the mystery of God', i.e. all the mysteries of God declared by all the prophets (v. 7). Nothing will be hidden - everything will be revealed to everybody when Jesus returns.

---

455   *Silencing the Witnesses*, pp. 316-319.
456   The Greek, *biblaridion*, refers to the inner bark of the papyrus plant. Kittel, pp. 106-107.

John is then told to take the little book, the open scroll, and eat it:

> 9. "Take it and eat it; it will make your stomach bitter, but in your mouth it will be sweet as honey...
> 11. "*You must prophesy* again concerning many peoples and nations and tongues and kings." (Rev 10:9-11*)

John's 1st century Jewish audience would have recognised this unusual command because Ezekiel received a similar command in the 6th century BC, to eat a scroll with a message causing 'lamentations, mourning, and woe' to Israel (Ezek 2:9-3:3). Ezekiel was told what this signified:

> 10. ...He said to me, "Son of man, *take into your heart* all My words which I will speak to you and *listen* closely." (Ezek 3:10*)

Everything God says should taste "sweet as honey" (v. 9) to us because every word is precious; we should listen and take it into our hearts even when it leads to bitterness and grief. God Himself grieves at the death of every individual:

> "As I live!" declares the Lord GOD, "I take no pleasure in the death of the wicked, but rather that the wicked turn from his way and live. Turn back, turn back from your evil ways! Why then will you die, O house of Israel?" (Ezek 33:11)

Jeremiah often wept as he prophesied.[457]

Just as Ezekiel ate and then prophesied God's judgement on Israel, John was to eat and then prophesy God's judgement on the whole world (Rev 10:11) - the 7th Trumpet will be the end of 'this present evil age' (Gal 1:4).

---

[457] Jeremiah 8:21, 9:1, 13:17, 23:9.

The Third Woe

The coming of the King to judge the world will be the third woe for unbelievers but blessed relief for those of us who love Him, angels and humans:

> 15. Then the seventh angel sounded; and there were loud voices in heaven, saying, "The kingdom of the world has become the kingdom of our Lord and of His Christ; and He will reign forever and ever." (Rev 11:15*)

In 1741, this text was set to music by Frederick Handel and Charles Jennens[458] in the magnificent *Hallelujah Chorus* of their oratorio *Messiah* which became one of the best-known and most frequently played choral work in Western civilisation.

John sees the response in heaven is pure worship and gratitude:

> 16. And the twenty-four elders, who sit on their thrones before God, fell on their faces and *worshiped* God,
> 17. saying, "We give You *thanks*, O Lord God, the Almighty, who are and who were, because You have taken Your great power and have *begun to reign...*" (Rev 11:16-17*)

At last!

Utterly convinced that our reigning over the earth has been an abject and irredeemable failure, we will be delighted to welcome Jesus back as the only one fit to reign. His enemies, however, will not welcome Him because He will hold us accountable for what we have done:

> 18. "And the nations were enraged, and Your wrath came, and the time came... to reward Your bond-servants the prophets and the saints and those who fear Your name..., and *to destroy those who destroy the earth.*" (Rev 11:18*)

---

[458] Handel wrote the music to Jennens's lyrics which he had compiled from throughout the Scriptures. The rest of the chorus is from Revelation 19:6 & 16.

"Every Eye…"

The first six trumpets were to tell us the significance of what we see occurring in the earth, sea, freshwater, and sky but most people will still not understand. Not so with the seventh. The seventh will be His visible reappearance and no one will misunderstand that:

> "And then the sign of the Son of Man will *appear* in the sky, and then *all the tribes of the earth will mourn,* and they will see the SON OF MAN COMING ON THE CLOUDS OF THE SKY with power and great glory." (Matt 24:30*)

When Jesus quotes the phrase from Daniel 7:13, capitalised here in the NASB, He predicts the utter dismay that His appearing will cause to unbelievers of every people-group on earth. Sixty-five years later, John rephrases this, beginning with an exhortation for us to look:

> BEHOLD, HE IS COMING WITH THE CLOUDS, and *every eye* will see Him, even those who pierced Him; and *all the tribes of the earth will mourn* over Him. So it is to be. Amen. (Rev 1:7*)

John specifies that 'every eye will see Him', even unbelieving Jews and Gentiles who will mourn their newly revealed situation. He finishes by commenting that this is exactly how it should be.

Through the ages some have claimed that Jesus has already returned invisibly or metaphorically. For example, Charles T. Russell (1852-1916) founded the Jehovah's Witnesses in the belief that Jesus had returned invisibly in 1874 and began ruling in 1914.[459] In 19th century Persia, Bahá'u'lláh (1817-1892) founded the Bahá'í Faith, thinking that he was Jesus returned; in 1954 in Korea, Sun Myung Moon (1920-2012) founded the Unification Church, claiming that he was 'to carry

---

459 www.jw.org/en/bible-teachings/questions/daniel-4-bible-chronology-1914, 3 Mar, 2023.

out Christ's unfinished task'.[460] New Age teacher Benjamin Creme announced that Jesus had 'taken up residence in the Indian-Pakistani community of London' in 1997 as a man called Maitreya, the World Teacher.[461]

However, Jesus made it plain He would not be coming invisibly, metaphorically, or mysteriously but visibly and literally:

> 25. "Behold, I have told you in advance.
> 26. "So if they say to you, 'Behold, He is in the wilderness,' do not go out, or, 'Behold, He is in the inner rooms,' do not believe them.
> 27. "For just as the lightning comes from the east and flashes even to the west, *so will the coming of the Son of Man be.* (Matt 24:25-27*)

There will also be no mistaking the immediate aftermath.

The Resurrection

He will raise and judge the dead:

> 18. "...and the time came for *the dead to be judged*, and the time to reward Your bond-servants the prophets and the saints and those who fear Your name, the small and the great, and to destroy those who destroy the earth." (Rev 11:18*)

We will look at this properly in Book 7, *Kingdom Come: Justice for All* - for now we are simply focussing on the trumpet proclaiming Jesus' return as the King and "Judge of all the earth" (Gen 18:25).

Paul described this day to the Thessalonians:

> For the Lord Himself will descend from heaven with a shout, with the voice of the archangel and with *the trumpet of God*, and *the dead* in Christ *will rise* first. (1 Thess 4:16*)

---

460 www.britannica.com/biography/Sun-Myung-Moon, 3 Mar, 2023.
461 https://share-international.org/summary-for-new-readers, 4 Mar, 2023.

In other words, the living will not be the only ones to see His return - the dead will too, from their resurrected bodies, just as Job prophesied and Handel and Jennens' *Messiah* celebrates:

> 25. "As for me, I know that my Redeemer lives,
> And *at the last* He will take His stand on the earth.
> 26. "Even after my skin is destroyed,
> *Yet from my flesh I shall see God*;
> 27. Whom I myself shall behold,
> And whom *my eyes will see* and not another..."
> (Job 19:25-27*)

Paul carefully notes the order - the conscious spirits and souls of all who have died trusting in Jesus will return with Him:

> For if we believe that Jesus died and rose again, even so God will bring *with Him those who have fallen asleep* in Jesus. (1 Thess 4:14*)

'Fallen asleep' means their bodies have not been conscious and resurrection is, by definition, the reuniting of their conscious spirits and souls with their unconscious bodies (cf. Jas 2:26).

What then of those who do not need resurrection? Paul continues:

> Then we who are alive and remain will be caught up together with them in the clouds to meet the Lord in the air... (1 Thess 4:17)

We will need a different kind of resurrection to be transformed:

> 51. Behold, I tell you a mystery; we will not all sleep, but we will all be *changed*,
> 52. in a moment, in the twinkling of an eye, at *the last trumpet*; for *the trumpet will sound*, and the dead will be raised imperishable, and we will be *changed*. (1 Cor 15:51-52*)

This 'change' at 'the last trumpet' is because 'this perishable must put on the imperishable, and this mortal must put on immortality' (1 Cor 15:53).

We will look at this properly in Book 7 so for now, let us focus on 'the last trumpet'.

'The Last Trumpet'

As noted in Chapter 2, every culture old and new has horns or trumpets but the seventh and last trumpet had a particular significance to the Jews in John's 1st century audience.

In their festivals, major days and events were not only introduced by trumpets but also set up by repetitions of sevens to build extraordinary climaxes. Every year, for example, the Feast of Weeks or Pentecost[462] was established as the climax of seven Sabbaths (Lev 23:15-21); Jubilee was the climax of seven Sabbath years (Lev 25:8-34). Their holiest day, Yom Kippur or Day of Atonement, was in the seventh month which was heralded as unique by the Feast of Trumpets on its first day (Lev 23:24-25).

However, two particular events help us understand the 7th Trumpet: the conquering of Jericho and the proclamation of Jubilee.

(i) Conquering Jericho

As I mentioned in Chapter 2, every Jew, every Jewish teenager in the 1st century would have recognised Paul's description of the last trumpet because of their nation's astonishing and much-celebrated victory at Jericho in 1406 BC. I recognised it myself, from being ten years old in 1960 when our radios played Jimmie Rodgers' 'Joshua Fit the Battle o' Jericho',[463]

---

462 Pentecost comes from the Greek word meaning fifty.
463 Recorded by Roulette Records (R4234), the song is thought to have been written early in the 19th century by slaves in America's South rejoicing in faith that one day they would escape from slavery.

here in the uttermost parts of the earth 3,500 years later.

Jericho was famous for its fortifications which dated back to 8000 BC. Today, archaeologists conclude:

> Jericho was surrounded by a great earthen rampart, or embankment, with a stone retaining wall at its base. The retaining wall was some 12-15 ft [4-5 m] high. On top of that was a mudbrick wall 6 ft [2 m] thick and about 20-26 ft [6-8 m] high (Sellin and Watzinger 1973: 58). At the crest of the embankment was a similar mudbrick wall whose base was roughly 46 ft [14 m] above the ground level outside the retaining wall.[464]

God had led Joshua and the Hebrews through today's Jordan to the Jordan River, directly opposite Jericho, to at last enter the Promised Land.

His plan for the battle had sevens everywhere:

> "...*seven* priests shall carry *seven trumpets* of rams' horns before the ark; then on the *seventh* day you shall march around the city *seven times*, and the priests shall blow the trumpets. (Josh 6:4*)

Nothing was to happen for the first six days of marching, nor for the first six circuits on the seventh day. However, on the seventh circuit on the seventh day, when the seven priests blew the seven rams' horns, everyone was to shout:

> "It shall be that when they make a long blast with the ram's horn, and when you hear *the sound of the trumpet*, all the people shall *shout* with a great shout; and the wall of the city will fall down flat, and the people will go up every man straight ahead." (Josh 6:5*)

---

[464] In 1957, British archaeologist Kathleen Kenyon famously rejected the Biblical account but she had misdated her findings. Today, 'the archaeological evidence supports the historical accuracy of the Biblical account in every detail. Every aspect of the story that could possibly be verified by the findings of archaeology is, in fact, verified' (https://biblearchaeology.org/research/conquest-of-canaan/3625-the-walls-of-jericho, 15 Feb, 2023).

The peoples' voices were an essential but carefully restrained element:

> "You shall not shout nor let your voice be heard nor let a word proceed out of your mouth, until the day I tell you, 'Shout!' Then you shall shout!" (Jos 6:10)

It was at that moment that the seemingly impregnable walls of Jericho 'fell down flat' (Josh 6:20), except for the area where Rahab and her family lived.[465]

(ii) Seven meaning 'rest'

As noted in Chapter 2 and Book 5,[466] sevenfold or seven times is often used in the Scriptures as a metaphor meaning:

> justly, completely, or perfectly. It originates from the seventh day, the Sabbath, when God rested from all His works – He had finished Creation to the state of [absolute] goodness or perfection, i.e. nothing was wrong or lacking (Gen 1:31).[467]

However, when seven referred to days and years, it meant that Israel were to stop working, to rest from their own good works and trust instead in what God would do (Heb 4:9-10).

The fall of Jericho's walls was not due to any work that Israel did - they just had to walk - but entirely due to the supernatural intervention of God while they obeyed His command.

In the same way, in Revelation we see that God is laying siege to the whole world - its walls will come tumbling down at the 7th Trumpet and a great shout from Jesus, our Joshua,[468] and from the archangel (1 Thess 4:16). I believe,

---

465 https://biblearchaeologyreport.com/2019/05/25/biblical-sites-three-discoveries-at-jericho, 15 Feb, 2023.
466 *Threshing Hour*, Appendix A - Seven, Ten, and Seventy, pp. 209-210.
467 *Gotta Serve Somebody*, p. 147.
468 Jesus is the Anglicised Greek equivalent of Joshua, the Anglicised Hebrew

though, we will all be shouting, marvelling, and worshipping at our being resurrected or transformed 'in the twinkling of an eye' (1 Cor 15:52) - could anyone remain silent at such a moment? Then will follow the half an hour of absolute silence predicted by the 7th Seal.

The 7th Trumpet will indeed be "the third woe" for unbelievers but not for the rest of us:

> ...when He comes to be glorified in His saints on that day, and to be marveled at among all who have believed (2 Thess 1:10*)

(iii) The Year of Jubilee

Every fifty years in ancient Israel, they were to blow a trumpet:

> 9. "You shall then sound *a ram's horn* abroad on the tenth day of the seventh month; on the Day of Atonement you shall sound a horn all through your land.
> 10. "'You shall thus consecrate the *fiftieth year* and *proclaim a release through the land to all its inhabitants*. It shall be a jubilee for you, and each of you shall return to his own property, and each of you shall return to his family."
> (Lev 25:9-10*)

The annual Day of Atonement was for forgiveness of sins but this fiftieth Day of Atonement was to proclaim forgiveness of all debts, freedom from slavery,[469] and the regaining of any lost family land (v. 10), ensuring that every generation could have a fresh start in the Promised Land.

It was to be carefully measured out:

> 8. "You are... to count off seven sabbaths of years for yourself, seven times seven years, so that you have the

---

of *Yehoshua*, which means 'The LORD is salvation', hence the angel telling Joseph, "you shall call His name Jesus, for He will save His people from their sins" (Matt 1:21).

[469] In ancient Israel as in the British Empire more recently, debtors could sell themselves into indentured servitude for up to six years (Ex 21:2).

> time of the seven sabbaths of years, namely, forty-nine years..." (Lev 25:8)

This forgiveness in the fiftieth year was due to the atonement but also because it was founded on the seven Sabbatical years when Israel were to stop working, to rest from their own good works and trust instead in what God would provide (Lev 25:2-7).

This Messianic prophecy was to predict that when Jesus returns, He will be proclaiming our Jubilee, our freedom from all sins and debts, and our regaining of our lost heavens and earth, but in their new form.

Which leads us to consider the trumpet ancient Israel were to use.

(iv) The ram's horn

Israel usually used two silver trumpets but, as you can see above, on these two occasions at Jericho (Jos 6:5) and at Jubilee (Lev 25:9), they were to use a shofar, or ram's horn, which wonderfully predicts the unique work of Messiah.

When Abraham was commanded by God to offer up Isaac as a burnt offering, he was actually being asked to star in an extraordinary drama.[470] Abraham was to play the role of our Father who so loved the world that He gave His only-begotten Son to die so that we could gain eternal life (John 3:16).

Isaac's role as Jesus was twofold. First, he and a ram foreshadowed Jesus' death:

> 13. Then Abraham raised his eyes and looked, and behold, behind him *a ram* caught in the thicket by *his horns*; and Abraham went and took the ram and offered him up for a burnt offering *in the place* of his son. (Gen 22:13*)

Abraham delighted in God's provision:

---
470 *The Red Heifer's Ashes: Mysteries of Ancient Israel*, pp. 29-31.

> 14. Abraham called the name of that place The LORD Will Provide, as it is said to this day, "In the mount of the LORD it will be provided." (Gen 22:14)

Isaac's second part was to foreshadow Jesus' resurrection 'on the third day' (Gen 22:4), as we are told in Hebrews:

> 17. By faith Abraham, when he was tested, offered up Isaac, and he who had received the promises was offering up his only begotten son…
> 19. He considered that God is able to raise people even from the dead, from which *he also received him back as a type*. (Heb 11:17-19*)

The horns of rams, goats, and bulls symbolised the strength and power of these animals (Num 23:22, Deut 33:17) so Biblical visions often include horns to portray kings and kingdoms.[471] We have seen throughout this series that the dragon of Revelation 12 and the beast of Revelation 11, 13, and 17 have ten horns on their seventh head to symbolise all the kings and kingdoms of the earth finally uniting with the beast (Rev 17:12).

In Abraham's case, however, the ram being caught by its horns foreshadows Messiah being taken captive for our sins. As Isaiah prophesied:

> All of us like sheep have gone astray,
> Each of us has turned to his own way;
> But the LORD has caused the iniquity of us all
> To fall on Him. (Isa 53:6)

The Son of God became "the Lamb of God who takes away the sins of the world" (John 1:29 & 34):

> 3. For what the Law could not do …God did: sending His own Son in *the likeness of sinful flesh* and *as an offering for sin*, He condemned sin in the flesh (Rom 8:3*)

---

[471] E.g. Daniel 7:24, 8:20, 17:12; Zechariah 1:18-19.

The Last Trumpet being a shofar proclaims that the Lamb has "all authority in heaven and on earth."[472]

"A Great Trumpet"

Lastly, consider Jesus' final public address:

> 29. "But immediately after the tribulation of those days THE SUN WILL BE DARKENED, AND THE MOON WILL NOT GIVE ITS LIGHT, AND THE STARS WILL FALL from the sky, and the powers of the heavens will be shaken.
> 30. "And then the sign of the Son of Man will appear in the sky, and then all the tribes of the earth will mourn, and they will see the SON OF MAN COMING ON THE CLOUDS OF THE SKY with power and great glory.
> 31."And He will send forth His angels with A GREAT TRUMPET and THEY WILL GATHER TOGETHER His elect from the four winds, from one end of the sky to the other.
> (Matt 24:29-31*)

He is drawing together a number of Old Testament prophecies, as capitalised here in the *NASB*. In v. 29, He is quoting from Isaiah, Jeremiah, Ezekiel, and Joel;[473] in v. 30, from Daniel;[474] in v. 31, from Isaiah again:

> It will come about also in that day that *a great trumpet* will be blown, and those who were perishing in the land of Assyria and who were scattered in the land of Egypt will come and worship the LORD in the holy mountain at Jerusalem. (Isa 27:13*)

In context, Isaiah had just been predicting the resurrection of the dead (Isa 26:19), Judgement Day (Isa 26:20-21), the end of Satan (Isa 27:1), and the threshing of the harvest (Isa 27:12), as covered in Book 5.[475] Jesus was telling the

---

472   Matthew 28:18. We also see this prefigured in the shofar's blast on the third day at Mt Sinai (Ex 19:13 & 16).
473   E.g. Isaiah 13:10, 24:21-23; Jeremiah 4:23-28; Ezekiel 32:7-8; Joel 2:10, 30-31, 3:15; Amos 5:20.
474   Daniel 7:13.
475   *Threshing Hour.*

disciples that He would be fulfilling all of these prophecies, just as the enormous angel of Revelation 10 announced.

Summary

(i) The angel astride the earth and the sea and reaching to the clouds announces to the three areas of man's dominion that the 7th Trumpet will be the last, just as Paul wrote of the 'last trumpet' to the Thessalonians and Corinthians.

(ii) Jewish disciples would have readily recognised the seven trumpets' parallel with Joshua and Israel's conquering of Jericho and with the wonderful freedom and restoration of their Year of Jubilee, proclaimed with the sounding of the shofar, i.e. ram's horn.

(iii) Both events were the climax of a series of sevens, extrapolating from Israel's weekly Sabbath rest when Israel were to stop working and trust in God's work. All of these were Messianic prophecies, proclaimed by the shofar which was in itself a Messianic prophecy.

(iv) The 7th Trumpet is God's trumpet proclaiming Jesus' second coming to put everything right. This will be the third woe for unbelievers but a marvel and a delight to all who believe!

19
Twenty-Two Signs
"When You See..."

In Chapters 6 and 8, I described the seven trumpets as signs of the time of Jesus' return - the first six were to alert us to be ready for the 7th Trumpet, His visible reappearance.

In Chapters 9-13, I explained how I believe those first six are being fulfilled in our time.

In this chapter, we will see them in context with twelve other signs of the times covered in Books 1-5 and I will comment on just three more that I have not yet covered so this will be mostly summary.

As you will see, ten of the twenty-two have already been fulfilled, ten are in progress, leaving only two yet to come.

"Recognise..."

Remember, Jesus told His 1st century disciples to watch for a specific sign to escape the destruction of Jerusalem which was still forty years away:

> "...*when you see* Jerusalem surrounded by armies, *then recognise* that her desolation is near. Then those who are in Judea must *flee* to the mountains, and those who are in the midst of the city must *leave*... (Luke 21:20-22*)

The sign of that time was the Roman siege: "When you see..., then recognise... [then] flee... [or] leave" Jerusalem. Today, as covered in Book 5,[476] we only have to leave Babylon the Great so if we are truly trusting in Jesus and His atoning death for our sins, if we are filled with the Holy Spirit, and if we are walking with Him daily, we are ready.

---

[476] *Threshing Hour*, pp. 109-129.

However, we are also supposed to be watching for *all the signs* of His return.

In Chapter 17, I noted that the 6th Trumpet can only be seen and recognised as fulfilled by those who believe abortion is the killing of human beings in utero; those who do not believe this will remain unaware of this sign occurring.

In the same way, the three signs regarding Israel's miraculous restoration (Signs 1, 2, and 16 in the chart over the page) can only be seen and recognised by those who believe the Scriptures are predicting restoration; those who instead believe that the Church has superseded or replaced[477] Israel in the promises of God, or that they are all fulfilled[478] in Jesus, will remain unaware of the significance of what has been happening since 1948!

These can be summarised as relating to:

(i) Israel and the Jews (1, 2, 13-16)

(ii) The natural realm (3-8)

(iii) The Gentile nations (9, 11-14, 18)

(iv) The Church (10, 17)

(v) Everyone (18-22)

The sons of Issachar were renowned for being 'men who understood the times, with knowledge of what Israel should do' (1 Chron 12:32). However, there are twenty-two signs of the times that we are all supposed to see and recognise as in the following chart. I covered the first, second, and sixteenth signs (Israel's restoration, the regaining of Jerusalem, and the coming of Elijah) as well as the eleventh (the gospel going to

---

477 As in Supersessionism or Replacement Theology. I refuted this idea in Book 1, *Dancing in the Dragon's Jaws*, pp. 53-65, 184-185.

478 Fulfilment Theology. In quoting 2 Corinthians 1:20, these scholars fail to see that Jesus is not the sole recipient or fulfilment but actually the guarantor of the everlasting land promises to Israel (*Dancing in the Dragon's Jaws*, pp. 61-65), just as He is for every Jew or Gentile who trusts in God's promises to them.

"When You See..."			
A = Fulfilled B = In progress C = Yet to come	A	B	C
1. The fig tree in leaf (Matt 24:32-34) - Israel, 1948	✓		
2. Jews regaining Jerusalem (Luke 21:24) - 1967	✓		
3. 1st Trumpet - ⅓ Trees on Earth (Rev 8:7)	✓		
— "All the green grass" (Rev 8:7)		✓	
4. 2nd Trumpet - ⅓ Sea-life, ⅓ Ships (Rev 8:8-9)	✓		
5. 3rd Trumpet - ⅓ Freshwater (Rev 8:11)	✓		
6. 4th Trumpet - ⅓ Sun, moon, and stars (Rev 8:12)	✓		
7. 5th Trumpet - Locusts (Rev 9:1-11)	✓		
8. 6th Trumpet - ⅓ Mankind killed (Rev 9:18)	✓		
9. ⅓ "all the nations", spirit of antichrist (Dan 7:24-26)	✓		
10. The Great Apostasy (2 Thess 2:3, 1 Tim 4:1)	✓		
11. Gospel to "all the nations" (Matt 24:14)		✓	
12. The Great Tribulation (Rev 7:14)		✓	
13. The demonic frogs croaking (Rev 16:13-14)		✓	
14. "All the nations" against Jerusalem (Zech 12:3)		✓	
15. Great Revival in Israel (Zech 12:10, Rev 11:13)		✓	
16. The Coming of Elijah (Matt 17:11)		✓	
17. Great Revival in the churches (Jas 5:7-8)		✓	
18. Great Delusion in the world (2 Thess 2:11)		✓	
19. The mark of the beast (Rev 13:16-17)		✓	
20. "All these things" (Matt 24:33)		✓	
21. The Antichrist, 'man of sin' (2 Thess 2:3)			✓
22. 7th Trumpet - Jesus' return (Matt 24:30-31)			✓

Fig (xi) Twenty-two signs

"all the nations") in Book 1;[479] the third to the eighth (the first six trumpets) in Chapters 8-17 here; the ninth (1/3 of "all the nations" being subdued by the spirit of antichrist) in Book 2;[480] the tenth and twelfth (the Great Apostasy and

---
479 *Dancing in the Dragon's Jaws*, pp. 58, 117-148, 175-176.
480 *Slouching Towards Bethlehem*, pp. 69-73.

the Great Tribulation) in Book 5;[481] the thirteenth (the frog-like demons tempting the world's leaders to take Jerusalem from the Jews) in Book 5;[482] the fourteenth (the gathering of "all the nations" around Jerusalem) in Books 1, 2, 4, and 5; the fifteenth and sixteenth (the Great Revival in Israel, and the coming of Elijah) in Books 1, 4, and 5; the nineteenth (the mark of the beast) in Book 3;[483] the twenty-first (the Antichrist) in Books 2 and 5, and the twenty-second (Jesus' return) in all five books.

That leaves only the seventeenth, eighteenth, and twentieth signs (the Great Revival in the churches, the Great Delusion, and "All these things") to be covered now.

The Great Revival

In Book 4,[484] I showed from Revelation 11 that God has always foreknown and planned for a great revival in Israel just before Jesus returns, that 90% of the nation will turn to Jesus, and, I believe, we are seeing the beginnings of that revival today.

God has also foreknown and planned for a great revival among the Gentiles too. In the 1st century, James used a farming metaphor to teach the disciples to be patient:

> 7. Therefore be patient, brethren, until the coming of the Lord. The farmer waits for the precious produce of the soil, being patient about it, until it gets the early [i.e. autumn] and late [i.e. spring] rains.
> 8. You too be patient; strengthen your hearts, for the coming of the Lord is near. (Jas 5:7-8*)

James' audience would have known that Moses had promised Israel:

---

481   *Threshing Hour*, pp. 83-89, 163-179.
482   Ibid, pp. 39-47.
483   *Gotta Serve Somebody*, pp. 109-112.
484   *Silencing the Witnesses*, pp. 280-302.

> "He will give the rain for your land *in its season*, the *early and late rain*, that you may gather in your grain and your new wine and your oil." (Deut 11:14*)

As mentioned in Chapter 6, Israel's "early rain" usually begins in mid-autumn, i.e. October and their "late rain" usually ends in mid-spring, i.e. April.

James was reminding us all that just as every natural harvest has its seasons, so too does God's spiritual harvest of the earth (Jesus also spoke of the fig tree's leaves appearing in the spring to herald the coming summer of His return).

What then should we expect to see?

As I see it, God's spiritual "early rain" began with the outpouring of the Holy Spirit on the Day of Pentecost in 30 AD. This lasted some three hundred years and was followed by a long spiritual winter due to the Great Apostasy, as I covered in Book 5.[485] However, over the last one hundred years, there has been a major outpouring of the Holy Spirit which I believe is God's spiritual "late rain". In 2014, Pew Research reported:

> With nearly 300 million followers worldwide, including many in Africa and Latin America, Pentecostalism is now a global phenomenon. But present day Pentecostalism traces its origins to a religious revival movement that began in the early 20th century.[486]

American Pentecostals often refer to this movement as the Latter Rain Revival, believing it began with the spiritual gift of speaking in tongues described in 1 Corinthians 12-14 in 1901 in Topeka, Kansas, or in 1906 in Azusa St, Los Angeles.[487] However, as I noted in Book 2,[488] these meetings

---
485 *Threshing Hour*, pp. 163-179.
486 www.pewresearch.org/fact-tank/2014/11/14/why-has-pentecostalism-grown-so-dramatically-in-latin-america, 4 Mar, 2023.
487 www.britannica.com/topic/Pentecostalism, 5 May, 2023.
488 *Slouching Towards Bethlehem*, p. 163, footnote 270.

were preceded by a Pentecostal revival in Armenia in 1855, renowned for dreams and prophecies as described in Acts 2, which had spilled over from southern Russia.

The traditional denominations initially rejected these manifestations but most today accept them as legitimate for believers. The Pew report continues:

> Starting in the late '60s...the Catholic Church embraced charismatic Christianity. That has been the church's primary response to Pentecostal inroads.[489]

Today, Charismatic/Pentecostal churches are common throughout the West. Meanwhile in China, where in 1949 Mao Zedong had outlawed any kind of Christianity, the underground church has grown a hundredfold:

> Over the past four decades, Christianity has grown faster in China than anywhere else in the world. Daryl Ireland, a Boston University School of Theology research assistant professor of mission, estimates that the Christian community there has grown from 1 million to 100 million.[490]

In 2012, Pew were reporting:

> Christians number 2.2 billion, or about one-in-three (32%) people worldwide. About half of all Christians are Catholic (50%). An estimated 37% of Christians belong to the Protestant tradition, broadly defined to include Anglicans as well as independent and nondenominational churches. The Orthodox Communion, including the

---

[489] www.pewresearch.org/fact-tank/2014/11/14/why-has-pentecostalism-grown-so-dramatically-in-latin-america, 5 May, 2023.
[490] www.bu.edu/articles/2023/why-is-christianity-growing-in-china, 6 May, 2023. In *Dancing in the Dragon's Jaws* (p. 130), I quoted a news report of 130 million but I now see that as exaggerated. Also corrected in *Gotta Serve Somebody*, p. 158, footnote 173.

Greek and Russian Orthodox, make up 12% of Christians.[491]

That was one third of the world's population then but I believe we are going to see many more believers yet as the Holy Spirit continues to rain on us.

The Great Delusion

We are also to expect and recognise a great delusion just before the Lord returns.

In Books 2[492] and 5,[493] I commented on Paul's description of this in conjunction with the Antichrist:

> 8. Then *that lawless one* will be revealed whom the Lord will slay with the breath of His mouth and bring to an end by the appearance of His coming;
> 9. that is, the one whose coming is in accord with the activity of Satan, with all power and signs and false wonders,
> 10. and with all the deception of wickedness for those who perish, because *they did not receive the love of the truth* so as to be saved. (2 Thess 2:8-10*)

The Antichrist's 'deception of wickedness' (v. 10) with 'power and signs and false wonders' (v. 9) will not be unjust because it follows God's offer to every one of us a truly extraordinary, supernatural 'love of the truth' (v. 10). This love, Jesus says, comes from:

> "...the Spirit of truth, whom the world cannot receive, because it does not see Him or know Him, but you know Him because *He abides with you* and *will be in you*." (John 14:17*)

---

491 Europe (558 million), Latin America-Caribbean (531 million), Sub-Saharan Africa (517 million), Asia-Pacific (287 million), and North America (267 million). www.bc.edu/content/dam/files/centers/jesinst/pdf/Grim-globalReligion-full.pdf. p. 17. 6 May, 2023.
492 *Slouching Towards Bethlehem*, pp. 196-199.
493 *Threshing Hour*, pp. 42, 179-182.

He promised that:

> "...the Spirit of truth... will guide you into all the truth... and He will disclose to you what is to come." (John 16:13)

John therefore assured us:

> 20. ...you have *an anointing* from the Holy One, and you all know....
> 26. These things I have written to you concerning those who are trying *to deceive you*.
> 27. As for you, *the anointing* which you received from Him *abides in you*, and you have no need for anyone to teach you; but as *His anointing teaches you about all things*, and is true and is not a lie, and just as it has taught you, you abide in Him. (1 John 2:20, 26-27*)

Receiving this love of the truth is always humbling and often embarrassing because it begins with us having to accept God's perfectly accurate assessment of us as sinful:

> 8. If we say that we have no sin, *we are deceiving ourselves* and *the truth is not in us*...
> 10. If we say that we have not sinned, we make Him a liar and His word is not in us. (1 John 1:8-10*)

If we willingly deceive ourselves regarding ourselves, we will be easily deceived by others:

> 11. For this reason God will send upon them *a deluding influence* so that *they will believe what is false*,
> 12. in order that they all may be judged who did not believe the truth, but took pleasure in wickedness.
> (2 Thess 2:11-12*)

Some may ask, however, if it is God sending 'a deluding influence' (v. 11), how is that our fault? Paul is not saying God is the source of the delusion; he is describing His sovereignty in allowing the natural consequences of us rejecting the truth.

The Deluding Influence

We see this illustrated in Micaiah's vision regarding the wicked king Ahab:

> 19. Micaiah said, "Therefore, hear the word of the LORD. I saw the LORD sitting on His throne, and all the host of heaven standing by Him on His right and on His left.
> 20. "The LORD said, 'Who will entice Ahab to go up and fall at Ramoth-gilead?'...
> 21. "Then a spirit came forward and stood before the LORD and said, 'I will entice him.'
> 22. "The LORD said to him, 'How?' And he said, 'I will go out and be a deceiving spirit in the mouth of all his prophets.' Then He said, 'You are to entice him and also prevail. Go and do so.'
> 23. "Now therefore, behold, *the LORD has put a deceiving spirit* in the mouth of all these your prophets; and the LORD has proclaimed disaster against you."
> (1 Kin 22:19-23*)

Ahab had wanted to capture the city of Ramoth-gilead (vv. 3-4) and the false prophets were flattering him by confirming his desire (v. 6, 10-13). However, he already suspected that Micaiah would thwart him (v. 8) and Micaiah did indeed prophesy that he would lose the battle and his life (vv. 15-17). When Ahab complained (v. 18), Micaiah explained the false prophecies of the other prophets but ascribes it all to the sovereignty of God.

Ahab had the choice to either accept what God was saying to him through Micaiah or the deceiving spirit through the false prophets and he foolishly chose what he most wanted to hear.

Today God is offering the whole world the choice between the gospel of Jesus and the gospel of the spirit of antichrist and it really is our choice.

Political Delusion

In the 20th century we saw this delusion regarding a number of antichrists and their sinfulness in the national politics of Hirohito's Japan, Stalin's Russia, Mussolini's Italy, Hitler's Germany, Mao's China, Kim Il Sung's Korea, and Pol Pot's Cambodia.

We can also see it throughout the 1,400 years of Muhammad's Arab-Islamic Empire - his followers widely accept child-brides as normal because he married 'Aishah at age 6 and had sexual intercourse with her when she was aged 9.[494]

However, this perverse delusion is today infecting international politics through the United Nations. For decades, the International Children's Emergency Fund (UNICEF) tried to protect children, declaring that:

> Child marriage threatens the lives, well-being and futures of girls around the world... [Defined as] any formal marriage or informal union between a child under the age of 18 and an adult or another child.[495]

However, on 8 March, 2023, another UN organisation called UNAIDS launched its new '8 March Principles' which include 'Principle 16: Consensual Sexual Conduct' and states:

> Enforcement may not be linked to the sex/gender of participants or *age of consent* to marriage. Moreover, sexual conduct involving persons below the domestically prescribed minimum age of consent to sex may be *consensual in fact, if not in law*.[496]

---

494 As narrated by 'Aishah, recorded by al-Bukhari 3894, Muslim 1422 (https://islamqa.info/en/answers/124483/how-old-was-aishah-when-she-married-the-prophet, 8 Dec, 2023).
495 www.unicef.org/protection/child-marriage, 6 May, 2023.
496 www.documentcloud.org/documents/23785476-8-march-principles-final-printer-version-1-march-2023-1, p. 22, 7 Feb, 2024. Emphasis added.

While this is rightly aimed at decriminalising teenage promiscuity,[497] it fails to uphold UNICEF's aims and does not define any age as too young. Also, as noted in Book 5,[498] the UN Human Rights Council (UNHRC) refuses to even consider female genital mutilation, child marriages, and the stoning of women because Islam or Muhammad might be criticised.

If the Antichrist is a Muslim and their predicted Mehdi, as I believe, any criticism of his wickedness may well be dismissed as Islamophobia.

Moral Delusion

It also seems that 21st century morals and values will be determined by whoever controls the technology companies determining what we can see, read, or hear.

Rejecting 'the love of the truth' as God Himself defines it has led our society into irrational and often bizarre dogmas, even the redefining of 'truth'. For centuries truth has been defined and understood as:

1. Conformity to fact or actuality.
2. Reality; actuality.
3. The reality of a situation.[499]

Today, young people are being taught that we can each have our own 'truth' instead of our own perception or perspective on anything. What we believe can be 'our truth', even if it bears no resemblance to fact, actuality, or reality.

---

497   The punishments for sexual immorality are often misunderstood by Christians because, as I showed in *Silencing the Witnesses* (p. 258), while the Law of Moses criminalised sexual sins (Lev 18), the New Covenant condemns them but decriminalises them (1 Cor 6:9-11, Gal 5:19-21). The New also decriminalises Sabbath-breaking and occult practices such as witchcraft and heresy (ibid. pp. 116-117) but not murder, theft, rape, child molestation - these remain crimes to be punished by every government (Rom 13:1-4).
498   *Threshing Hour*, p. 158.
499   *The American Heritage® Dictionary of the English Language*, 5th Edition.

In Biblical terms, we have returned to 'the days of the judges' when 'every man did what was right in his own eyes' (Judg 17:6), ignoring the will of God as revealed by the Holy Spirit and the Scriptures.

Sexual Delusion

We are being told, at least in the West, that we now need at least sixty-eight terms to describe gender identity and expression.[500] Of course, there have always been issues with human sexuality. As noted in Chapter 8, Jesus taught that:

> "...there are eunuchs who were *born that way* from their mother's womb; and there are eunuchs who were *made eunuchs by men*; and there are also eunuchs who *made themselves eunuchs* for the sake of the kingdom of heaven..." (Matt 19:12*)

Biblically, eunuchs were impotent or castrated males who were unable to procreate and therefore could be trusted to look after royal harems and court business (Est 2:3, Jer 38:7, Acts 8:27).

Some, however, are 'born' eunuchs in that they are intersex, as defined by the United Nations Human Rights High Commissioner:

> Intersex people are born with sex characteristics (including genitals, gonads, and chromosome patterns) that do not fit typical binary notions of male or female... between 0.05% and 1.7% of the population is born with intersex traits.[501]

Others have been 'made' eunuchs by castration or, as with some of my friends, by trauma caused by molestation in

---

500 www.healthline.com/health/different-genders, 6 May, 2023.
501 www.unfe.org/wp-content/uploads/2017/05/UNFE-Intersex.pdf, 7 Feb, 2024.

childhood. Still others 'make themselves' eunuchs, living celibate lives to serve the Lord.[502]

Still others have a psychological condition called gender dysphoria, which is 'the discomfort or distress a person can feel when there is a mismatch between their body and their gender or sense of self.'[503] We should therefore always be loving and compassionate with all of our neighbours.

However, none of this changes the definition of male or female.

Despite this certainty, we are today living in a philosophical and emotional minefield created by an ideology fuelled by academia which causes even jurists to equivocate. In 2022 in the USA, prospective Supreme Court Justice Ketanji Brown Jackson was asked, "Can you provide a definition for the word 'woman'?" and she replied "I can't... I'm not a biologist."[504] Legacy newspapers *The New York Times*[505] and *The Washington Post*[506] lauded her astounding courage and patience while *USA Today* solemnly reported:

> Scientists, gender law scholars and philosophers of biology said Jackson's response was commendable, though perhaps misleading.... they note that *a competent biologist* would not be able to offer a definitive answer either. *Scientists agree* there is no sufficient way to clearly define what makes someone a woman, and with billions of women on the planet, there is much variation.[507]

---

502   Discussed in *Threshing Hour*, pp. 236-238.
503   https://mentalhealth.org.nz/conditions/condition/gender-dysphoria,6May, 2023.
504   Judge Ketanji Brown Jackson, in reply to Senator Marsha Blackburn at her Senate Confirmation Hearing on 23 March, 2022.
505   www.nytimes.com/2022/03/23/us/politics/ketanji-brown-jackson-woman-definition.html, 6 May, 2023.
506   www.washingtonpost.com/lifestyle/2022/03/25/ketanji-brown-jackson-woman, 6 May, 2023.
507   www.usatoday.com/story/life/health-wellness/2022/03/24/marsha-blackburn-asked-ketanji-jackson-define-woman-science/7152439001, 6 May, 2023.

So no one - no scientist, law scholar, philosopher of biology, or biologist -knows!

Judge Brown Jackson, however, had earlier referred to the First Lady, her mother, her sisters-in-law, her mother-in-law, her daughters (whom she called "girls"), as well as to Judge Constance Baker Motley, "the first African American woman to be appointed to the federal bench".[508] She obviously knows what women and girls are but did not want to offend anyone regarding transgender issues and rights.

Sports Delusion

Transgender issues are now beginning to impact women's sports. These were created for good reason:

> If you know sport, you know this beyond a reasonable doubt: there is an average 10-12% performance gap between elite males and elite females. The gap is smaller between elite females and non-elite males, but it's still insurmountable and that's ultimately what matters.[509]

For example, in 2017 the fastest woman on earth was Tori Bowie. She was US, Olympic, and World Champion with her 100 metre best of 10.78 seconds and her 200 metre best of 21.77. However, in that year, her best times were beaten 19,002 times by men and boys - 10,009 over 100 metres and 8,993 over 200 metres![510]

In 2017, Allyson Felix was the world's fastest woman over 400 metres with a best time of 49.26 seconds but in that year, men and boys beat her time 13,898 times. In the 800, 1500, 3000, and 5000 metres, men and boys beat the fastest women's times over 24,500 times. In high jump, long jump, triple jump, and pole vault, men and boys surpassed women's world records on 13,963 occasions!

---

508   https://edition.cnn.com/2022/03/21/politics/ketanji-brown-jackson-hearing-opening-statement-transcript/index.html, 6 May, 2023.
509   Duke Law Center for Sports Law and Policy. https://law.duke.edu/sports/sex-sport/comparative-athletic-performance, 6 May, 2023.
510   Ibid.

In conclusion:

> Not only did hundreds and thousands of males outperform the best results of the elite females, they did so thousands and tens of thousands of times. (Yes, again, that's the right number of zeros.)[511]

We see the same results in every sport that requires physical strength such as weight-lifting, swimming, boxing, wrestling, soccer, rugby, tennis, golf, archery, javelin, shot-put etc.

Being compassionate for transgender athletes does not mean denying human anatomy and physiology, no matter what ideology may demand.

"All These Things"

Like the shepherd boy in the fable who falsely cried "Wolf!" too many times before the wolf actually attacked his sheep, many have tried to guess the time of the Antichrist and the Lord's return and lost credibility.

As I noted in Books 2[512] and 3,[513] for centuries Eastern Orthodox and Protestant leaders have believed the Pope of their day was the Antichrist; in the 19th century, many thought it was Napoleon Bonaparte; in the 20th, Benito Mussolini, Adolf Hitler, Henry Kissinger, or Ronald Reagan.

In jumping to their conclusions, however, they ignored the most obvious sign of Jesus' return. He told the disciples:

> 33. so, you too, *when you see all these things, recognise* that He is near, right at the door.
> 34. "Truly I say to you, *this generation* will not pass away until all these things take place. (Matt 24:33-34*)

We are not to 'recognise' that He is near until we 'see *all* these things' - one or two, or five or ten, or fifteen signs of the times are not enough. Only when we see twenty-one signs in

---

511 Ibid.
512 *Slouching Towards Bethlehem*, p. 49.
513 *Gotta Serve Somebody*, pp. 123-125.

the same 'generation', i.e. one hundred year period,[514] should we expect the twenty-second, "the sign of the Son of Man… in the sky, …coming on the clouds of the sky with power and great glory" (Matt 24:30).

The early 19th century missionaries arriving in New Zealand and the South Pacific islands may have thought that bringing the gospel for the first time to the "remotest part of the earth" from Jerusalem (Acts 1:8) would fulfil the eleventh sign, i.e. of the gospel reaching "the whole world… and then the end will come" (Matt 24:14). However, there were many unreached people groups between Jerusalem and Wellington, our capital city, that are only now being reached.

The first, second, and sixteenth signs (i.e. Israel becoming a sovereign nation, the Jews regaining Jerusalem, and the coming of Elijah) could not be seen until 1948 and 1967. The signs of the first six trumpets have likewise only appeared in the last one hundred years.

I believe we are that generation that "will not pass away until *all these things* take place".

Summary

(i) I have listed twenty-two signs of the times that we are supposed to look for and recognise as such. I see ten as being fulfilled in the last 80-100 years, ten as presently in progress, and only two as yet to appear - the Antichrist and Jesus' return.

(ii) Every reader needs to check for themselves if I have rightly explained these signs from the Scriptures and secondly, if I have rightly observed what is happening around us. We also need to keep an eye on the latest data.

---

514 See Chapter 6, "This Generation".

20
The Seven Bowls
Tipping Point

> Then I saw another sign in heaven, great and marvelous, seven angels who had seven plagues, which are the last, because in them the wrath of God is finished... seven golden bowls full of the wrath of God... (Rev 15:1 & 7)

We have now come to the tipping point - God is at last stepping in to stop all further sin.

Those who do not know Him may question His timing, as Peter warned:

> 3. Know this first of all, that in the last days mockers will come with their mocking, following after their own lusts, 4. and saying, "Where is the promise of His coming? For ever since the fathers fell asleep, all continues just as it was from the beginning of creation." (2 Pet 3:3-4)

But He has delayed for one reason:

> 9. The Lord is not slow about His promise, as some count slowness, but is patient toward you, not wishing for *any* to perish but for all to come to repentance. (2 Pet 3:9*)

He has been waiting until everyone has received every possible opportunity to turn to Him.

As noted in Chapter 2, God's anger is never uncontrolled - it is His righteous response to injustice and always restrained by His love and patience. We also saw there that these bowls of wrath are *phiales*, i.e. libation bowls, and readily recognisable to John's 1st century audience because they were used in worship by the Romans, Greeks, and Jews.

However, the Jewish disciples would have seen a particular significance because these were the holy vessels of their Temple (1 Chron 28:17) and I showed how John paraphrases Daniel's rebuke of Belshazzar for his blasphemous use of these golden bowls (Rev 9:20, Dan 5:23). It was Daniel's interpretation of the famous 'writing on the wall' that signalled the end of the Babylonian Empire (Dan 5:5-31) so the disciples would have been delighted by John's vision, knowing that the writing is on the wall for the whole world.

So what else would they have known that we may not know today?

Contents Matter

Firstly, these golden bowls were originally to hold blood for atonement or wine for rejoicing.

(i) Blood

The Law of Moses required that every sacrificial animal be killed 'at the doorway of the Tent of Meeting' (Ex 29:11, Lev 1:3, 3:2) with its blood poured out at the base of the bronze altar (Lev 1:5). In Chapter 4, I showed that the 5th Seal's martyrs 'underneath the [heavenly] altar' therefore signified that, despite their being put to death as criminals by the Romans, God accepted the very precious sacrifice of their lives and He will vindicate them on the Last Day for everyone to see.

In Chapter 11 regarding the 6th Trumpet, we saw that Israel's sin offerings required a small amount of that blood to be smeared on the horns of the golden incense altar:

> "He shall put *some of the blood* on the horns of the [golden incense] altar which is before the LORD in the tent of meeting; and *all the blood* he shall pour out at the base of the [bronze] altar of burnt offering which is at the doorway of the tent of meeting." (Lev 4:18*)

This is where the golden bowls came in - the priests used them at the bronze altar to catch some of the blood of the sin offering for the golden altar. This was because blood had to be shed to atone for sins (Lev 17:11, Ezek 18:14) and its presence on the golden altar's horns proved a death had taken place (Ex 12:13). This signified that justice had been done for the offerors so that their sins could be forgiven and forgotten (Isa 43:25).

(ii) Wine

The Law required libations, drink offerings of wine, to accompany all burnt and grain offerings (Num 28:7, 31), also using golden bowls:

> "You shall make its dishes and its pans and its *jars* and its *bowls* with which to pour *drink offerings*; you shall make them *of pure gold*. (Exo 25:29*)

The Law's drink offerings were poured out on top of the animal sacrifices on the bronze altar (Phil 2:17) while the blood of sacrifices for sin was poured out at its base (Ex 29:12; Lev 4:7-34).

One and a half thousand years later, Jesus fulfilled this foreshadowing at the Last Supper:

> And when He had taken a cup [of wine] and given thanks, He gave it to them, saying, "Drink from it, all of you; for this is My blood of the covenant, which is *poured out* for many for forgiveness of sins." (Matt 26:27-28*)

As Paul explained to the Romans, Jesus' crucifixion was:

> displayed publicly as a propitiation [i.e. atoning sacrifice] in His blood [i.e. His death]… so that He [the Father] would *be just* and *the justifier* of the one who has faith in Jesus. (Rom 3:25-26*)

In other words, this New Covenant ritual was to forever remind us that His blood was poured out 2,000 years ago to show the world that God is perfectly 'just' and we drink His wine because He is our 'justifier' who has forgiven our sins as a result.[515]

Wine was also to celebrate. When the psalmist wrote of how God provides, he also described His purposes:

> 14. He causes the grass to grow for the cattle,
> And vegetation for the labor of man,
> So that he may bring forth food from the earth,
> 15. And *wine which makes man's heart glad*,
> So that he may make his face glisten with *oil*,
> And food [lit. *bread*] which sustains man's heart.
> (Psa 104:14-15*)

Ancient Israel's basic diet of bread, wine, and oil was to sustain and make them happy.[516]

We see then that the Law's golden bowls were firstly to illustrate that justice had been done and atonement made through God's forgiveness, and secondly, to provide sustenance and gladness.

(iii) Wrath

In Chapter 2, I also showed that John's vision of the bowls of wrath contains three metaphors familiar and reassuring to the Jewish disciples in his audience: God's 'pouring out' of

---

515 Paul also used the prophetic drama of the libation to illustrate his ministry, writing to the Philippians that 'I am being poured out as a drink offering upon the sacrifice and service of your faith' (Php 2:17. Also 2 Tim 4:6). Of course, this was not to make atonement but he was soon to die for urging the Gentiles to 'present their bodies' to God (Rom 12:1, 15:16) as prefigured in Israel's burnt offering (Lev 1). To complete the picture, Paul's accompanying 'grain offering of fine flour' (Lev 2:1) was his presenting them with the gospel (Luke 8:11), 'seasoned' with the salt of 'grace' (Lev 2:13, Col 4:6).

516 Jesus has also given us spiritual equivalents of bread, wine, and oil to sustain and make us happy. I explain all on our website (https://emmausroad.org.nz/bread-wine-oil-hands).

wrath, targeted 'cups' of wrath, and 'seven' meaning justly, completely, or perfectly.

They knew, and Gentile disciples were learning, that God is always perfectly just and only pours out His wrath on those who deserve it while all who are forgiven are spared His wrath. As Paul wrote to the Romans:

> And we *know* that the judgment of God *rightly* falls upon those who practice such things (Rom 2:2*)

He therefore warned the Romans to remain repentant in order to be spared on that day:

> 5. But because of your stubbornness and unrepentant heart you are storing up wrath for yourself in *the day of wrath* and revelation of the *righteous judgment of God*,
> 6. who WILL RENDER TO EACH PERSON ACCORDING TO HIS DEEDS:
> 7. to those who by perseverance in doing good seek for glory and honor and immortality, eternal life;
> 8. but to those who are selfishly ambitious and do not obey the truth, but obey unrighteousness, wrath and indignation. (Rom 2:5-8)

There is no ambiguity here: those who persevere 'in doing good' and 'seek for glory and honor and immortality' will receive 'eternal life' (v. 7); those who do not will receive God's 'wrath and indignation' (v. 8). Justice will be perfectly impartial:

> 9. There will be tribulation and distress for every soul of man who does evil, of the Jew first and also of the Greek,
> 10. but glory and honor and peace to everyone who does good, to the Jew first and also to the Greek.
> 11. For *there is no partiality with God*. (Rom 2:9-11*)

Temporal cf. Eternal Judgement

John's Jewish audience would also have known the difference between God's temporal judgements, i.e. made within time, and His eternal judgements, made in and for eternity.

Temporal judgements demonstrate what is coming - we are to learn from them and change our behaviour; eternal judgement is for eternity and therefore final and irreversible. This will not occur until 'the Last Day' (John 6:39-40, 12:48), i.e. the last day of this era, which we will consider when we come to Revelation 20 in Book 7.[517]

We are all supposed to learn from how God dealt with Israel, as Ezekiel prophesied:

> "Therefore, thus says the Lord GOD, 'Behold, I, even I, am against you, and I will execute *judgments* among you *in the sight of the nations*." (Ezek 5:8*)

The Scriptures present a long record of temporal judgements against Israel and surrounding nations and cities as well as individuals. We find that:

(i) God executes temporal judgements as examples, confirming His standards before we face His eternal judgement.

(ii) Some are redemptive; others punitive of the irredeemable.

(iii) Others, however, are His refusing to intervene, leaving us to face the consequences of our sinful behaviour.

Obvious temporal judgements include the Fall, the Flood, the confusion of languages at Babel, the destruction of Sodom and Gomorrah, the plagues on Egypt, and the genocide of the Canaanites. The most profound of all, however, is the Crucifixion.

---

517 *Kingdom Come: Justice for All.*

Let us consider some of these.

'Example' Judgements

Some are specifically described as examples to forewarn us of what is inevitably going to happen to all of us at any time:

(i) The wilderness

In 1 Corinthians 10, Paul urges all of us who are Gentiles to learn the reasons for God's judgements, just as the ancient Jews did, from His judgements of Israel. The Hebrew slaves had begun their new life with spectacular signs and wonders after fleeing Egypt: they saw the Sea parted and were led by a pillar of cloud by day (vv. 1-2); they were fed manna from heaven and rocks split apart to provide water in the desert.[518]

> 5. Nevertheless, with most of them God was not well-pleased; for they were laid low in the wilderness.
> 6. Now these things happened as *examples* for us, *so that we would not crave evil things as they also craved.*
> (1 Cor 10:5-6*)

Reading on, we find that He judged His people for idolatry (v. 7), immorality (v. 8), testing Him (v. 10), and complaining (v. 10). The guilty died in the wilderness, missing out on the Promised Land, and we are to learn from this:

> 11. Now these things happened to them as *an example*, and they were *written for our instruction*, upon whom the ends of the ages have come.
> 12. Therefore let him who thinks he stands take heed that he does not fall. (1 Cor 10:11-12*)

'Example' here (vv. 6 & 11) is *tupos* in Greek and gives us our English word 'type' which means a shape or repeated pattern,

---

[518] He explains that these events prefigured our spiritual life, beginning with Jesus being the Rock that was struck to provide us with the Holy Spirit (1 Cor 10:4).

as on the *type*faces of a *type*writer which place the letters on the paper. Paul is explaining that we are all facing or will soon face these same temptations to leave God and His ways:

> 13. No temptation has overtaken you but such as is *common to man*; and God is faithful, who will not allow you to be tempted beyond what you are able, but with the temptation will provide the way of escape also, so that you will be able to endure it. (1 Cor 10:13*)

In these temporal judgements, we see God's attitude to these sins in His first nation ahead of His eternally judging "all the nations", i.e. every individual, on that Day.

(ii) Noah's Flood

We are also to learn from God's attitude to the sins of the world before the Flood:

> For if God did not… spare the ancient world, but preserved Noah… with seven others, when He brought a flood upon the world of the ungodly… then the Lord knows how to rescue the godly from temptation, and to keep the unrighteous under punishment for the day of judgment (2 Pet 2:4-5, 9*)

However, the issues were complicated by the presence of fallen angels and their hybrid children:

> 4. The *Nephilim* were on the earth in those days, and also afterward, when *the sons of God* came in to the daughters of men, and they bore children to them. Those were the mighty men who were of old, men of renown.
> 5. And the LORD saw that the wickedness of man was great on the earth, and that *every intent of the thoughts* of his heart was *only evil continually*.
> 6. The LORD was sorry that He had made man on the earth, and He was grieved in His heart…
> 8. But Noah found favor in the eyes of the LORD.
> (Gen 6:4-8*)

The Scriptures reveal that these 'sons of God'[519] were 'angels who did not keep their own domain, but abandoned their proper abode' (Jude 6) to have sexual intercourse with 'the daughters of men'; their hybrid children were called Nephilim,[520] 'the mighty men who were… men of renown' (v. 4).

Bizarrely, these demigods were worshipped in most ancient cultures.

In Graeco-Roman mythology, they were renowned for every kind of evil and immorality including murder, lying, theft, adultery, rape, incest, and bestiality - Zeus, the king of the Greek gods,[521] betrayed Hera,[522] his sister and wife, with the goddess Leto[523] who gave birth to Apollo[524] and Artemis;[525] he also assumed the form of a swan to seduce or rape Leda, a Spartan queen and mother of Helen of Troy. And he was the greatest of their gods!

The ancients did believe some, the Titans, were thoroughly evil, even though they reigned in what was called the Golden Age, and Zeus locked them up in Tartarus, i.e. the Greek underworld:

> Tartarus, the infernal regions of ancient Greek mythology. The name was originally used for the deepest region of the world, the lower of the two parts of the underworld, where the gods locked up their enemies. It gradually came to mean the entire underworld. As such it was the opposite of Elysium, where happy souls lived after death.[526]

---

519 Satan is named among 'the sons of God' in Job 1:6 and 2:1.
520 From the Hebrew verb 'to fall', Nephilim means 'a *feller*, that is, a *bully* or *tyrant*' (Strong's H5303). It is often translated as "giants" because the Septuagint has the Greek as *gigantes*.
521 The Romans accepted the Greek pantheon but changed their names so Zeus became Jupiter.
522 Greek goddess of marriage, called Juno by the Romans.
523 Greek goddess of motherhood, called Latona by the Romans.
524 Greek god of music, also called Apollo by the Romans.
525 Greek goddess of hunting, known by the Romans as Diana.
526 *Encyclopedia Britannica* www.britannica.com/topic/Tartarus, 24 Aug, 2022.

Peter uses this Greek expression when describing God's judgement of the sinful angels and humans in the Flood:

> ...God did not spare *angels* when they sinned, but *cast them into hell* [Grk verb, *tartaroo*, to cast into Tartarus] and committed them to *pits of darkness*, reserved for judgment; and did not spare the *ancient world*, but preserved Noah... (2 Pet 2:4*)

So what the Greeks called Titans, Peter includes in his description of 'angels' who 'sinned'. Jude also writes of fallen angels being 'kept in eternal bonds under darkness for the judgment of the great day' (Jude 6).

The Scriptures therefore record that only eight humans, Noah and his wife, their three sons and their wives, survived the Flood and, emerging from the ark on Mt Ararat, became the necessary new beginning for the human race without these angelic hybrids. Similarly, Egyptian mythology from Hermopolis has the Ogdoad (a group of eight gods, arranged in four couples) appearing on a mountain which rose out of primordial waters and creating the human race.[527]

The Crux

While the pagan mythologies agree with the Scriptures' historical record that there was a supernatural conflict that ended in cataclysmic judgement, they give very different reasons for it and therefore very different lessons to be learned.

(i) Punishment of the Titans

In Greek mythology, during what they called the Golden Age, Zeus condemned his father Cronus and the Titans to Tartarus for devouring his siblings and usurping Gaia, the primordial goddess of the earth, and Uranus, the primordial

---

527 https://ancientegyptonline.co.uk/ogdoad, 28 Aug, 2023.

god of the sky.[528] As noted above, however, Zeus was notoriously immoral. The Greeks and Romans therefore learned nothing from this judgement except that the gods are cruel, immoral, and capricious.

(ii) The Flood

In stark contrast, the Scriptures record the Flood as an historical event which demonstrates that God is perfectly righteous and consistent, judging men and angels for their wicked behaviour, intentions, and thoughts.

We need to learn the correct message of these judgements from the Scriptures, as Paul and Peter urged us in their very last letters (2 Tim 3:15-17, 2 Pet 1:16-21).

Sodom and Gomorrah

Jude the Lord's half-brother also spelled out the lessons we are to learn from not only the Flood judgement (v. 6) but also God's judgement of Sodom and Gomorrah:

> 6. And *angels* who did not keep their own domain, but abandoned their proper abode [before the flood], He has kept in eternal bonds under darkness for the judgment of the great day,
> 7. just as Sodom and Gomorrah and the cities around them, since they *in the same way as these indulged in gross immorality* and went after strange flesh, are *exhibited as an example* in undergoing the punishment of eternal fire. (Jude 6-7*)

The judgement of these cities was not by water this time but by fire, to be 'exhibited as an example' (v. 7), a type or foreshadowing of the 'eternal fire' (v. 7) of 'the judgment of the great day' (v. 6).

To this day, tourists marvel at the sulphur balls found there

---

528 https://ancientpal.com/why-did-zeus-imprison-the-titans, 26 Aug, 2022.

which are 98% pure sulphur, i.e. significantly more pure than naturally occurring sulphur and found nowhere else on earth, while scientists argue about a possible meteorite strike.[529]

So what exactly are we supposed to learn from this 'exhibit' and 'example' of God's temporal judgement? Most already know of the 'gross immorality' of 'Sodom and Gomorrah and the cities around them' (Jude 7) - homosexuality used to be called 'sodomy'. However, in Ezekiel, the Lord explains that Sodom's primary sin was their utterly self-indulgent lifestyle:

> "Behold, this was the guilt of your sister Sodom: she and her daughters had *arrogance, abundant food* and *careless ease*, but she *did not help* the poor and needy" (Ezek 16:49*)

The attempted rape of the two angels sent to rescue Lot and his family was only the last straw. Prior to His judgement, God had discussed it with Abraham (Gen 18:17-33), telling him:

> "The outcry of Sodom and Gomorrah is indeed great, and their sin is exceedingly grave" (Gen 18:20)

We are therefore to learn that God judged their "arrogance", "careless ease", and neglect of the "poor and needy".

Jesus also spelled this out in His parable of the sheep and goats where the rejected "goats" are those who neglect to feed the hungry and thirsty, show hospitality to strangers, clothe the naked, tend the sick, and visit those in prison (Matt 25:31-46).

---

[529] www.timesofisrael.com/evidence-of-sodom-meteor-blast-cause-of-biblical-destruction-say-scientists, 15 May, 2023.

The Canaanite Genocide

Two aspects of God's character are often misunderstood:

> Behold then the kindness *and* severity of God
> (Rom 14:22*)

Misunderstand His kindness and we can think that He is like a Father Christmas who would never judge anyone; misunderstand His severity and we worry that, like human tyrants everywhere, He is unjust.

The Hebrew slaves saw His kindness when He liberated them from slavery in Egypt, the most powerful empire in the Middle East in the 15th century BC, and promised them a land of their own, free from tyranny. However, they also saw His severity with the Egyptians and their gods (Ex 12:12) and knew that was well-deserved justice.

They were also about to see His 'take no-prisoners' judgement of Canaan and learn the reason why, as well as why they had been in Egypt for over four hundred years: they *had to wait* until the Amorites[530] were beyond redemption. As God explained to Abraham:

> 13. "Know for certain that your descendants will be strangers in a land that is not theirs, where they will be enslaved and oppressed *four hundred years*.
> 14. "But I will also judge the nation whom they will serve, and afterward they will come out with many possessions.
> 15. "As for you, you shall go to your fathers in peace; you will be buried at a good old age.
> 16. "Then in the fourth generation they will return here, for *the iniquity of the Amorite is not yet complete."*
> (Gen 15:13-16*)

---

530 This generic term, used interchangeably with Canaanite, includes the Kenites, Kenizzites, Kadmonites, Hittites, Perizzites, Rephaim, Amorites, Girgashites, and Jebusites (Gen 15:18-21) as well as the Hivites (Ex 23:23, 34:11).

In Abraham's time, Melchizedek,[531] the godly priest-king of Jerusalem, had welcomed him in the name of the Lord (Gen 14:18-20); 'four hundred years' and 'four generations' later,[532] Melchizedek's place has been taken by Adonizedek[533] who was a bitter opponent of God and Israel (Josh 10:1-5).

God warned Israel not to be like the Canaanites:

> 24. "Do not defile yourselves by any of these things; for by all these the nations which I am casting out before you have become defiled.
> 25. "For the land has become defiled, *therefore I have brought its punishment upon it,* so the land has spewed out its inhabitants." (Lev 18:24-25*)

Their defiling behaviour included incest (Lev 18:6-18), adultery (v. 20), child sacrifice (v. 21), homosexuality (v. 22), and bestiality (v. 23), as well as male and female temple prostitution (Deut 23:17).

There may therefore have been a medical as well as a moral reason for this judgement.

Richard Willcox (1912-1985) was a world-renowned venereologist[534] who recognised that 'the practice of such idolatry would be followed by retribution in the form of venereal disease'.[535] Writing in the British Medical Journal,[536] he diagnosed gonorrhoea and syphilis from the Scriptures' descriptions (Lev 15:2-12, Deut 28:27-28) and the drastic remedy, to the disastrous plague of Moab (Num 25:9, Deut 4:3).

---

531 Melchizedek translates as 'King of Righteousness' (Heb 7:2).
532 Abraham was one hundred years old when he finally sired Isaac, the promised heir (Gen 17:1).
533 Adoni-zedek translates as 'Lord of Righteousness' (Strong's H139).
534 Senior Assistant Medical Officer, Department of Venereal Diseases, St. Mary's Hospital, London; Physician in Charge, Department of Venereal Diseases, King Edward VII Hospital, Windsor; adviser in venereology to the British War Office as well as the World Health Organization.
535 R. R. Willcox, *Venereal Disease in the Bible*, p. 29. https://sti.bmj.com/content/25/1/28, 2 Nov, 2023.
536 Ibid, pp. 29-32.

We also see the patience of God.

When He made the covenant with Abraham, He warned him that his descendants would have to wait over 400 years in Egypt (Gen 15:13-15):

> "Then in the fourth generation they will return here, for *the iniquity of the Amorite* is not yet *complete*." (Gen 15:16*)

History records that they waited 430 years in Egypt (Ex 12:40) until the Amorites were beyond redemption.

Redemptive Judgements

God's judgement of Adam and Eve and their descendants aimed to redeem us from eternal separation from Himself. The curse of mortality, sickness, hatred, and hardship are the natural consequences of leaving the One who is immortal, healthy, loving, and caring - we are supposed to see for ourselves the effects of our separation and turn back to Him.

(i) Every individual

As Paul explained to the Athenians, God has set limitations on us all:

> 26. "...He made from one man every nation of mankind to live on all the face of the earth, *having determined* their *appointed times* and *the boundaries* of their habitation,
> 27. *that they would seek God*, if perhaps they might *grope for Him and find Him*..." (Acts 17:26-27*)

Every nation and/or empire has 'appointed times' to flourish and wane and 'boundaries' to their spread and power (v. 26) so that every individual will look beyond those. Despite any intellectual conclusions we may come to, we all have an inner sense that death is not normal. Solomon describes how God has created this inner dilemma in mankind:

> He has made everything appropriate in its time. He has also *set eternity in their heart*… (Ecc 3:11*)

Many of us have experienced the chilling recognition of our own mortality and begun to "seek God" as a consequence, feeling around as in the dark until we "find Him" (v. 27). Paul continues:

> …though He is not far from each one of us;
> 28. for *'in Him we live* and move and exist', as even some of your own poets have said, 'For we also are *His children*.'" (Acts 17:27-28*)

Paul is simply appealing to what they already sense as expressed by two of their most famous poets, Epimenides of Crete and Aratus of Cicilia.[537]

Alcoholics Anonymous have helped countless individuals out of addiction through their Twelve Step program which begins with them facing consequences:

> 1. We admitted we were powerless over alcohol—that our lives had become unmanageable.
>
> 2. Came to believe that a Power greater than ourselves could restore us to sanity.[538]

The next steps they found were to judge themselves accurately:

> 3. Made a decision to turn our will and our lives over to the care of God as we understood Him.
>
> 4. Made a searching and fearless moral inventory of ourselves.
>
> 5. Admitted to God, to ourselves, and to another human being the exact nature of our wrongs.

---

[537] Paul obviously knew Epimenides' poetry, also quoting him to Titus (Titus 1:12), and of Epimenides' connection to the Athenian altar to the unknown god (Acts 17:23). See Diogenes Laertius, *Lives of Eminent Philosophers*, R.D. Hicks, Ed., Chap 10, v. 110. www.perseus.tufts.edu/hopper/text?doc=Perseus%3Atext%3A1999.01.0258%3Abook%3D1%3Achapter%3D10, 15 May, 2023.

[538] https://alcohol.org/alcoholics-anonymous, 18 Aug, 2022.

> 6. Were entirely ready to have God remove all these defects of character.
> 7. Humbly asked Him to remove our shortcomings. [539]

This is just as Paul explained to the Corinthians:

> 31. But if we judged ourselves rightly, we would not be judged.
> 32. But *when we are judged*, we are *disciplined* by the Lord so that we will *not be condemned* along with the world. (1 Cor 11:31-32*)

As considered earlier, Paul was urging them to learn from God's judging of His first nation Israel in the wilderness (1 Cor 10:1-13).

These temporal judgements are to discipline us in order to redeem us.

(ii) Non-intervention

Sometimes, God's judgement is to not intervene. He want us to learn cause and effect so, as every good human parent does from time to time, He leaves us to face the consequences of our actions or behaviour. In Chapter 8, I gave the example of Paul's explanation, though often misunderstood, to the Romans regarding idolatry:

> 18. For *the wrath of God is revealed* from heaven against all ungodliness and unrighteousness of men who suppress the truth in unrighteousness… (Rom 1:18*)

Paul spelled out this idolatry:

> 22. Professing to be wise, they became fools,
> 23. and exchanged the glory of the incorruptible God for an image in the form of corruptible man and of birds and four-footed animals and crawling creatures. (Rom 1:22-23)

---

539   https://alcohol.org/alcoholics-anonymous, 18 Aug, 2022.

How is God's wrath 'revealed' here? He lets us follow our own hearts:

> 24. Therefore God *gave them over* in the lusts of *their hearts* to impurity, so that their bodies would be dishonored among them...
> 26. *For this reason* God gave them over to degrading passions; for their women exchanged the natural function for that which is unnatural,
> 27. and in the same way also the men abandoned the natural function of the woman and burned in their desire toward one another, men with men committing indecent acts and receiving in their own persons *the due penalty* of their error. (Rom 1:24-27*)

'The due penalty' (v. 27) is getting our own way. If we do not want to think properly, He *lets* us:

> 28. And just as they did not see fit to acknowledge God any longer, God *gave them over* to a *depraved mind*, to do those things which are not proper,
> 29. being filled with all unrighteousness, wickedness, greed, evil; full of envy, murder, strife, deceit, malice... (Rom 1:28-29*)

In my own life, until I was twenty-three, I paid the due penalty of facing the consequences of my own stupidity.

As a devout atheist and evolutionist, at age seventeen and 'professing to be wise', I threw aside the standards of my upright parents and family. After six years, I was as broken-hearted and humiliated as the prodigal son (Luke 15:11-19) but was just as generously welcomed and restored by God and my family (Luke 15:20-32).

More to be feared is God not judging us as His people because He has given up on us. The writer to the Hebrews quotes Proverbs 3:11-12 to encourage us:

> 5. ... "MY SON, DO NOT REGARD LIGHTLY THE DISCIPLINE OF THE LORD, NOR FAINT WHEN YOU ARE REPROVED BY HIM;
> 6. FOR THOSE WHOM THE LORD LOVES HE DISCIPLINES, AND HE SCOURGES EVERY SON WHOM HE RECEIVES."
> 7. It is for discipline that you endure; God deals with you as with sons; for what son is there whom his father does not discipline?
> 8. But *if you are without discipline*, of which all have become partakers, then *you are illegitimate children and not sons*. (Heb 5-8*)

If God is still disciplining us, still correcting, reproving, or rebuking us, that is wonderful evidence that we are indeed His children.

(iii) The Crucifixion

Although temporal, it is also eternal because it was done 'once for all' (Heb 9:12) for eternity:

> ...Christ, who *through the eternal Spirit* offered Himself without blemish to God... (Heb 9:14*)

On the cross, Jesus drank 'the cup of the wine of wrath' of God (Jer 25:15, Matt 26:39) for all the sins of all mankind for all time! In this one stupendous event, God demonstrates His justice in punishing all sin while providing a vindication for all who trust in Him:

> ...displayed publicly... to demonstrate *His righteousness*... at the present time, so that He would *be just* and *the justifier* of the one who has faith in Jesus (Rom 3:25-26*)

All of these temporal judgements were redemptive but although the seven bowls of wrath are temporal, they are not redemptive – they are the final judgement of mankind's arrogant, selfish, and greedy government of our dominion, the land, sea, and sky of the old earth.

Summary

(i) The seven golden bowls were a familiar image to John's 1st century audience, whether Roman, Greek, or Jewish, because they all used them in worship. The Jews, however, had a history of God using these temple bowls as a metaphor for His wrath being poured out.

(ii) The metaphor signifies that atonement was no longer being made but justice was being administered where it was due so it was not randomly applied but targeted.

(iii) The Jews had also had it explained to them throughout their sacred historical record, the Scriptures, why God was judging and how to avoid His judgements through atonement.

(iv) They also knew that temporal judgements were aimed at redemption, forewarnings of final judgements and the Last Day when He will hold every individual accountable for the life they have lived.

(v) The Crucifixion was the ultimate demonstration of God judging justly while simultaneously justifying all who believe in Jesus as our atoning sacrifice.

(vi) All warnings completed, every opportunity given, God will then end every aspect of mankind's dominion of the old earth.

21
Bowl by Bowl
Hoping for Repentance

As we saw in Chapter 8, the first four trumpets are to alert us to what we are doing to ourselves in four areas of our dominion: the earth, the sea, the freshwater, and the earth's atmosphere. The first four bowls affect the same four areas.

In the Temple, the golden bowls were to hold either blood from the sacrifices or wine poured out as a libation but John's bowls are specifically a metaphor for God pouring out His wrath in each area:

> 1. Then I heard a loud voice from the temple, saying to the seven angels, "Go and pour out on the earth the seven bowls of the wrath of God." (Rev 16:1)

For believers, this will not be as appalling as it seems because as we will see, the bowls will be targeted and very brief, the second and third bowls occurring instantaneously when 'the present heavens and earth' are replaced by the 'new heavens and a new earth'.

The First Bowl

The first *trumpet* was to sound the alarm when mankind has destroyed a third of the trees on the earth. Accordingly, the first *bowl* is God's judgement on mankind on the earth:

> 2. So the first angel went and poured out his bowl *on the earth*; and it became a loathsome and malignant sore *on the people* who had *the mark of the beast* and who *worshiped his image*. (Rev 16:2*)

As you can see, however, the judgement is targeted at only those bearing the mark of the beast.

(i) Those marked

The beast is the first beast of Revelation 13:1-10 which, as I showed in Book 2,[540] is the seven-headed 'principality and power' formed by the Gentile empires that had ruled and would rule over Israel.[541] Governing authorities are called to be 'servants of God' in upholding justice (Rom 13:1-7) but this principality became a Feral State,[542] demanding worship of itself - in John's day, the Romans had personified their Empire as *Dea Roma*, lit. the Goddess Rome.

This may seem odd today until we learn that 'worship', from the Old English word 'worth-ship', means to give ultimate worth or value to something. Whatever we most value, we are actually 'worshipping' e.g. Mammon, i.e. money, rather than God (Luke 16:13) or, in this case, obeying the State rather than God (Acts 4:19).

The beast's living 'image' (Rev 13:14-15) is any human believed to embody that State; in John's day, the Romans had deified their emperors. Beginning in Pergamum early in the 1st century BC, they worshipped *Dea Roma et Augustus*, i.e. the Roman Empire and Augustus Caesar[543] - 'the beast and his image'.

Two thousand years later, in the 20th century, we can see the Japanese worshipped the Empire of the Rising Sun and Emperor Hirohito; the Italians worshipped the Italian State and Mussolini; the Russians worshipped the Rodina and Stalin;

---

540 *Slouching Towards Bethlehem*, pp. 36-48, 92-102.
541 Explained by the angel as "five have fallen (Egypt, Assyria, Babylon, Medo-Persia, and Greece), one is (Rome), the other has not yet come (All the nations)" in Revelation 17:10.
542 I coined this term from John's description of a beast, in contrast to the secular term 'rogue state' which is a state or nation acting outside of the accepted international norms and policies.
543 Ibid, pp. 98-102.

the Germans worshipped the Third Reich and Hitler.[544]

In our day, in this last hour, I believe the principality and power of the blasphemous Feral State is manifesting as the seventh head with its ten horns in the United Nations - it is no accident that many want it to be the highest authority on earth. I also believe that its living image will be the Antichrist who will emerge from the Islamic nations.[545]

Those obeying the beast and its image will bear the ownership 'mark of the beast' in direct contrast to those trusting in Jesus who bear the mark of God's ownership on their hand and forehead, as covered in Book 3.[546]

(ii) The sore

The 'loathsome and malignant sore' - is it literal or metaphorical?

In Chapter 7, I summarised the ten judgements God passed on the Egyptians for enslaving the Hebrews. The sixth was 'boils breaking out with sores… on all the Egyptians' (Ex 9:9-10), causing some of them to repent and believe Moses when he warned of the seventh plague, the hailstorm. The 1st Bowl's sores may therefore be literal.

However, it seems more likely to me that this sore is a metaphor for the public and very painful regret of unbelievers, as experienced throughout Germany during World War II when Hitler's Third Reich began its death spiral. Some afflicted by the 1st Bowl may also repent when they see the consequences of their trusting in the Antichrist.

Either way, as will become obvious with the other six bowls, this judgement will not last very long.

The Second Bowl

The 2nd Trumpet was to sound the alarm at what we have done to and on the sea, killing a third of its living creatures

---

544 Ibid, pp. 103-107.
545 *Slouching Towards Bethlehem*, pp. 153-173, 212-221; *Threshing Hour*, pp. 45-46.
546 *Gotta Serve Somebody*.

and destroying a third of the ships. Accordingly, the 2nd Bowl strikes the sea:

> The second angel poured out his bowl into the sea, and it became blood like that of a dead man; and every living thing in the sea died. (Rev 16:3)

Is this literal or metaphorical? It is obviously metaphorical to turn the sea into blood, which is a metaphor for death, but literally 'every living thing' there will die. It will occur instantaneously when the old heavens and earth pass away, as Peter explained:

> 7. But by His word *the present heavens and earth* are being reserved for fire, kept for the day of judgment and destruction of ungodly men…
> 12. …[on] the day of God, because of which *the heavens will be destroyed* by burning, and *the elements will melt* with intense heat!
> 13. But according to His promise we are looking for *new heavens and a new earth*, in which righteousness dwells. (2 Pet 3:7-13*)

John saw that the new earth will not have a sea:

> Then I saw a new heaven and a new earth; for the first heaven and the first earth passed away, and *there is no longer any sea*. (Rev 21:1*)

In Biblical days, the sea was also referred to as the abyss, as noted in Book 4:

> The abyss, from the Greek, *abussos*, meaning 'bottomless', means the depths of the sea and, in Hebrew thinking, symbolised the place of the dead (Rom 10:7, Rev 20:13) and of evil spirits (Luke 8:31, Rev 9:11). Accordingly, the dead are raised from 'the sea' as well as from 'death and Hades' (Rev 20:13) and 'there is no longer any sea'

in the new heaven and new earth (Rev 21:1). I see this as symbolic, signifying not that God will change His mind about saltwater or surfing but that evil will no longer have a hiding place. The sea also symbolises "peoples and multitudes and nations and tongues" (Rev 17:15. Also Dan 7:3 & 17), i.e. ungodly Gentiles.[547]

'The sea' also symbolised where Leviathan lives so Isaiah writes of Judgement Day as:

> ... that day [when] the LORD will punish *Leviathan* the fleeing serpent,
> With His fierce and great and mighty sword,
> Even Leviathan the twisted serpent;
> And He will kill *the dragon* who lives in *the sea*. (Isa 27:1*)

Leviathan was the Hebrew name for the fire-breathing dragon (Job 41:1-34), as covered in Book 1, so there being no sea simply means there will be no place for Leviathan, evil spirits, demons, and the dead. We will look at this again in Book 7, *Kingdom Come*.

The 2nd Bowl literally and instantly ends life in the sea but also signifies that evil will have nowhere to hide.

The Third Bowl

The 3rd Trumpet was to sound the alarm at what we have done to a third of our freshwater; the 3rd Bowl takes that to its logical conclusion:

> 4. Then the third angel poured out his bowl into the rivers and the springs of waters; and they became blood.
> (Rev 16:4)

Is this literal or metaphorical? As with the 2nd Bowl, it is obviously metaphorical, but with the literal passing away of

---

547 *Silencing the Witnesses*, p. 219, footnote 259; *Slouching Towards Bethlehem*, p. 21.

the old heavens and earth, there will again be no more need for this 'old' water.

The 3rd bowl illustrates the perfect justice of it all, as John hears in a heavenly dialogue:

> 5. And I heard the angel of the waters saying, "Righteous are You, who are and who were, O Holy One, because You judged these things;
> 6. for they *poured out the blood* of saints and prophets, and You have given them *blood to drink*. They deserve it."
> 7. And I heard the altar saying, "Yes, O Lord God, the Almighty, true and righteous are Your judgments."
> (Rev 16:5-7*)

Again the judgement is targeted at the guilty, those who have killed the 'saints and prophets' (v. 6). And again, this will be virtually instantaneous.

The Fourth Bowl

We saw that the 4th Trumpet was to sound the alarm on the darkening of a third of the sun, moon, and stars which seems to be due to air pollution by day and artificial light pollution by night creating today's phenomenon of global dimming:

> 12. The fourth angel *sounded*, and a third of *the sun* and a third of the *moon* and a third of the *stars* were struck, so that *a third* of them would be *darkened* and the day would not shine for a third of it, and the night in the same way.
> (Rev 8:12*)

Here in Revelation 16, the 4th Bowl similarly targets the sun but increases its heat:

> 8. The fourth angel poured out his bowl upon the sun, and it was given to it to scorch men with fire.
> 9. Men were scorched with fierce heat; and they blasphemed the name of God who has the power over

these plagues, and they did not repent so as to give Him glory. (Rev 16:8-9)

This judgement is not fatal - no one is killed by it - but it is targeted at the unrepentant in hope that they would repent even at the last minute (v. 9).

So what of those already repentant? Abraham was a friend of God and when they were discussing His imminent judgment on Sodom and Gomorrah, Abraham confidently asked:

> 23. "Will You indeed sweep away the righteous with the wicked? ...
> 25. "Far be it from You to do such a thing, to slay the righteous with the wicked, so that the righteous and the wicked are treated alike.
> Far be it from You! Shall not the Judge of all the earth deal justly?" (Gen 18:23-25)

Obviously He will "deal justly".

Isaiah had a similar prediction to the 4th Bowl:

> The light of the moon will be as the light of the sun, and the light of *the sun* will be *seven times brighter*, like the light of seven days, on the day the LORD binds up the fracture of *His people* and heals the bruise He has inflicted. (Isa 30:26*)

This sevenfold increase in the sun's light is actually healing for 'His people' and metaphorically, an increase in spiritual enlightenment day and night.

So is the 4th Bowl's heating up the sun literal or metaphorical?

If literal, we know that when Nebuchadnezzar had the blazing furnace heated *'seven times* more than it was usually heated' (Dan 3:19*), its flames scorched and killed their executioners while Shadrach, Meshach and Abed-nego were not harmed at all. They were actually set free, their bonds burned up when the Lord appeared with them in the fire (Dan 3:23-27).

However, as we will see with the 5th Bowl, the hotter sun could be a metaphor in counterpoint to that. The Davidic Covenant included a promise:

> "His descendants shall endure forever
> And *his throne as the sun* before Me. (Psa 89:36*)

This promise to Jesus of His throne being 'as the sun' would therefore be not only truly glorious but also enlightening to all His subjects and they too will reflect His glory:

> "Thus let all Your enemies perish, O LORD;
> But let those who love Him be like the rising of *the sun in its might*." (Jdg 5:31*)

Solomon's general wisdom would therefore have an end-time fulfilment:

> ...the path of the righteous is like the light of dawn,
> That shines brighter and brighter until the full day.
> (Prov 4:18)

The 4th Bowl being metaphorical could therefore mean that in the last hour, Jesus and His disciples will produce so much light that unbelievers will find it very painful.

The Fifth Bowl

The 5th Trumpet was to sound the alarm about a season of a plague of demonic locusts tormenting all without the mark of God and who worship the beast; the 5th Bowl increases the torment for the beast's followers as his kingdom becomes 'darkened':

> 10. Then the fifth angel poured out his bowl on *the throne of the beast*, and *his kingdom became darkened*; and they gnawed their tongues because of pain,

> 11. and they blasphemed the God of heaven because of their pains and their sores; and they did not repent of their deeds. (Rev 16:10-11*)

As noted in Chapter 7, this is an obvious parallel with the ninth plague of the Exodus which lasted three days: Clearly supernatural, the 'thick darkness' came with a sense of dread - "a darkness which may be felt" (Ex 10:21) - but only for the Egyptians. Again, God's plan is that unbelievers will repent (Rev 16:11) as the beast's true nature becomes more and more apparent.

In the antichrist regimes of 20th century - Hitler's Germany, Stalin's Russia, Mao's China - as these tyrants neared their end, they became increasingly unhinged. I commented on the 1st Bowl that the spell was broken for the Germans when Hitler died but many had come to their senses earlier.

Albert Speer, for example, had been Hitler's closest friend but when he learned of Hitler's orders to destroy Germany's infrastructure ahead of the advancing Allied troops, he countermanded those orders. At the Nuremberg trials, he was sentenced to 20 years in Spandau Prison where the Protestant chaplain, Georges Casalis described him as "the most guilt-ridden, the most tortured man I had ever met[548]... By the time I left Spandau [in 1950], I saw him as the most repentant."[549]

Mao Zedong's designated successor, Liu Shaoqi, similarly tried in 1962 to overturn Mao's Great Leap Forward in which the collectivisation of small farms caused widespread famine and the deaths of 43 million Chinese peasants.[550] Liu worked with General Secretary Deng Xiaoping to rescue

---

548 Gitta Sereny, *Albert Speer: His Battle With Truth*, London; Macmillan, 1995, pp. 22-23.
549 Ibid, p. 13.
550 Frank Dikötter, *Mao's Great Famine: The History of China's Most Devastating Catastrophe, 1958-1962*, New York; Bloomsbury and Walker Press, 2010. Also Jung Chang and Jon Halliday, *Mao: The Unknown Story*, London; Jonathan Cape, 2005, pp. 456-457.

the economy and import grain to combat the famine but in 1968, he was imprisoned and died the following year. Deng Xiaoping survived the purges to become President (1978-1989), posthumously "rehabilitating" Liu in 1980 and overturning Mao's disastrous economic policies.[551]

Stalin's murderous regime was not exposed until after he died with Nikita Khrushchev finally denouncing his appalling excesses in 1956.[552]

Tragically, however, while these successors partially repented in denouncing the antichrist of their time, they continued to 'blaspheme the God of heaven' (Rev 16:11). It seems this will be repeated in the time of the coming Antichrist.

The Sixth Bowl

The 6th Trumpet was to sound the alarm about the effects of mankind's warfare and technology on a third of the world's population; the 6th Bowl allows mankind to gather for our last ever war at Har-Magedon:

> 12. The sixth angel poured out his bowl on the great river, the Euphrates; and its water was dried up, so that the way would be prepared for the kings from the east.
> 13. And I saw coming out of the mouth of the dragon and

---

[551] *Encyclopedia Britannica* notes that 'Deng restored China to domestic stability and economic growth after the disastrous excesses of the Cultural Revolution. Under his leadership, China acquired a rapidly growing economy, rising standards of living, considerably expanded personal and cultural freedoms, and growing ties to the world economy. Deng also left in place a mildly authoritarian government that remained committed to the CCP's one-party rule even while it relied on free-market mechanisms to transform China into a developed country' (www.britannica.com/biography/Deng-Xiaoping, 22 Feb, 2023). His reforms increased their GDP by over 8% per year for thirty years and China now has the second largest economy in the world. Although Deng presided over the crackdown on the Tiananmen Square democracy protest in 1989, he also freed many Christians from prison, financially compensating them for wrongful imprisonment. I met one underground church leader who was released after 25 years and given an apartment in Shanghai.

[552] www.historytoday.com/archive/months-past/stalin-denounced-nikita-khrushchev, 22 Feb, 2023.

> out of the mouth of the beast and out of the mouth of the false prophet, three unclean spirits like frogs…
> 16. And they gathered them together to the place which in Hebrew is called Har-Magedon. (Rev 16:12-16*)

As I established in Book 5, *Threshing Hour: Armageddon & Babylon the Great*, this war will be for the control of just one city, Jerusalem. That is why the 6th Bowl is poured out on the Euphrates River, the northern boundary of the land God promised to Abraham, Isaac, and Jacob and their descendants as an everlasting possession. We will look at this battle again when we come to Revelation Chapter 20 in Book 7, *Kingdom Come*, where it is also called the Battle of Gog and Magog (Rev 20:7-9).

This last-ever battle which seems to be fast approaching will be the ultimate rebellion against God and therefore leads to the seventh and last bowl of wrath.

The Seventh Bowl

We now come to the last:

> 17. Then the seventh angel poured out his bowl upon the air, and a loud voice came out of the temple from the throne, saying, "It is done." (Rev 16:17)

As noted in Chapter 1, the effect will be catastrophic:

> 18. And there were flashes of *lightning* and sounds and peals of *thunder*…
> 21. And huge *hailstones*, about one hundred pounds each, came down from heaven upon men; and men blasphemed God because of the plague of the hail, because its plague was extremely severe. (Rev 16:18 & 21*)

The seventh plague on Egypt was an unprecedented 'very heavy hail' which struck down everything still out in the field, 'both man and beast... every plant... and shattered every tree' except 'in the land of Goshen, where the sons of Israel were' (Ex 9:25-26). What John sees are huge, 30 kg blocks of ice.

When the five Canaanite kings came against Joshua and Israel's army, God rained down 'large hailstones from heaven' and 'there were more who died from the hailstones than those whom the sons of Israel killed with the sword' (Jos 10:11).

The 7th Bowl will also have a staggering effect on the earth and sea:

> 18. ...and there was *a great earthquake*, such as there had not been since man came to be upon the earth, so great an earthquake was it, and so mighty...
> 20. And *every island* fled away, and *the mountains* were not found. (Rev 16:18 & 20*)

'Every island' and mountain disappearing means the end of the physical world and, as covered in Book 5, the end of the whole spiritual 'world' known as Babylon the Great:

> 19. The great city was split into three parts, and the cities of the nations fell. Babylon the Great was remembered before God, to give her the cup of the wine of His fierce wrath. (Rev 16:19)

The Jewish disciples would have readily remembered the original 'Babylon the Great' (Dan 4:30) also being split into three by Darius the Mede (Dan 6:2) when it fell in 539 BC. The fall of this Babylon will be the end of what Jesus called "the present age" (Mark 10:30) and Paul, 'this present evil age' (Gal 1:4).

Jewish History 101

As frightening as this 7th Bowl may seem for us today, the Jewish disciples in John's 1st century audience would have recognised it as their coming vindication and liberation - this is just what happens when God Himself steps into a battle. They actually celebrated His thunderstorms, lightning, hailstones, and earthquakes throughout their national history.

As covered in Book 5,[553] the prophetic name of the Last Battle - Har-Magedon - comes from Israel's famous victory over Sisera's invading armies at Megiddo. As Deborah described it:

> 4. "LORD, when You went out from Seir,
> When You marched from the field of Edom,
> *The earth quaked*, the heavens also dripped,
> Even the clouds dripped water.
> 5. "The *mountains quaked* at the presence of the LORD,
> This Sinai, at the presence of the LORD, the God of Israel…
> (Jud 5:4-5*)

Not only did the earth shake but the heavens joined in:

> 19. "…At Taanach near the waters of Megiddo…
> 20. "*The stars fought* from heaven,
> From their courses they fought against Sisera.
> 21. "The torrent of Kishon swept them away,
> The ancient torrent, the torrent Kishon." (Jud 5:19-21*)

John's 7th Bowl, however, is on a much vaster scale. This time the earthquake causes *every* mountain and *every* island to disappear; this time the storm has hailstones so huge that God's enemies will simply not survive at Har-Magedon, i.e. Jerusalem.

John's Jewish audience would also have celebrated at every Passover their ancestors being protected from the hailstones of the Exodus and, forty years later, the Canaanite armies being destroyed by hailstones in the Promised Land (Jos 10:9-11).

---

553   *Threshing Hour.*

Comparing these historic episodes to Revelation's 7th Bowl, some argue that John's earthquake and hailstones will be metaphorical but I believe they may be literal.

Haggai's Prediction

Haggai was one of the last of Israel's prophets and in 520 BC (Hag 1:1), he predicted that the earth's last earthquake will be uniquely cataclysmic:

> 6. "For thus says the LORD of hosts, 'Once more in a little while, I am going to shake *the heavens* and *the earth, the sea* also and *the dry land.*
> 7. "'I will shake *all the nations*; and they will come with *the wealth of all nations*, and I will fill this house with glory...'" (Hag 2:6-7*)

"All the nations" here means that every single human being, both the living and the resurrected dead, will metaphorically pay tribute to Him by admitting that He is indeed King of kings and Lord of lords.

As for the shaking, the author of Hebrews gives us the inspired interpretation *as understood* by John's 1st century Jewish audience:

> 26. ...He has promised, saying, "YET ONCE MORE I WILL SHAKE NOT ONLY THE EARTH, BUT ALSO THE HEAVEN."
> 27. This expression, "Yet once more," denotes *the removing of those things which can be shaken*, as of created things, so that those things which cannot be shaken may remain.
> 28. Therefore, since we receive a kingdom which cannot be shaken, let us show gratitude... (Heb 12:26-28*)

Those disciples would therefore have recognised John's description of the 7th Bowl as exactly fulfilling Haggai's prophecy that the heavens, 'the dry land' with all its cities and its highest mountains, and 'every island' in the sea will be 'removed':

> 18. and there was a great earthquake, such as *there had not been* since man came to be upon the earth, so great an

earthquake was it, and so mighty...
19. ...and *the cities of the nations fell*...
20. And *every island fled away*, and *the mountains were not found*. (Rev 16:18-20*)

Summary

(i) The seven bowls of wrath are God's final temporal judgements before He judges for all eternity, targeted at unbelievers to bring about last-minute repentance.

(ii) The 1st Bowl produces painful sores on the followers of the Antichrist. While these may be literal, I believe they are more likely to be a metaphor, signifying his followers facing the awful consequences of their choices, and some will turn to Jesus.

(iii) The 2nd Bowl ends all life in the sea but also signifies there will be nowhere for evil to hide.

(iv) The 3rd Bowl turns our freshwater not into literal blood but signifies the end of all life there, metaphorically targeting all who have spilled blood.

(v) The 4th Bowl on the sun only affects the unrepentant if literal; if metaphorical, it signifies that Jesus and believers will produce so much light that unbelievers will find it unbearable.

(vi) The 5th does not affect believers but reveals the Antichrist's darkness to all of his followers on the earth.

(vii) The 6th Bowl is the releasing of all the forces, demonic and human, to gather for the Last Battle for Jerusalem.

(viii) The 7th Bowl is God destroying all of these forces from the heavens above and the earth and sea beneath them when Jesus returns as the King of Kings and Lord of Lords.

Epilogue

This book surveys the seven seals, seven trumpets, and seven bowls of the Book of Revelation which graphically illustrate the temporal judgements of God.

The seals reveal it is the Father's will to let us face the consequences of our misrule of the earth and to not intervene until Jesus returns as the true and worthy King.

The trumpets are to warn us of where we have come to when we have destroyed a third of our dominion of the earth, the sea, the freshwater, and the first 'heaven' or atmosphere, caused extraordinary torment, and killed a third of mankind. When we have fulfilled the first six, which is the number of man, the seventh will announce Jesus' return.

The bowls are God at last intervening in time before His eternal judgement.

In all of these, we can see the extraordinary insight of Elihu, trusting in the character of our God:

> 10. "Therefore, listen to me, you men of understanding.
> *Far be it from God to do wickedness,*
> *And from the Almighty to do wrong.*
> 11. "For He pays a man according to his work,
> And makes him find it according to his way.
> 12. "Surely, God will not act wickedly,
> And the Almighty will not pervert justice. (Job 34:10-12*)

As our Creator, He has every right to give up on us:

> 13. "Who gave Him authority over the earth?
> And who has laid on Him the whole world?
> 14. "If He should determine to do so,
> If He should gather to Himself His spirit and His breath,
> 15. All flesh would perish together,
> And man would return to dust." (Job 34:13-15)

Hopefully, this book has illustrated God's awesome love and patience while He has waited for us to learn from our sinfulness and foolishness, to turn to Him for His justice and forgiveness.

In the next and last book in this series, Book 7, *Kingdom Come: Justice for All*, we come to the last three chapters of the Bible, Revelation 20-22, and consider where we will all go from here.

Bibliography

Books

Carlé, Graeme.
>1998. *Because of the Angels: Unveiling 1 Corinthians 11:2-16*. Auckland: Emmaus Road Publishing
>2001. *The Red Heifer's Ashes: Mysteries of Ancient Israel,* Auckland, Emmaus Road Publishing

2011. *Dancing in the Dragon's Jaws: The Mystery of Israel's Survival,* Auckland: Emmaus Road Publishing
2012. *Slouching Towards Bethlehem: The Rise of the Antichrists,* Auckland: Emmaus Road Publishing
2014. *Gotta Serve Somebody: The Mystery of the Marks & 666,* Auckland: Emmaus Road Publishing
2017. *Silencing the Witnesses: Jerusalem & the Ascent of Secularism,* Auckland: Emmaus Road Publishing
2023. *Threshing Hour: Armageddon & Babylon the Great,* Auckland: Emmaus Road Publishing

Dikotter, F. 2020. *Mao's Great Famine: The History of China's Most Devastating Catastrophe, 1958-62*, New York; Walker & Co

Erickson, Millard J. 1998. *A Basic Guide to Eschatology: Making Sense of the Millennium*, Grand Rapids, MI: Baker Books.

Garnsey, P. 2000. The Land, in *Cambridge Ancient History: The High Empire A.D. 70–192*. Cambridge University Press

Guy, Laurie. 2004. *Introducing Early Christianity: A Topical Survey of Its Life, Beliefs & Practices*, Downers Grove, IL: InterVarsity Press
2009. *Making Sense of the Book of Revelation,* Oxford: Regent's Park College with Smyth & Helwys Publishing
2016. *Unlocking Revelation,* Bletchley, UK: Paternoster Press

Hendriksen, W. 1986. *More than Conquerors: An Interpretation of the Book of Revelation*, Grand Rapids, MI; Baker Book House

Jeremiah, D, 2008. *What in the World is Going On? 10 Prophetic Clues You Cannot Afford to Ignore*, Nashville, TN; Thomas Nelson

Kennedy, Jonathan. 2023. *Pathogenesis: How Germs Made History*, London: Torva

Kenyon, Paul. 2019. *Dictatorland: The Men Who Stole Africa*, London; Head of Zeus Ltd

LaHaye, Tim & Jenkins, Jerry B.
    1999. *Apollyon: The Destroyer is Unleashed*, Wheaton, Ill; Tyndale Publishing House
    1999. *Are We Living in the End Times? Current Events Foretold in Scripture… And What They Mean*. Wheaton, Ill: Tyndale House Publishers
    1999. *Assassins (Assignment: Jerusalem, Target: Antichrist)*, Wheaton, Ill; Tyndale House Publishers

Lindsey, Hal, with Carlson, Carole C. 1970. *The Late, Great Planet Earth*, Grand Rapids, MI; Zondervan

Miller, Nathan. 1995. *War at Sea - A Naval History of World War II*, New York; Scribner

Murray, Douglas. 2018. *The Strange Death of Europe: Immigration, Identity, Islam*, London; Bloomsbury Continuum

Sebag-Montefiore, Hugh. 2006. *Dunkirk: Fight to the Last Man*, New York; Viking

Sereny, Gitta. 1995. *Albert Speer: His Battle With Truth*, London; Macmillan

Shotter, D. C. A, 2005. Augustus Caesar, New York: Routledge, 2nd edition

Terraine, John. 1989. *Business in Great Waters: The U-Boat Wars, 1916-1945*, London; Leo Cooper

Thurston, Robert W. 1998. *Life and Terror in Stalin's Russia, 1934-1941*. Yale University Press,

Virgil. 37-29 BC. *The Works of Virgil*, Vol 2, trans. Dryden, 1792.

Westcott Allan Ferguson et al, *American Sea Power Since 1775*, Chicago; J.B. Lippincott Company

Wilkinson, Toby. 2015. *The Nile: Travelling Downriver Through Egypt's Past and Present*, New York; Knopf Doubleday Publishing Group

Willmott, H. P., *The Last Century of Sea Power: From Port Arthur to*

Chanak, 1894–1922, Volume 1, 2009. Indiana University Press
Wright, N.T. *Revelation for Everyone*, Louisville, KY; Westminster John Knox Press, 2011

Books Online

Diogenes Laertius, *Lives of Eminent Philosophers*, R.D. Hicks, Ed. www.perseus.tufts.edu/hopper/text?

Josephus, Flavius. *Antiquities of the Jews*. www.academia.edu/32013960/Complete_Works_of_Josephus_pdf
 The Wars of the Jews. www.gutenberg.org/files/2850/2850-h/2850-h.htm

Memnon of Heraclea, *History*. www.attalus.org/translate/memnon2.html,

Partington, J.R. *A History of Greek Fire and Gunpowder*. https://archive.org/details/historyofgreekfi00part/page/3

Pliny the Elder *The Natural History*, Book 2, www.perseus.tufts.edu/hopper/text?doc=Plin.%20Nat.%202.110&lang=original

Plutarch, *Lives: The Life of Crassus*. https://penelope.uchicago.edu/Thayer/E/Roman/Texts/Plutarch/Lives/Crassus*.html
 The Life of Sulla, https://penelope.uchicago.edu/Thayer/E/Roman/Texts/Plutarch/Lives/Sulla*.html#ref43

Ramsay, W.H. 1994. *The Letters to the Seven Churches of Asia, and Their Place in the Plan of the Apocalypse*. www.ccel.org/ccel/Ramsay/letters.i.html

Strabo, *Geography* Book XVI. www.perseus.tufts.edu/hopper/text?doc=Perseus%3Atext%3A1999.01.0239%3Abook%3D16

Tacitus. Publius Cornelius. c. 100 AD. *The Histories*. www.gutenberg.org/files/16927/16927-h/16927-h.htm#BOOK_V

Thucydides, *History of the Peloponnesian War*, Book 4. www.perseus.tufts.edu/hoppertext?doc=urn:cts:greekLit:tlg0003.tlg001.perseus-eng3

Bible Translations

Authorised (AV) or *King James Version (KJV)*, 1611. Oxford: Oxford University Press
Christian Standard Bible (CSB), 2012. Nashville, TN: B&H Publishing
Contemporary English Version (CEV), 1995. Philadelphia, PA: American Bible Society
Darby Bible (DBY), 1890.
English Standard Version (ESV), 2001. Wheaton, IL: Crossway
New American Standard (NASB), 1970. La Habra, CA: The Lockman Foundation
New International Version (NIV), 1978. Grand Rapids, MI: Zondervan Bible Publishers
New King James Version (NKJV), 1992. Nashville, TN: Thomas Nelson Publishers
New Revised Standard Version (NRSV), 1989. New York: American Bible Society
Revised Standard Version (RSV), 1971. New York: Collins
Schofield Reference Bible, 1909. Oxford University Press
The Jewish Study Bible, ed. Adele Berlin and Marc Zvi Brettler. 2004. Oxford University Press
The Kingdom New Testament (A Contemporary Translation), 2011. N.T. Wright. New York: HarperOne Publishers
The New Oxford Annotated Bible (New Revised Standard Version with the Apocrypha), Augmented 3rd College Edition, 2001. New York: Oxford University Press
Zondervan (NASB) Study Bible, 1999. Grand Rapids, MI: Zondervan

Commentaries

Barnes, Albert. 1832. *Notes on the Whole Bible*. Ada, MI: Baker Books 19th edition, 1983
Calvin, John. *Commentaries*. c. 1557. www.ccel.org/ccel/calvin/commentaries.i.html
Cambridge Bible for Schools and Colleges, ed. J. J. Perowne. 1914. University Press.

Gill, John. *Exposition of the Entire Bible*. c. 1746. https://biblehub.com/commentaries/gill/revelation/9.htm

MacDonald, William. 1995. *Believer's Bible Commentary*, ed. Arthur Farstad, Thomas Nelson Publishers, Nashville

Thayer, Joseph. 1889. *A Greek-English Lexicon of the New Testament*. New York; Harper & Brothers

Dictionaries & Encyclopaedias

An Expository Dictionary of New Testament Words, W.E. Vine. 1975. London: Oliphants

Anchor Bible Dictionary. 1992. New York; Doubleday

Athenian Democracy: Edinburgh Readings on the Ancient World. ed. P. J. Rhodes. 2004. Oxford University Press

Concise Oxford Dictionary, 1985. Oxford University Press

Encyclopaedia Britannica online www.britannica.com

Illustrated Bible Dictionary (also known as *Easton's Bible Dictionary*), 3rd ed. London: T. Nelson & Sons

International Standard Bible Encyclopedia. 1915. Chicago Howard-Severance Co

NAS Exhaustive Concordance of the Bible, 1981. Nashville, TN: Holman

The American Heritage Dictionary of the English Language, 5th Ed. 2011. Boston, MA: Houghton Mifflin

The Exhaustive Concordance of the Bible, James Strong, 1890. New York: Abingdon Press

Theological Dictionary of the New Testament, Kittel & Friedrich, abridged by Geoffrey Bromley. 1990. Grand Rapids, MI: William B. Eerdmans Publishing Co

Newspaper & Magazine Articles

Borschel-Dan, Amanda. (2018, November 22). Evidence of Sodom? Meteor blast cause of biblical destruction, say scientists. *Times of Israel*. www.timesofisrael.com/evidence-of-sodom-meteor-blast-cause-of-biblical-destruction-say-scientists/

Dastagir, Alia E. (2022, March 24). Marsha Blackburn asked

Ketanji Brown Jackson to define 'woman'. Science says there's no simple answer. *USA Today.* www.usatoday.com/story/life/health-wellness/2022/03/24/marsha-blackburn-asked-ketanji-jackson-define-woman-science/7152439001/

Hesse, Monica. (2022, March 25). Ketanji Brown Jackson did define 'woman' at her confirmation hearing. *The Washington Post.* www.washingtonpost.com/lifestyle/2022/03/25/ketanji-brown-jackson-woman

Holland, Eva. (2018, May 16). Where the doomed, beloved polar bear is still a dangerous predator. *Smithsonian Magazine.* www.smithsonianmag.com/science-nature/doomed-beloved-polar-bear-dangerous-180969092/

Hulse, Carl & Weisman, Jonathan. (2022, March 23).Ketanji Brown Jackson survives a final bruising day of questions. *The New York Times.* www.nytimes.com/2022/03/23/us/politics/ketanji-brown-jackson.html

Lyons, Leonard. (1947, January 30). Loose-leaf notebook. *The Washington Post.*

Remembering Auschwitz. (1995, January 26). *The New York Times.* www.nytimes.com/1995/01/26/opinion/remembering-auschwitz.html

Report on David Lloyd George, British Prime Minister. (1936, September 17). *The Daily Express.*

Stalin ordered massacre of Polish officers in 1940, Soviet paper says. (1990, March 22). *Los Angeles Times,* www.latimes.com/archives/la-xpm-1990-03-22-mn-1021-story.html

Twain, Mark. (1906, September to 1907, December). Chapters from my autobiography. *North American Review.*

Yardley, Jonathan. (2007, December 27). In a time of posturing, Didion dared slouching. *The Washington Post.*

Articles & Pamphlets

How Did People Die in the Holocaust? 24 Jan 2012. www.bbc.co.uk/newsround/16700249

Venereal Disease in the Bible. R. R. Willcox. 25 Jan, 1928. British Medical Journal. https://sti.bmj.com/content/25/1/28

Index

Numbers

1260 days 13
144,000 apostles 13, 45, 78-81, 87, 174
1st Century Jewish Teenager Approach 19-20, 27-28, 33, 88, 106
24, TV drama analogy 24
42 months

A

Aaron, High Priest 107-108
'A time, times and half a time' metaphorical meaning of 13
Abominations 38, 168
'Abomination of desolation' 95, 203, 244
    timings in the Gospels 203
Abram, the patriarch 101
Abraham,
    bargain re Sodom 308, 323
    covenant of 101, 109-110
    descendants as stars 154
    in Canaan 309-311
    inheriting the land 231, 327
    offering Isaac 277-278
Abyss, the 188, 191
    angel of 153, 176
    definition of 320
Air, the 16, 119
    atmosphere 15-16, 34, 40, 327
    definition 121
    forces 145, 249
    meeting the Lord in 34, 272
    pollution 142, 160-162, 322
    signs in 148, 158-162

Alexander the Great, 52, 239-240
Altar
    bronze 44, 47, 71, 240-242, 244, 298-299, 322
    golden 71, 106-109, 228-231, 238, 298-299
    pagan 35-36, 312
Ambiguity, deliberate 102-103
Angels 98, 128, 148, 269, 279, 308
    as fallen stars 153
    Because of the Angels 153
    fallen 153, 162, 304-307
    offspring demigods 304-307
    the four 77-78, 222, 227-231, 238, 259, 263
    the seven 15, 40, 106, 123, 297, 317
Antichrist, the 55, 212, 284, 287, 295, 332
    competing regimes of
    Eastern Orthodox view 295
    Historical guesses 295
    Historicist view 166-168
    Muslim Mahdi 263, 291, 319
    Preterist view of 55
    sign of 11, 284, 296
Antichrist, the spirit of 59, 122, 183, 289
    in 20th century regimes 146, 290, 325-326
    in Christian regimes 295
    in Islam 283, 290-291
    in Roman Empire 59
Antiochus IV Epiphanes 154, 244-245
Apostasy, definition 155
    Esau's 156

Apostasy, the Great 43, 283, 285
  the end of 285
Apostles 13, 45, 78-81, 87, 174
  definition of 78
Armageddon 11, 158, 261-262
  See Har-Magedon & Megiddo
Assyrian Empire 13, 51-53, 95-118, 172, 230-231, 318
Augustine of Hippo 27
Augustus Caesar 56-59, 318
Axis Powers 145-147, 249

B

Babylonian Empire 36, 49-53, 63, 154, 172, 230-231, 247, 298
  as "destroying mountain" 137-138, 144-145
Babylonian Talmud 165-166
Bacon, Sir Francis 101
Beasts, domestic 13-15, 119, 328
Beast, John's first 158, 174, 278, 324-327
  identity of 13, 59, 318-319
  misidentification of 168
  seventh head of 158
  the mark of 284, 317-318
Beast, John's second
  identity of 13, 59, 318-319
Beasts, wild 62-63, 121
  damnatio ad bestias 70-72
Beatles, the 102, 193
Belshazzar 36-38, 154, 298
Bergman, Ingmar 81-82
Bethlehem, prediction 91-92
  Yeats's poem 211-212
Burning mountain 136-137, 147
Byzantine Empire 169
  famine 65
  fire ships 225-226, 238-239

C

Canaanites, genocide of 110, 302, 309-311, 328-329
Catholicism - see Roman Catholicism
China 145, 161
  abortion 256
  antichrist regimes 325-326
  army 223
  deserts 129-132
  evangelism 79-80, 286
  famine eradication 67
  famines 64-68, 258
  fish-farming 38
  gunpowder 225
  invasion of 251
  road toll 248
Climate Change 207-208, 214-216, 248
Cousteau, Jacques 11-12, 88, 124

D

Daniel, the prophet 29, 36-37
  prediction of Messiah 92, 102-105
  spirit of antichrist 122
Daniel, Book of
  Chapter 5 - 36-37, 298
  Chapter 7 - 120, 122, 168, 183, 233, 270, 278-279
  Chapter 8 - 154
  Chapter 9 - 92, 102-105, 174
  Chapter 12 - 29, 101-102
David, King 17-18, 197-200, 229, 231-232, 234-235, 247
  covenant of 91, 324
Dea Roma 318
Dea Roma et Augustus 59, 318

Death tolls
    abortion 255-257
    Belgian Congo 251
    Cambodian 251
    China 64, 66, 251, 258, 325
    drugs 205-206
    famines 66-67
    guns 252
    Holocaust 259-260
    Islam 65, 251
    last 100 years 261
    Pakistan 251
    plagues 65-70
    Poland 258
    road deaths 248-249
    Rome 61, 65
    scorpions 176
    Turkish genocides 251
    Ukraine 258
    USSR 60, 66, 258
    WWI 65, 251
    WWII 65, 251
Deification 13
Deluding influence 289-295
Devereux, Dr. Stephen 67
Devil, the - see Satan
Diamond, Jared 69
Didion, Joan 211-212
Dispensationalist view 26
Domitian 176
Doomscrolling 211-212
Dragon - see also Satan
    manifesting in Gentile empires 13, 278, 321, 327

E

Eagle 163-164
Earthquakes 17-18, 329-330
    as metaphors 17-19, 26
    the last 16, 21-23, 74, 328

Eastern Orthodoxy 295
Elijah, the prophet 53, 93, 236, 246
    the mystery of 97, 283-284, 296
Elisha, the prophet 53, 93, 236, 246
Emperor - see Roman emperors
Emperor-worship 13, 59, 72, 251, 318
Euphrates River 58, 222-223, 227-231, 237, 239-242, 245, 262-263, 326-327
European colonisation 69

F

Feral State, definition of 318-319
Fig tree
    Messianic sign 96-101, 105, 285
First Century Jewish Teenager Approach - see "1st Century"
Forty-two months, metaphorical meaning of 13
Fresh water 148-162, 247, 270, 317, 321-333
Frogs 112-113, 327

G

Generation, definition of 100-102
    every 33, 117-118, 155, 267, 276
    evil 94
    fourth 101, 309-311
    last 267
    power 12, 124
    The Anxious Generation 209
    "this generation" 100-102, 104, 295-296

Gentiles 259-261, 265, 270, 284, 303
   'the times of the...' 13-14, 174
Germany 61, 65, 145-147, 290, 319, 325
Global Warming 160, 207-208, 248
Gore, VP Al 213-214
Great Pacific Garbage patch 140-141
Greek Fire 225-226, 238, 239-247, 249, 265
Gunpowder 224-225, 247

H
Haggai, the prophet 330-331
Haidt, Jonathan 209
Hailstones 16-18, 27, 327-330
Har-Magedon 14-16, 27, 39, 76, 89, 105, 158
   location of 14, 326-327
   meaning of 329
Hendriksen, William 171, 227
Herod Antipas 93
Herod the Great 92
Herodotus 52-53, 111
Hirohito, Emperor 145, 290, 318
Hitler, Adolf 145, 249, 290, 295, 325
   role in the Holocaust 259
   worship of 319
Holocaust, the 259
Horn, the eleventh 183
Horns, the ten 122, 158
   place on heads 278, 319
Horsemen
   200 million 222-238
   colours of 235-237
   meaning of 246-247, 262-265
   of fire 235-238
   Parthian 55-58
   Persian 52
   the Four 45-47, 54, 73
   Zechariah's 49-51
Horses 45-62, 114,
   colours of 50, 61-62
   equestrian skills 55-58
   horses of fire 53, 236-237
   locusts 164-171, 180-181, 191
   serpent-tails 252-253, 259
Hus, Jan 188

I
Incas 134
Incense 106-108, 119, 229
Incense altar 71, 106-107, 229, 298
India
   abortion 256
   eradication of famine 67
   groundwater 131
   invasion of 64-65
Inquisition, the 196
Interpretations of Revelation
   Dispensationalist 26, 227
      definition of 26
   Futurist 19, 42, 55, 169-171, 178-180, 185, 188, 191
      definition of 26
   Historicist 19, 42, 55, 166-168, 171, 178, 180, 183-185, 191, 225-226, 235
      definition of 26
   Idealist 19, 42, 55, 171, 180, 186-191
      definition of 27-28
   Preterist 19, 42, 55, 75, 165-166, 171, 180, 85, 191, 226-227, 231, 236
      definition of 25

Iran 58, 239, 263
Iraq 58, 230-231, 239, 263
Islam
    empire of 64-65, 166-169, 180
    impact on UN 290-291
    revival of 262-263, 290-291
Israel
    global dimming 159
    gospel to 174
    in exile 51, 63, 137
    promises of land 43-44
    relevance to Revelation 12-20, 33, 88-101, 302-303, 315, 318, 329
    restoration of 49-54, 101, 103-104, 282-285
    sign of the times 282-285, 296

J

Jacob, patriarch 90-91, 109-110, 154, 327
Jenkins, Jerry 26, 170, 180, 188, 192, 224-225
Jeremiah, David 223-224
Jericho 33, 89, 98, 105, 273-277, 280
Jerusalem 92, 229, 279, 296
    as a sign 14, 39, 83, 281-284
    as Har-Magedon 16, 27, 76, 327-329, 331
    fall in 63 BC 244
    fall in 70 AD 43-44, 54, 95-97
    fall in 586 BC 36, 63, 247
    New 45, 79, 157
    Preterist view of 19, 25, 75, 165-166, 178, 226-227, 231, 238
    restoration of 49-53, 103-105
    ruled by Melchizedek 310
John the Baptist 92-93, 181
John Paul II, Pope 196

Jonah, the prophet 95
    the sign of 94
Jordan River 92, 104, 274
Jordan, the Hashemite Kingdom of 172, 274
Josephus, Flavius 166, 187, 226, 244

K

Kennedy, Dr. Jonathan 67-69
Kim Il Sung 290

L

LaHaye, Tim 26, 170, 180, 186, 188, 192, 224-225
Left Behind series 26, 170, 180, 186, 192, 198, 224-225, 261
Leviathan 321
Libations 35, 297- 300, 317
Locusts
    antidote to demonic 217-221
    demonic 153, 164-178, 182-192, 203-206, 253, 324
    desert 115-116, 174, 179-186
Luther, Martin 168

M

Mao Zedong 66, 79-80, 258, 286, 290, 325-326
Maori 100
Martyrs 44, 47-48, 79-73, 298
Medo-Persian Empire 13, 37, 51-53, 137, 318
Meggido 28, 329
Mercury levels 11-12, 88, 131, 136, 138, 147, 151-152
Midnight Oil 208
Millennium, the 19
Mithridates 242-246
Moses, the prophet 103, 108-119,

136, 179-180, 191, 253, 284, 319
  Law of 71, 291, 298,
  Tabernacle of 36
Muhammad 168, 290-291
Mussolini, Benito 145, 290, 295, 318
Mystery of Elijah 97
  of God 267
  of resurrection 34, 272-273
  of the locusts 164-202
  of the Nile 112

N

Naphtha 225, 239-242, 247-249, 263-265
National Geographic 125, 140-141
Nebuchadnezzar, king 36, 230, 323
Nehemiah 118, 240-242
Nero, Emperor 55, 96
New Zealand 43, 100, 143, 152, 204, 217, 296
New World 69
New World Order 204
New York Times 131, 250
Noah, the patriarch 121, 304, 306
  the covenant of 266-267
  the days of 262, 264

O

Orthodox Churches 188, 286, 295

P

Palestine 263
Parable of
  fig tree 96-99
  sheep and goats 308
  unforgiving servant 195-196
  wedding feast 86

Passover, Festival of 17, 28, 113, 117, 166
  Jesus' fulfillment 110, 175
Parthian Empire 55-58, 73, 231
  shot 55-57
Patera - see phiale
Pergamum 59, 243-245, 318
Phiale 35-36, 297
Plagues, the Ten 111-117
Pliny the Elder 240-242
Polar bears 213-214
Popes 180, 295
  Boniface I 166
  Eulalius 166
  John Paul II 196
Population, world 260-261
Porteous, Bishop Beilby 258
Preterist view 19, 25, 42, 55, 75, 165-166, 171, 178, 180, 185, 191, 226-227, 231, 236
Principalities and powers 45, 158, 318-319
Protestants in China 80
Protestant views 26, 166, 196, 286, 295

R

Rapture, the 225, 261
Redemptive judgements 311-316
Reformers, the 26, 168, 188
Revelation presuppositions
  burning questions 42-45
  Jewish advantage 19-20, 27-28, 33, 88, 105-106, 232-233, 273-280
Roman Catholic Church
  apologies by 187-188, 196
  Charismatic view 286
  Historicist view of 26, 166-168, 180, 183-185

in China 80
Post-Reformation 25-26
Roman emperors 13, 59-60, 67-68, 72, 318
   Augustus Caesar 56-59, 318
   Claudius II 68
   Galerius 58
   Hostilianus 68
   Justinian 68
   Lucius Verus 67
   Marcus Aurelius 59-60, 67
Roman Empire
   circuses 70, 72
   famines 60-61, 65
   Pax Romana 58-60, 73
   plagues 67-68
Russia 64, 146, 290, 318, 325
   abortion 255
   famines 65-66
   fresh water 150, 152
   global dimming 159
   oil discovery 263
   Orthodox Church 286
   revival in 285
   Russo-Japanese War 143
   Stalin's massacres 258

S

Samaritans 118
Satan, enemy of God 188, 280
   as roaring lion 35
   authority of 90, 109
   Century of 250-252
   dwelling place of 188
   fall of 153-154
   false wonders of 287
   handing over to 200-202, 221
   political machinations of 13
   son of God 305
Scorpions 70, 171, 175-176, 178, 185, 189, 253
   horses' tails 165-170
Sea, the 78, 266-267
   end of 319-321, 331
   Green 61
   Mediterranean 52
   metaphorical meaning of 321
   overfishing 138-139
   pollution of 136, 140-142
   Red Sea 116, 303
   rising levels 208, 213-216
   signs in 11-12, 88, 98, 120-122, 136, 147
Serpents - also snakes 70
   horses' tails 234, 247, 252-253, 259, 265
   Messianic miracle 111
   metaphor for Satan 321
Seven, meaning of 15
Ships, sinking 142-144
Signs of the times
   of His return 11, 96-98, 281-296
   of Messiah 90-94
   of the seasons 98-101
   of the siege of Jerusalem 95-96
Silence 81-86
Simone, Nina 76
Sodom and Gomorrah 307-308
Solomon, King 51, 156-158, 231
   Song of 183, 232
   Temple of 36, 137, 230, 247
   wisdom of 311-312, 324
Stalin, Joseph 66, 145, 258, 290, 325-326
Strabo 239
Sudan 172
Sulphur 160, 224-225, 235-239, 307-308

T

Tacitus, Cornelius 226
Temple Mount, the 203
Thucydides 239
TikTok Frenzies 209-211
Time, magazine 11, 210, 214, 216
Timing of seals, trumpets & bowls 21-28
Titus, the apostle 312
Titus, Roman general, later emperor 165-166, 227, 231
Torturers 195-198, 202, 221

U

United Nations, the
    as the seventh head 219, 283
    reports by 205, 252, 255, 290-292
USA
    abortion 256
    delusions 293-295
    neutrality in WWII 145
    opioid crisis 206
    road toll 248
    ship building 144
USSR
    abortion 256
    oil discovery 263
    treaty with Hitler 145-146

V

Vengeance, the days of 96
Vespasian 55

W

Watercutter, Angela 210-211
Wildfires 127-129
World Health Organization (WHO) 205
World Wildlife Fund (WWF) 139, 151-152
Wormwood 148, 153-158, 162
Wrath of God 132-135
Wright, N. T. 227-228, 232-233, 235-236, 247

Z

Zechariah, the prophet 39, 137
    chariots 51-53
    horse 58
    horsemen 49-51
    scroll 48-49
Zefferelli, Franco 82
Zion 83

Other Books by Graeme Carlé

Available from:

Emmaus Road Publishing
PO Box 38-823 Howick
Auckland 2014
New Zealand

Website: www.emmausroad.org.nz

Books & eBooks
Amazon
Barnes & Noble
Kindle
Kobo
Koorong
Nook
and more...

Book 1 in the Revelation series

Dancing in the Dragon's Jaws

The Mystery of Israel's Survival

Graeme Carlé

Why is the Book of Revelation so misunderstood?

Wasn't its whole point to give revelation? Well, in typically Jewish manner, yes and no.

The Book of Revelation was written as an apocalypse, a Jewish literary genre which also includes the extraordinary Books of Daniel and Zechariah. Profound truths were concealed from outsiders and opponents using elaborate symbolism, to be understood only by those properly taught – as Jesus explains in Matthew 13:10-13.

The apostle John's original 1st century audience, having been led by Jewish Christians, would have readily understood his imagery from Jewish history. His plagues echo the ten plagues of Israel's exodus; his seven trumpets resonate of the Old Testament battle for Jericho.

Many think the keys to unlocking the Book of Revelation are lost. Not so. We still have Old Testament history and, for those who know where to look, full explanations of its symbols in the New Testament. What we need is the humility to learn from the 1st century Jewish believers the mysteries of the woman, the Messiah, the dragon, the comings of Elijah, and 'the times of the Gentiles'. From these we can understand God's continuing purpose for Israel.

ISBN 978-09582746-5-4

Book 2 in the Revelation series

Slouching Towards Bethlehem
The Rise of the Antichrists

Graeme Carlé

The lost keys of Revelation?

It is often thought today that the keys to understanding the Book of Revelation have been lost and are irretrievable – but they're not. They were just buried under centuries of rubble created by the Gentile church's foolish attempts to distance itself from its Jewish foundations. If, like any archaeologist, we dig carefully we can rediscover them.

In *Dancing in the Dragon's Jaws*, we found one key to understanding Revelation chapter 12 is the metaphorical "time, times, and half a time" and we unlocked the last 4,000 years of Jewish history.

This book, *Slouching Towards Bethlehem*, unlocks Revelation chapter 13 and the last 2,000 years of the Christian era, with startling results. Not only can we now understand the forces shaping history and the deaths of some 270 million in 20th century genocides but we can also project the future of Israel and the Middle East.

ISBN 978-0-9582746-8-5

Book 3 in the Revelation series

Gotta Serve Somebody
The Mystery of the Marks & 666

Graeme Carlé

Are you confused about the mark of the beast?

You're not alone. The Mark and the number 666 have been controversial for centuries. Scholars and laymen alike have offered numerous interpretations, calculations and wild guesses but most predictions have failed to materialize. Some say we just have to wait.

In this book, Graeme uses the keys recovered in the first two of his series (*Dancing in the Dragon's Jaws* and *Slouching Towards Bethlehem*) to unlock the symbols and 'times' of the infamous and misunderstood mark in human history.

Instead of waiting for a world government or a global banking system that may never eventuate, Graeme believes and shows that The Mark is already here - and has been for the 2,000 years! We've just not recognized it.

It's actually the beast's *counterpart* of marks that God Himself placed on the forehead and hand of His people at the exodus and in the wilderness, with a numbering system of names as described in the Book of Numbers.

We don't need a profound theological education or esoteric enlightenment but we do need a basic grasp of Jewish History and the Old Testament, as understood by 1st Century Jewish believers in Jesus of Nazareth.

ISBN 978-0-9582746-9-2

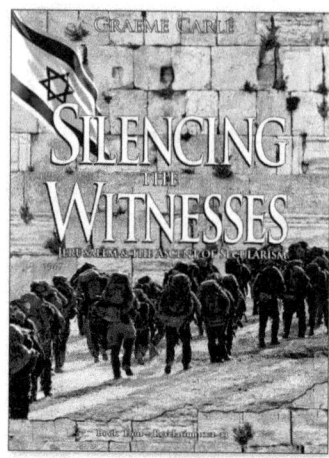

Book 4 in the Revelation series

Silencing the Witnesses
Jerusalem & the Ascent of Secularism

Graeme Carlé

Moses and Elijah back from the dead?

The most popular interpretation of Revelation 11 today is *literal* – that Moses and Elijah are soon to reappear in the streets of Jerusalem as witnesses, to preach for three and a half years, then be killed by a metaphorical beast (a man called the Antichrist) before being resurrected again after three and a half days.

The most common academic view today, however, is that these are all *metaphorical* images, referring to the church being persecuted initially by the Romans, today by the whole world, but ultimately vindicated.

In this book, Graeme takes the metaphorical approach but from a Jewish perspective. The Early Church was, after all, led by Jewish disciples and/or Gentiles taught by Jewish disciples. He shows how the two witnesses would have been understood by John's 1st Century audience to be the Law and the Prophets, making essential connections with Jesus' parable of the rich man and Lazarus, and with Paul's two Jerusalem's in Galatians 4.

In doing so, Graeme surveys the effects of the Law over 4,000 years of Jewish history, how it still applies to every Jew not under the New Covenant, and how it is relevant for all of us today.

ISBN 978-0-9941058-2-0

Book 5 in the Revelation series

Threshing Hour
Armageddon & Babylon the Great
Graeme Carlé

Dreading Armageddon & the Great Apostasy?

In 1973, we were taught the world is heading for a cataclysmic war but believers in Jesus were not to worry because we would be raptured, whisked away before it began. For those left behind, however, a charismatic world leader would emerge and broker a seven-year peace-treaty between Israel and the Arab nations. This would then disintegrate into World War III in which two-thirds of the Jews would be massacred, i.e. double the toll of the Holocaust.

This is not going to happen. Har-Magedon is a prophetic name for Jerusalem, used by John and inspired by Zechariah, to reveal that this battle will be an overwhelming victory for Israel, preceded by an outpouring of the Holy Spirit in which 90% will become 'Jews for Jesus', as explained in Book 4, *Silencing the Witnesses*.

As for Babylon the Great, in the 16th century Luther, Calvin, and the Reformers believed it was the Roman Catholic Church, the all-powerful European institution in their day. However, so much changed in the 20th century with the Second Vatican Council (1962-1965) and Benedict XVI pronounced that Luther was right all along!

In this book, Graeme shows that Babylon the Great is much older than Catholicism - almost as old as Creation - as well as much larger and more pervasive than we may have suspected.

ISBN 978-1-7385820-0-6

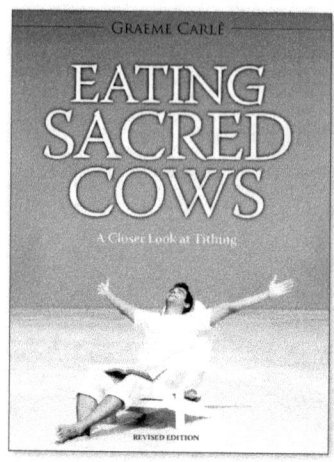

Eating Sacred Cows
A Closer Look at Tithing

Graeme Carlé

To tithe or not to tithe?

Tithing is one of the most misunderstood and abused aspects of modern day religion, and there are fine Christian leaders on both sides of the issue. Images of tele-evangelists and pastors living extravagant lifestyles can fuel resentment and mockery, but the defence is often that God's 'prosperity' ideal is being upheld (at least for the receiver of tithes).But what of the givers?

Many Christians testify how God has blessed them for tithing, but many others are disappointed, often too ashamed to speak openly in case they are 'letting God down'. Sermons on tithing almost always quote Malachi's rebuke of ancient Israel, "You are cursed for you are robbing God! Bring the whole tithe into the storehouse…" (Malachi 3:8–9). But what exactly did Malachi mean? Doesn't God still want us to tithe? Well, not in the way we are usually taught today.

Citing Biblical texts about tithing that are rarely, if ever, referred to by those teaching tithing to fund the church, Graeme shows instead how God wants us to receive a revelation of His goodness as we take time off to enjoy annual holidays. He also wants us to be generous, giving freely to those in need rather than tying up our resources in unnecessary church assets. Find out for yourself how to stand firm in your freedom and enjoy being generous!

This newly revised version expands the original by 50%.

ISBN 978-0-9941058-1-3

The Red Heifer's Ashes
Mysteries of Ancient Israel

Graeme Carlé

Israel's best-kept secret

This 3,500-year-old ritual is considered by Orthodox rabbis to be the greatest mystery of the Law of Moses. It is also essential to the rebuilding of the Temple in Jerusalem for which many today are hoping, including many Christian end-time preachers, and only became possible when Israel regained the Temple Mount in 1967. The ashes were to sanctify water sprinkled on worshippers to cleanse them from the defilement of death and that would include today's builders.

In all of Jewish history, only nine red heifers needed to be offered with the last of the ninth's ashes either disappearing when the Second Temple was razed in 70 AD or, as some historical sources indicate, running out at the beginning of the 4th century. However, in the 12th century, one of Israel's greatest sages Moses Maimonides taught that Messiah will come to offer the tenth. Many therefore believe we are living in that time.

The ritual, however, provides a truly astonishing revelation of Jesus of Nazareth as Messiah, who He was, why He had to die and be raised on the third day, and will return on the Last Day. This book unfolds the meaning of every detail as the reader follows a supernatural path through the whole of the Old Testament, just as the two disciples did on the road to Emmaus.

ISBN 0-473-08128-8

Born of the Spirit
A Study Guide for New Believers

Graeme Carlé

Growing in God

Jesus said that "it is enough for the disciple that he become like his teacher" (Matt 10:25) and that is always to be our goal - to become like Jesus. The question is, how can we be discipled by Jesus Himself, to be and to do what He wants, rather than limited by the teachings of any particular denomination?

For example, some do not practice water baptism and communion; others assume you become a Christian when you are sprinkled as baby; others know very little about the Holy Spirit and His gifts for us all; others do not understand that there is only one church and everyone who believes in Jesus belongs to it.

This interactive Bible study is for anyone who wants to develop their personal spirituality by checking the foundations of what Jude the Lord's youngest brother called 'the faith which was once for all delivered to the saints' (Jude 3). Avoiding all denominational allegiances, find out for yourself how God wants us to love, live and learn.

ISBN 978-0-9941058-1-3

Because of the Angels
Unveiling 1 Corinthians 11:2-16

Graeme Carlé

Lost in Translation

This text has been completely lost to the church today, dismissed as Paul's 1st century cultural baggage regarding veils and hairstyles. Ironically, our response was actually our 20th century cultural baggage because it had become unfashionable for women to wear hats and men to keep their hair short.

We then ended up in the right practice of discarding hats and veils and not worrying about hair length but for the wrong reason, while those concerned for the integrity of the Scriptures often retained hats, veils, and hair length for the right reason but with the wrong understanding of the text.

Paul was divinely inspired to write it, as Peter explained:

> ...our beloved brother Paul, according to the wisdom given him, wrote to you, as also in all his letters... in which are some things hard to understand, which the untaught and unstable distort, as they do also the rest of the Scriptures, to their own destruction.
> (2 Pet 3:15-16)

We have to humble ourselves and learn what Paul was trying to teach the Greeks 'according to the wisdom given him'. The key to understanding this passage is recognising its 1st century Jewishness: Paul was using Old Testament metaphors of 'head' and 'covering' and New Testament revelations of the fall of Satan and spiritual warfare.

ISBN 0-473-04955-4

www.ingramcontent.com/pod-product-compliance
Lightning Source LLC
Chambersburg PA
CBHW072146070526
44585CB00015B/1022